GIRL GUIDES
THE EDINBURGH STORY

GIRL GUIDES
THE EDINBURGH STORY

COMPILED AND EDITED BY
JOAN WARRACK AND PEGGY GREENING

FOREWORD BY
H.R.H. THE DUKE OF EDINBURGH
K.G., K.T.

Cover design by DOROTHY STEEDMAN
Illustrations by FIONA BARBER and JIM DONALDSON

The use of photographs from
The Scotsman, George Outram
and D. C. Thomson is gratefully
acknowledged.

Printed in Scotland by
Macdonald Printers (Edinburgh) Limited
Edgefield Road, Loanhead, Midlothian EH20 9SY

It is difficult to believe that becoming a Girl Guide was ever looked upon as rather daring and unconventional. This book is full of unexpected and interesting sidelights on the development of Guiding in Edinburgh.

It left me with two particular impressions. The enthusiasm of the response to the challenge of Guiding from the earliest days right up to the present and, secondly, the way in which the original challenge has been taken up and developed in so many different fields.

Guides who read this history will feel even more proud of their Movement than ever.

1976.

COUNTY PRESIDENTS

1912	Lady Brown
1913	Lady Fayrer
1922	Lady Maud Warrender
1935	Lady Constance Blackburn
1948	The Duchess of Hamilton and Brandon
1964	The Lady Primrose (now The Countess of Rosebery)

HONORARY PRESIDENT

From 1920   The Lord Provost of the City of Edinburgh

COUNCIL CHAIRMEN

1920	Lord Stevenson
1950	Mrs J. L. Hope
1965	Mrs G. C. Patterson
1974	Mrs G. Chiene

COUNTY COMMISSIONERS

1916	Mrs Laurie
1918	Miss Lilias Dalmahoy
1938	Miss Verona Wallace Williamson, O.B.E., J.P.
1950	Miss Doris Morison Inches, O.B.E.
1960	Mrs Jean Keppie
1970	Mrs Kath Wilkie

The County President

I am very proud to be associated with this book, and with the people it is by and about. I hope it will be read and enjoyed by many, certainly not only by Guides, for it has something to offer to all of us who cry "Not now—it's too late" and "Not now—there isn't time." "Now" is our only chance, the usable instant between past and future. This book is about its use.

All through there is a feeling of the adequacy and adaptability of the Guide Movement to the needs of its Members. It is full of gems—details of organisation, great occasions, recaptured moments of individual or group participation; memories of people learning to listen to one another, to think for themselves, to explore life and to enjoy life. And throughout is the faith that the Movement will develop "the way we want it" and therein lies its strength and value. Guiding will answer in the future to the demands of "Now" just as it did in the past.

Dendre Rosebery

Dalmeny 1977

In 1977

A BROWNIE says:

"I look forward to going every week to meet up with Tawny, Snowy and Brown Owl and my friends. It means an awful lot to me. I like the outings and picnics, helping people across roads, helping Mummy, and trying to do what someone says straight away. We take badge tests, and even to get everything ready is quite hard.

"Every Brownie round the whole wide world has a special part to play, whether it is small or big we do it. I think it is great fun, and we are all a bit of the story."

A QUEEN'S GUIDE says:

"Be prepared, as a few dedicated girls were at the beginning, and they, with many more since, have prepared others to follow their example.

"The Guide Movement is not an old-fashioned institution, it continues to develop around the needs of modern girls, whether we are shy or independent, tactless or sensitive. Guiding helps us to mix, not only in our patrols but in the whole community, and gives us a training for living.

"We all know the personal pride in passing the Enrolment Challenge, an Interest Badge, or in working on a Patrol project, but we may not have realised how different the challenges were years ago.

"This book tells us so much—from tiny details, through funny happenings, to the effect that world events have had upon a Patrol Leader. Through it all, we see the important part that Camping plays, perhaps because under an open sky sharing the work and fun together it is easier to understand the simple truth and love on which the Guide Laws, Motto and Promise are based."

THE RANGER GUIDES of a newly-formed Unit say:

"This book is fascinating, it has given us an insight into the adventure and enjoyment that lie behind the faded photographs. How lucky new Guides will be to read all this when they first join their Patrols.

"More than anything we have seen that Guiding has been, and we hope always will be, a challenge and fun. In this Unit we hope to follow the example set us so that we too can look back with pride and say—*we began it.*"

Editorial Introduction

The idea of collecting memories and photographs arose in 1974. This book has grown out of that idea because of the interest and encouragement of Edinburgh Guides of all generations; from the mass of material which flowed in after appeals in the Press and on the Radio, and through the personal contacts made by the Story Committee which was formed in 1976. The Chairman was Joan Warrack and the members were Shelagh Cuthbertson, Dorothy Donaldson, Jane Gibson, Doris Inches, Hilda Noble and Marjorie Rose. They all set to work to sift and sort all this information and to seek more from the scrap-books, records, log books and minutes of meetings over six decades. Having agreed on the framework of the book, each member wrote some chapters, and friends wrote other chapters.

In August 1976 Peggy Greening was co-opted on to the Story Committee, and her fresh approach was invaluable when editing began. For three months people and paper flowed in and out of the "Book room" in the Chairman's home; hard work and concentration, mixed with mirth, ensured that the typescript went to the printers on time.

Fun and friendship were rarely more apparent than in the making of this book, and the phrase "Do you remember?" occurred so often it nearly became a sub-title. Many memories were evoked, and the Committee much regrets that all were not able to be included, and it begs forgiveness for any mistakes which may have been made. It is hoped that readers will remember other happy times and perhaps old friendships will be renewed as a result.

It would be good if it were possible to thank everyone by name who has helped; there were the contributors, young and old, the writers, the illustrators and designers, the typists who transformed the handwritten words into clear typescripts, the sorters of photographs and readers of scripts and proofs; finally all the husbands who gave moral support.

In particular, the Story Committee would especially like to thank Miss Wallis Myers, the Archivist at Commonwealth Headquarters, for her encouragement and for checking the whole script for historical errors. Also John Bruce, who steered the story along the production line to become this book.

All have shared in making a book which the Committee hopes is worthy of the girls and women who followed the Founder's ideals, and his advice to "laugh while you work"; and whose work and play and care for each other are the subject of *The Edinburgh Story*.

Contents

Chapter   *Page*

1.   The Girls Began It . . .   1
Stories from the Guides of 60 years ago.

2.   The Chief Guide   9
Lady Baden-Powell's visits to Edinburgh Guides from 1917 to 1962.

3.   Laying the Foundations   14
First committee and companies in 1909. Uniform. First name, constitution and appointment of County Commissioner in 1916. Formation of Council.

4.   Brownie Guides   21
First packs. Activities, programmes, meetings, competitions. Pack Holidays from 1930 to the 1970s.

5.   Guides.   30
The meeting, and changing programmes through the years. Special meetings. Meaning of the Promise.

6.   Ranger Guides   38
1917—Rangers formed, Cadets and V.A.D. follow. Sea and Air Rangers. Berck 1952. Ranger service to the community. Why be a Ranger?

7.   Extensions   51
1926—first companies and packs formed for handicapped girls. Post Guides. Budgets. Fernielaw, day camps. Handcrafts. C.H.Q. competition 1972.

8.   Local Associations and Trefoil Guilds   63
Stories of two Local Associations and the help given to the girls and Guiders. Formation of the Guilds and how the Guide spirit continues, though out of uniform.

9.   Badges and Training   70
First badges, testers' suggestions, Guiders' help. Queen's Guide Badge in 1945. New badges in 1968. Changing patterns of training from 1916. Qualifications required. Conferences. Duke of Edinburgh's Award Scheme. Guides' participation and story from the first Edinburgh Guide "Gold".

10.   Property—Heritable, Rentable and Moveable   86
      33 Melville Street and the Guide Hall. Gifford Cottage and Johnstoun-
      burn. Stanemuir. Colstoun Old Mill Cottage. The Minibus, and two
      letters "written" by it.

11.   Rallies, Events and Competitions   101
      Early rallies. Tree planting in 1935,1953 and 1973. B-P's Centenary Year
      1957. Spotlight on Guiding 1964. New Programme 1968. Jubilee Years.
      Shield Competitions.

12.   Organisation between the Wars   112
      Growth of Movement. Divisions and districts formed. The Executive
      and County Committees at work. Miss Dalmahoy retires.

13.   Guiding in Wartime, and Guide International Service   119
      First World War Service. Evacuation of children in Second World War,
      and start of "The Trefoil School". Randolph Canteen. Church of
      Scotland Mobile Canteens. War Service Badge. G.I.S. Training from
      1942. Guide teams in Europe from 1944 to 1950.

14.   Messengers—Banners, Pigeons and Scrolls   128
      Description of the County and Division Banners. Pigeon post. Scrolls
      of Friendship.

15.   Royal Visitors   134
      Lining the Royal routes. Princess Mary's visit in 1920 and to the Wet
      Rally in 1931. Youth Rallies.

16.   International   141
      1911—first links abroad. Visits to Europe and America. Guests in
      Edinburgh. Thinking Day. Badges. World Camps and World
      Conferences.

17.   Funds and Finance   152
      Early fund-raising. Handcraft Exhibition 1928. Subscriptions and
      administration. Fund-raising for the County and for others.

18.   More Organisation   158
      Activities in the County, its growth and development from 1938 to 1977.
      An appraisal from each of the four County Commissioners covering
      this period.

19.   Exploring the Arts   170
      Choirs, orchestras, pageants, song contests, competitions, Gang Show.

20.   Camping   175
      Early camps, licences, wartime camping, Trefoil camp site, permits.
      International Camps in 1960 and 1968. Canoeing, skiing and orienteering.

21.   The Trefoil School   186
      Polkemmet in 1945. Kirklands in 1951 until the school closed in 1976.

22.   Reaching Out   195
      Links with other societies. Co-operation with the Scouts. The Square
      Centre. Community Development. Publicity through the media.

1

The Girls Began It . . .

ONE OF THE GIRLS starts our story—

"In the summer of 1909, on a Sunday afternoon walk in Colinton, my sister Margaret and I suddenly met a number of Girl Scouts running and walking down the road—what a thrill. Each wore a brown blouse and skirt, a scarf knotted in front, a belt with a knife and whistle, a haversack and a broad brimmed hat. All of them carried poles but the leader's had a triangular flag flying on top! They told us they were practising 'Scouts Pace' and were the Sheltie Patrol attached to the 33rd Edinburgh Boy Scout Troop.

The 33rd Edinburgh Scout Troop.

"For some time many boys and girls had been practising the activities described in *Aids to Scouting,* a book written by General Robert Baden-Powell in 1899 for his young soldiers in South Africa (he had jotted down notes for it during the long waits whilst stalking bears in Kashmir when he was serving with the Indian Army!). Then in January 1908 came the first instalment of *Scouting for Boys* originally intended for use by any boys' organisation, but when so many boys banded together independently it became the handbook for the newly formed Boy Scout Movement.

"The six fortnightly parts were snapped up by enthusiastic

1

boys whose sisters secretly smuggled them under their pillows to read when their disapproving mothers were not looking.

"Edinburgh girls were no exception and, when we heard that the hero of Mafeking, B-P himself, was coming to the Lauriston Hall on 19th March 1909 to talk about the Boy Scout Movement, Margaret and I were in his large audience along with a few other enthusiastic girls. We were lucky because our mother was sympathetic towards the movement. At the end of his fascinating talk General Baden-Powell asked if any young *men* interested in forming Scout Troops would like to meet him in a small room behind the Hall. To our surprise up stood Molly Mellis Smith: she and her brother went through to meet the General—no one knows what he said to her, but she became the leader of the Girls' Patrol in the flourishing Boy Scout Troop led by her brother.

"I was delighted when Molly said I might join the Sheltie Patrol, but on the very day I joined she told me that we were not to be called Girl Scouts any more. What a blow—but all was well! So many girls all over the country had been playing the game he invented for boys that General Baden-Powell decided that the best thing to do was to form a Girls' organisation on similar lines.

"He chose to name it after a famous Indian regiment and also after the brave mountaineers of Switzerland—and so we became Girl Guides. Molly told us we were to wear brown tammies, not hats, and brown jerseys instead of blouses but otherwise 'we would be just the same as before' said in a firm tone!

"However, 'Sheltie' was considered rather unladylike and as two Patrols were now needed the names became Ling Heather and Bell Heather (rather to our disgust). We all embroidered our own emblems and I remember later on I had to make a Union Jack that looked the same on both sides for my 2nd Class test, and also had to learn all the bones in the body by heart by their Latin names.

"We met out of doors whenever possible, even in winter, in local gardens or in Colinton Dell; we lit fires (with two matches), cooked, tracked, sang songs of Scotland round the camp fire and I remember our turnip lanterns on Hallowe'en making a line of light as we wended our way along the river. We were so enthusiastic and dedicated to the job in hand, be it learning Morse code, signalling or practising first aid. We longed to put the latter to good use and many an old lady crossing the road must have wondered why we watched her so anxiously.

"If she had only known why—we were prepared to use each item of our uniform had she fallen and hurt herself. Our poles made a stretcher when two were pushed into coat or jersey sleeves (they were broom handles marked in feet and inches with a red hot wire); padded with our stockings the poles made splints for broken legs and our ties were triangular bandages for damaged arms and so on. . . .

"Everything was entered into with such enthusiasm and we badgered our young friends and relations to become leaders, but were rather fussy about whom we chose as we wanted our Movement to grow the way *we* wanted. Growing it certainly was—I was so excited when I actually met a girl I didn't know wearing a Guide badge, the now familiar Trefoil which was issued about May 1910. Until then we had used the Scouts' Fleur-de-Lys and their proficiency badges.

"Others, however, were not so pleased to see our badge (in fact we weren't approved of at all by some) and one headmistress of an Edinburgh school threatened to punish any girl wearing the Trefoil. Our families feared we would turn into tomboys and small boys hooted at us in the streets. However, B-P had asked his sister, Miss Agnes Baden-Powell, to organise the Girl Guides for him and her gentle influence persuaded many anxious mothers that the game of Guiding could be played by girls with advantage to all; the character training would lead to self control, resourcefulness and consideration for others, so making them better daughters, wives and mothers of the future.

"It took time to organise the new movement and it was a year after I had joined when, in July 1910, our company was registered in London as the 1st Midlóthian Girl Guide Company with Molly Mellis-Smith as the first Captain. We heard that 8000 Girl Guides were registered in companies in Great Britain that month— the girls really had started something! Molly was an inspiring leader with a keen sense of humour; she infected us all with her own love of adventure and outdoor exploration and through Scouting games she trained us to 'Be Prepared' to serve others. We tried very hard to achieve her high standards.

"By now we knew girls in the other Edinburgh companies, so it was exciting when all five paraded for the first time at a public event to march in the Procession through the city on the occasion of King George V's Coronation in June 1911. We met in Clarendon Crescent to form up and you can imagine how we studied one another. One company wore bright green uniform, one wore scarlet, two were in blue and we were still in our original brown. How proud we all were! Then in July we were amongst 400 Scottish Guides who lined the route as King George and Queen Mary drove through Edinburgh on their first visit after being crowned.

"To our great disappointment we were told in November that all companies would wear blue uniform so—off with the brown and on with the blue but back came our 'wide-awake' hats with broad brims. This official uniform gave us a nice bonus as all Guides in uniform could travel on Edinburgh trams and visit the Zoo for 1d.

"The way I became an officer was rather strange. There was to be a meeting of all the Edinburgh Guides in a garden which we were digging up to make vegetable plots and on that day our Captain developed chickenpox. She telephoned me as I was the Senior Patrol Leader, told me to turn up the left hand brim of my hat, fasten some hen's tail feathers in it and take the Company to the meeting as her Lieutenant. As Captain she wore cock's tail feathers in *her* hat! And so my Guiding days continued . . . looking back on them they seem to have been full of adventure, enthusiasm, happiness and dedication—what fun we had."

These are some of the memories of Catherine Hamilton Bruce, one of Edinburgh's first Girl Guides who has stayed in the Movement as Captain, Commissioner, then Guider in charge of the Trefoil School, and is now a member of the Council of the County of the City of Edinburgh Girl Guides.

In the squares and gardens of Edinburgh many girls were playing the Scouting game and here are some of their memories.

Alison Graham (née Christison) says:

"I remember how some of my friends and I read *Scouting for Boys* and we formed a Patrol, meeting in Moray Place Gardens. We made our own uniforms, shoulder knots, badges, etc., and had great fun trying to be Girl Scouts. Then we were allowed to join the 1st Midlothian Girl Guide Company at St George's West Church, which was even more fun.

"During the long summer holidays when all our family stayed on a farm at Killiehuntly, near Kingussie, my older sister Irene (who later became captain of the 17th Coy) and I formed the Peewit Patrol with the girls of the large family on the farm. The boys went off walking in the Cairngorms with my brothers, but we had wonderful times with the girls who loved this new game and they taught us a lot of country lore, whereas we told them of the world beyond the farm. Such happy days!"

Ina Armstrong and Jean Baillie were Guides in the 2nd Midlothian Coy., later becoming Captains of it. They brought photographs and mementoes for this book to the Guide office after an appeal in the *Evening News*. Though both in their 80s they climbed the stairs to the top of "No. 33" and told many tales

—of early meetings, picnics, rallies;

—of how Ina received a collapsible metal cup from Miss Agnes Baden-Powell and her autograph;

—of the Archerfield Camp in 1912 when they slept in a wagon and a striped tent;

—of marching in the funeral procession of their Lieutenant;

—of the family feeling they all had with Mina Brown, the Secretary, and how Lilias Dalmahoy knew every Patrol Leader's face and name throughout her 20 years as County Commissioner.

These two ladies with others, were invited to the A.G.M. in 1975 to see how the Movement they helped to begin had progressed.

Elizabeth Somerville (née Watson) tells us:

"On 12th September 1910, I was enrolled as a tenderfoot Guide in the 2nd Edinburgh Company of Girl Guides. I was only ten years old, and special permission had to be received from Miss Agnes Baden-Powell before I could be admitted to the Movement.

"It was a very happy company with a devoted and most competent Captain, Miss L. A. Robertson. We started off our meetings with marching and drill, and went on to do signalling—semaphore and Morse—and then first-aid. If there was any time over, we might have some singing or Indian club swinging, or talks about the Guide Movement.

"We also met on Saturday afternoons. If it was fine we went for a march. I *mean* march. We formed up in fours, and marched on the left side of the road. I very often played for the marching as I was also a piper, having had lessons since the age of seven.

"I remember one wet Victoria Day when we took a train to South Queensferry where a pinnace took us out to *H.M.S. Natal* which was lying in the Forth. We were greeted by the Captain and shown over the ship. We were also given a scrumptious tea. I was asked to play my bagpipes, which I did, and the Captain gave me a present of a box of chocolate biscuits and the ship's ribbon inscribed with the name *H.M.S. Natal.* He said I would be the ship's honorary piper. I wore the ribbon on my pipes whenever I went on parade with the Guides. Unfortunately *H.M.S. Natal* was blown up in a South of England dock during World War I.

"1911 was, of course, the year of the Coronation of George V when, during his visit, he laid the foundation stone of the Usher Hall. On one of his tours in the city he drove, with Queen Mary, slowly along Waterloo Place. Guides lined the Post Office side of the street and our company was among them. Only two of us were allowed to salute the King, one—a bugler from outside Edinburgh—

and myself. He graciously saluted us back and I could hardly stand still for pride. I was not quite 11 years old.

"When World War I broke out, I became involved in the Army Recruiting Campaign until the end of Voluntary Military Service in 1916. Later I helped the 6th Guide Company which met in Abbeyhill School and of which a friend of mine was Lieutenant and then for a time I was a lone Guide; but Guiding for me will always recall with gratitude those Wednesday evenings and Saturday afternoons with the 2nd Coy., where we were just one big family."

The 4th Midlothian Company was formed in October 1910 at St Serf's Church, Edinburgh. Miss Janet Tait was appointed Captain and Miss McCready Lieutenant. The Captain wore a beautiful cockade of feathers in her hat, and always carried a walking stick as part of her uniform. Quite a number of parents were interested to see what would come of it, but were afraid of the girls becoming tomboys, as the first few had asked if they might take their straight tight skirts up an inch or so, for climbing fences!

Margaret Lechler (Née Roberts) continues:

"In April 1911 I was allowed to join, to my great joy, and having

The 4th Company depart for camp in 1913.

passed my preliminary tests, I was enrolled on May 11th. In June King George V and Queen Mary arrived by train for an official visit to Edinburgh and the Girl Guides formed a Guard of Honour near Waverley Station. For the Royal Visit we had been issued with large rush hats (such as the Brownies wore later) and it was one of Edinburgh's windiest days. Just as the Royal Procession reached the top of the hill down to Holyrood Palace, a terrific blast of wind removed nearly all the hats and swept them down on to the railway line below.

"The railway men were wonderful and came panting up the steep slope with rescued hats but alas, quite a number had been crushed by an incoming train.

"When the Royal Procession had passed, we all marched up to Patrick Thomson's where the County Committee had arranged a splendid lunch for us all after which, with a few speeches, we were allowed to go home individually.

"In 1912 the Company had its first camp, sleeping in the village school at Romanno Bridge, and again in 1913, but no camping was allowed when the Great War began until in 1917, a large area camp was held at Ninemileburn to pick sphagnum moss for war wounds. It was strenuous but great fun.

"By now I had been promoted to Lieutenant and was later appointed Captain until I went out to India in 1922. Miss Ida Wooster was Captain for some years and when she left the district my sister, Phoebe Roberts, was appointed Captain.

"The title 4th Midlothian was later changed to 4th Edinburgh and Leith, and later to the 4th City of Edinburgh. I had the great pleasure of being with the present company for their 40th and 50th anniversaries."

Jennie Aitken says:

"What would the girls of today think if the only exciting events in their spare time were Sunday School, Bands of Hope, Sewing Bees, piano lessons, etc.? But that was to be changed for the better. In 1915 Marshall Street Baptist Church started a Scout Troop and the girls of the congregation, when they saw the fun the boys were having, demanded a similar organisation for themselves. Early in 1916 a Guide Company was formed and 32 girls joined with Miss F. Fleming as the first Captain. The Company was registered as the 19th Midlothian.

"As it was war time uniforms were scarce so some bought Scout navy blue serge shirts, cutting off part of the tail! Black shoes and stockings were worn, hair had to be in plaits with navy blue ribbon and the Guiders wore black lacing boots—even at camp! Oh, the 19th had a bugler—the first Company photograph in 1917 shows the Guide wearing the bugle on a cord.

"Guiding was taken very seriously in these early years—A Good Turn had to be done daily—sometimes at the Campfire the Guides were asked to say what Good Turns they had done during the past week (a bit embarrassing).

"The church Hall was used for winter meetings until the first week in March—all other meetings were held out of doors. We sometimes spent a whole day out. I remember once in 1917 the Guide Company met in George Square, formed fours, and *marched* to Cramond where we had the use of a private field and woodlands for the day, Captain pointing out items of historical interest, natural history, etc., on the way. On arrival at the field we had games based on what we had learned on our way! By the way, when marching along George IV Bridge, someone shouted at us, 'There goes Britain's last hope!' The day was spent in wide games, etc., and in the early evening we formed fours again and marched home from Cramond to George Square. In these early days no one appeared to have any pennies for tram fares so we marched everywhere, which we enjoyed and we were very proud of our smartness."

Elizabeth Baxendine says:

"Do you remember your enrolment? I pulled out the memory stop to find a picture of that night 65 years ago when I became a Girl Guide in a Portobello Company. I recaptured the thrill and solemnity of that moment when, standing in a semi-circle with my friends, we repeated the Promise and learned the secret pass words. Our Patrol Leader, with skirt down to her ankles, inspired us with awe and respect but the Captain was a goddess apart—SO OLD—twenty at least!

"We worked hard to master knots and acquire badges to be sewn on our sleeves with careful stitches and worn with pride. We went for route marches with poles and haversacks and a tail of small boys shrieking with mirth and shouting, 'See the lassie Scouts!' We were allowed to camp in a cottage in the country, sleeping on straw palliasses and cooking outside. I clearly remember cooking porridge on a wet morning—it tasted smoky and was full of lumps. I still like lumpy porridge!

"I remember when Miss Baden-Powell addressed us in the McEwan Hall; and the fervour and emotion aroused by so many of us singing 'Land of Hope and Glory'. I can never forget what Guiding meant to me in terms of friendship and the earliest lessons in the sharing of giving service to the community."

2

The Chief Guide

"Set an ideal and life becomes real"

HEAVEN MUST HAVE SMILED the day the young society girl seeking an ideal for living met Sir Robert Baden-Powell. Because that meeting gave us the future Chief Guide. She became an international figure, yet Edinburgh had a fair share of her attention. She first came in 1917 with her husband, but that day belonged to him, the Founder. Thereafter she came in her own right, helping his work of Scouting and Guiding.

In 1929 she spoke to a vast assembly of Guides from the East of Scotland area—Edinburgh Guides were allotted 100 places, and competition for them was keen. She also paid a flying visit to the very new Headquarters at 33 Melville Street.

In October 1936 the Chief Guide spoke at a luncheon given in her honour by the Council of Edinburgh Girl Guides. She referred to youth movements abroad which were started on Scout and Guide lines as in Italy and Germany but by then were run in nationalistic or military ways. She said the Guide Movement must not hide its light under a bushel but should come out more into the public eye. She spoke to a Conference later in the Music Hall reminding them that the first meeting of Girl Guides in Scotland was held there.

Lady Baden-Powell was back in Edinburgh a year later when the World Committee of the World Association met here; she was with the 20 members of the Committee from many nations who were entertained to luncheon in the City Chambers. The Lord Provost, Sir Louis Gumley, remarked, "In this country the Movement is so well established that I cannot think how we got on at all without it." He welcomed this international gathering, especially the French chairman, Mme. de Kerraoul, who remembered the Auld Alliance in her reply. Lady Baden-Powell said that it was the greatest delight of them all to have this chance of meeting in Edinburgh . . . she hoped Scotland might feel . . . that they had taken a share of laying foundations for lasting goodwill in the world.

When Lord Baden-Powell died in 1941, the loss to the world was enormous; Lady Baden-Powell, with great courage, continued his work, and travelled tirelessly to encourage and sustain Guiding throughout the world.

When Lady Baden-Powell was in Edinburgh in 1942 she handed over

9

the Guide Mobile Canteen at St Giles, an account of which is in the "Guiding in Wartime" Chapter.   She took part in a triumphant drive to 33 Melville Street, in the course of which she insisted on getting out of her carriage and talking to as many Guides as she could. Lady Baden-Powell attended the Scottish Conference of Commissioners and Guiders.   In her speech to the meeting she said "it was an unforgettable experience to return from Africa and find everyone so confident, so content, and so courageous everywhere."   She was told how well the Guides had done in the Services.   They were put into places of responsibility because they had gained that power of leadership, self reliance and strength of character which were bound up with the word "Guide".

On her next visit during the worst winter of the century, the Chief Guide spent 40 hours on her train journey from London, reaching Edinburgh early on a March morning in 1947.   The train was stuck in a snowdrift, another train came alongside and the intrepid lady climbed from the window of her carriage to that of the other.   (This story has become legendary.)   Fresh as ever, full of vigour, she spoke to an indoor Rally of Guiders, Patrol Leaders, Seconds and Rangers at the Assembly Hall, who gave her a tremendous welcome.   She entertained the girls with stories of her travels throughout the world—she told them how Guides in occupied countries had kept the spirit of Guiding alive, although underground; and how in Paris 40,000 Scouts and Guides had marched down the Champs Elysées when peace was declared.   Some had hidden their uniforms by burying them in the ground, and you can imagine with what pride they wore them openly once again.

In 1948 there was a Service in St Giles, and the Guides were there to welcome their Chief Guide—they surged forward in their enthusiasm to see her at close quarters and with her usual good humour Lady Baden-Powell had a word for the lucky ones near her, then she climbed the steps of the Cathedral to speak to all.   Later, the 1st Class Guide Club entertained her to tea at Edinburgh Headquarters.   During this visit she spoke to Local Associations and attended five receptions.

Girl Guides from all over Scotland, including Orkney, Shetland and the Hebrides, gathered in Edinburgh in June 1952 to meet the Chief Guide in the Usher Hall.   "A Pageant of Scotland" was presented in ten scenes and Edinburgh provided the "Grandmother" who opened the Book of the Pageant and read the stories, and also the last act which was of a Guide Company enrolling a new Guide.   Each of the other Counties acted a story or ballad, ranging from the dramatic, through the historic, to the humorous—the whole was directed by Greta Collyns.

Guides presented the Chief Guide with seven large bags, each one bearing a letter of the word—WELCOME—and containing reports of good turns done by Patrols; the Leaders had compiled the books.   Lady

Baden-Powell said that she would take them with her on her travels as messages of Guide friendship to other Guides in foreign countries. Colours were paraded from the Counties, and some of Edinburgh's

The Chief Guide outside St Giles

Queen's Guides carried the World Flag and County Banner. Carrying the responsibility for the whole evening, for arranging the church service at St Giles the next day, and for making welcome 132 Guides from all over Scotland, was Miss Inches who received the following message from Lady Baden-Powell:

"I cannot tell you how impressed I have been by all that I have seen and heard and felt of the great spirit of Guiding here in Edinburgh."

In 1959 the Chief Guide came to Edinburgh to address the Scottish Council at their H.Q. It was an open secret that Guides would be allowed to go to Waverley Station to greet her on arrival—provided they were present for roll calls at school and work. Just guess—yes the train was late—much 'phoning by Guides to schools and work, but nearly all stayed and gave her a great welcome. She wrote afterwards to the County Commissioner—"thrilled with all the arrangements made, and could you give me the names of the two Guides who carried my coat and baggage at the station!"

Although the visit was to Scotland, as the County on the spot Edinburgh had the privilege of helping Scottish Headquarters with hospitality, and Rangers and Cadets cooked and served a fork supper for the Chief Guide and visitors. Also some members of the Local Associations and Trefoil Guilds attended the evening meeting.

In 1962 Lady Baden-Powell arrived in Edinburgh once more, and this time the train was punctual! Guides were at the Assembly Hall to sing to her. They began:

> "Edinburgh, Lothians, Borders, Fife,
>   We're here to greet you
>   We're here to meet you—"

and indeed they were—all 2000 of them in the Hall and 2000 outside in the forecourt. When the Chief Guide left the Hall they sang "Will ye no' come back again?" The Guides outside pressed forward, all hoping to see the Chief close to them, and Mrs Keppie, the County Commissioner at that time, says, "She said quietly to me when the press of children became a little uncontrolled—'Now it is time to leave'—and with perfect timing we withdrew." Not only was this complete crowd control, but there was not one policeman needed.

Shelagh Cuthbertson writes:

"The foregoing is rather in the nature of a calendar of public appearances, in which it is difficult to give the tremendous personal touch which is so characteristic of the Chief Guide. For instance, at the opening of the Brownie House at Netherurd, an Edinburgh Brownie reported afterwards, 'She couldn't shake hands with us all, so she gave us each a finger to shake.' What a picture that conveys, the smile, the outstretched fingers, ten Brownies to shake hands instead of two!

"One of our Guiders went to a Conference in Belfast, and the guest of honour was the Chief Guide, radiating friendship and cheer. In the course of discussion our Guider mentioned the difficulty of finding a pictorial illustration of the aim of the Guide Movement—to draw all nations and creeds together in friendship. 'I know just the thing,' said the Chief Guide. 'I'll send it to you.' A large photograph of the Chief Guide holding the hands of a coloured and a white child, all smiling happily, arrived in Edinburgh before the Guider had even returned!

'Will ye no' come back again?
Better lo'ed ye canna be . . .'

How often must Lady Baden-Powell have heard Girl Guides of Scotland and Edinburgh sing those moving words? I vividly remember singing them in the Assembly Hall, and as we sang with all our hearts she threw out her arms, gave us that all-embracing smile, and we knew she would come back to each one of us—if not in person, perhaps her ideals would become a reality to us.''

3

Laying the Foundations

GIRLS HAD RESPONDED to General Baden-Powell's challenge and they lit the spark of Guiding in Edinburgh; but who fanned the tiny flame into the fire which has inspired more girls throughout six decades? How is it that in 1976 there are 11,000 Guides of all ages in uniform in Edinburgh, and countless thousands, both in the city and round the world, who can say, "Once a Guide, always a Guide," because they were Edinburgh Guides?

Organising any activity for girls was not a popular thing to do in Edwardian days, especially when it involved outdoor excitements like lighting fires and camping in tents, but Edinburgh was lucky in having a few far-sighted ladies and sympathetic mothers willing to help girls who had started the first Patrols. They called a public meeting in Lothian Road School on 15th June 1909, during which the first committee was formed which really helped to begin the movement in the City—and their successors have kept it on the move ever since.

Can it be just coincidence that the Girl Guide Movement took off in the same year that a man first flew across the Channel—heralding the air and space age? Women too had a vision and hoped that their Scout sons and Guide daughters would make an even more worthwhile contribution in future by following B-P's example within the movements he founded.

The experience gained in organising the Boy Scout movement proved very useful as Mr Laurence, the Scottish Scout Secretary, joined the Committee and his advice and help, especially in liaising with General Baden-Powell, was much appreciated by Miss Bremner, the Secretary, and the rest of the Committee. Within two weeks of their first meeting, they were hurriedly called together to consider proposals made by B-P for the suggested Girls' Movement (they had not intended to meet again until the autumn!) However, they obviously approved B-P's name for the new organisation as the handwritten minute for 28th June 1909 in the worn old book mentions Girl Scouts; the latter word is unfinished and crossed through and Guides added instead! The Committee did make some "corrections and additions" to the proposals and must have been pleased to see them incorporated in "The Scheme for Girl Guides" published in the Boy Scout Headquarters *Gazette* of November 1909. Edinburgh was one step ahead of this—it gave

"Practical suggestions for Organisation. Where it is desired to start

'Girl Guides', it would be best for ladies interested to form a committee. . .!!''

With all this encouragement, the girls and their leaders worked hard and gave the first public demonstration of Girl Guide work in June 1910 at Bruntsfield School. In July began the task of registering all the girls in Great Britain who had formed themselves into Patrols and Companies. To do this Miss Agnes Baden-Powell, now in charge of Girl Guides, borrowed £100 from her brother and rented a room in Boy Scouts Headquarters in London, asked two friends to help her and in the first month they registered 8000 girls in companies. Amongst these were the 1st Midlothian Coy. at St George's West Church and 2nd Midlothian Coy. at St Stephen's Church, Edinburgh. The 4th Coy. at St Serf's Church and the 8th Coy. at Haymarket soon followed. Other companies were formed and hard at work too, but were not registered until firmly established with officers to lead them.

The Committee in Edinburgh continued its work and in April 1911 it reformed and gave itself the first name, the "Midlothian Girl Guides Central Committee." All the Captains of companies were members, one of them, Miss Louisa Robertson of 2nd Coy., was Secretary and the first constitution was drawn up. This decreed that the committee should:

(1) Confer on practical points in connection with Companies.
(2) Appoint Examiners for Proficiency Badges.
(3) Be the sole means of obtaining badges from Scottish H.Q.
(4) Appoint Captains and help to form companies.
(5) Appoint Visitors to Companies who should not be a Captain or Lieutenant.

Girls were now indeed being supported by willing adults and the young Captains emphasise this in the appointment of "Visitors" who surely began the duties of future Commissioners.

The first "practical point" to be debated, not only in Edinburgh but through the length and breadth of Britain, was "Uniform."

If the 92 girls in the five Edinburgh companies paraded in four different colours in June 1911 for George V's Coronation Day, what was the rainbow-like effect of 400 Scottish Guides who lined the Royal route a month later?

A regulation uniform in blue had been designed and in true democratic fashion everybody's opinions were requested. In December 1911 six out of the eight Edinburgh Companies voted for the new blue uniform (guess who wanted brown!) and that is the colour worn by British Guides to this day.

Finance was the next practical problem for the Committee and the girls, also for the newly-formed Scottish Headquarters and London

Headquarters. After a great deal of debate, it was finally agreed that all members of the Movement would pay 3d per annum to Headquarters' Funds. The ladies on the Committee raised their own subscriptions to 2/6d per annum but many gave generous donations too. They also paid for all the Proficiency Badges gained by the Guides. Public support was not very strong and Miss Agnes Baden-Powell was invited to address a public meeting in February 1913 when the Guides demonstrated ambulance work, signalling and life in camp, and performed a play. £3 1/- was taken.

Numbers were not increasing very quickly at this time and one reason may have been that the Suffragette movement was becoming militant in the "Votes for Women" campaign. However, the girls were still very keen to be Guides, but more leaders were needed.

The first President of Midlothian Girl Guides, Lady Brown, had been elected in March 1912 and on her sudden death in January 1913 Lady Fayrer was appointed; she was the wife of Sir Joseph Fayrer, the Superintendent of the Royal Infirmary. Reorganisation of the Movement was being discussed at all levels and Lady Fayrer, the secretary Miss Robertson and Mrs Hamilton Bruce attended meetings at Scottish H.Q. representing the Midlothian Guides in discussions on the future growth of the Movement.

Literature for Girl Guides was now being published—in 1912 *The Handbook of the Girl Guides or How Girls can help to build up the Empire* gave the girls and their Captains a book of their own and standards for badges were laid down. In January 1913 the first *Girl Guide Diaries* were published by Letts.

Since 1910, *Home Notes* had printed two pages of Guide affairs, including a signed article by the President; those two pages in the weekly magazine must have looked odd between comic pages for children, advice to correspondents on love affairs and fashion pictures of ladies in trailing skirts, wasp waists and huge hats laden with fruit, flowers and feathers! The Guide pictures of camp, first aid, etc., and the uniform of shorter skirts, looser waists and plain felt hats seemed eccentric; but eventually, along with Scout uniform, it was to lead the trend towards more informal, casual clothing for everybody. The *Girl Guide Gazette* was planned to replace the pages in *Home Notes* and came out monthly from January 1914. A Scottish supplement was started in 1920, edited by Miss Anderson of North Division, and lasted some years. The *Gazette* is now called *Guider*. Nearer home, the *Leith Observer* published "Leith Girl Guide Notes" for many years and *The Scotsman* and *Evening News* have published many items on, and pictures of, Edinburgh Guide events.

In 1914, girls were taking part in camps, making a vegetable garden, taking badge tests, planning a cake and candy sale for

November and other exciting things. The Committee were planning to set up East and West Divisions in accordance with B-P's scheme for County and Division Commissioners, when, on 4th August, World War I began which shattered many more plans and dreams than these.

Once more a meeting was called hurriedly, this time to discuss how the Girl Guide Movement could contribute to the War effort. All the wheels were set in motion and the girls were in great demand to help in many ways. The Committee were careful to see that the Guides were not exploited as cheap labour and that all their activities were really worthwhile.

In 1915 a new Company in Leith was formed and Mrs Malcolm Smith was invited on to the Committee to represent Leith. A new company started in Penicuik and also three more in the City.

Miss Young had been Secretary for a while but now she handed over to Miss Mina Brown, daughter of the first President and a Committee member for years. She really organised the secretarial side in Edinburgh, she warranted the Captains and registered the companies; knew everybody from the start and always had a calm answer to every request and query. Mina Brown said years later:

"I often look back on the early days of Guiding with joy; we were like a family—There were eight companies then!"

She laid very good foundations for future secretaries.

Girls were joining the Guide companies in larger numbers and all work continued, with the Captains meeting regularly to organise the rallies and events which were held in spite of the War. There was great enthusiasm and dedication, good discipline and determination to do everything as well as possible and all was done with good humour— the girls wanted to be part of the war effort. Their little sisters were clamouring to join too and "Rosebuds" emerged in 1914, soon to fade and become "Brownies" the next year. The first girls were growing too old to be Guides and the Senior branch was started. All these changes added to the work of the Committee, now chaired by Mrs Boémé; and more changes were on the way.

In 1915 the Headquarters in London was reorganised, a Council was formed as an advisory body and a new Executive Committee, with Sir Robert Baden-Powell in the chair, was elected.

The system of appointing a Commissioner for each County was initiated and by 1916 the Founder's wife, Lady Baden-Powell, was taking an increasing share of the work of the Guide Movement. She wrote to people all over the country asking them to take an interest in the Guides of their own County by becoming Commissioners or members of local associations. In October the first conference was held in Matlock, Derbyshire, and a month later a meeting at Scottish Headquarters of representatives from all over Scotland decided that each Scottish County should have a Guide Commissioner. Because of their size, Edinburgh and Glasgow were designated as Guide "Counties"—so Midlothian separated from Edinburgh. After consulting Mrs Malcolm Smith, the new name became "The Edinburgh & Leith Girl Guides."

The 5th Coy. in Penicuik and 11th Coy. in Corstorphine went to Midlothian County, the latter now became the new 1st Midlothian, only to become 73rd Edinburgh in 1920 when the city boundaries were changed. This is a hazard to be faced whenever local authorities alter their areas and regionalisation in 1975 caused many such problems. The first County Commissioner for Edinburgh & Leith was Mrs Laurie who had tested the naturalist badge for four years; one who knew her says:

"Mrs Laurie was small, slight and auburn haired and full of energy; she was like a meteor flashing into the quiet Committee and gave herself utterly to work for the girls."

She also became Commissioner for Senior Guides on the Scottish Executive Committee formed at the first Scottish Conference in Perth in September 1917 and represented Girl Guides on the Advisory Committee on Juvenile Employment set up by the School Board. This latter appointment showed an early appreciation of the good training girls received in the Movement.

Official recognition of the Girl Guides by the Government had come on 24th September 1915 with the granting of the Charter of Incorporation. Royal recognition came in 1922 when King George V granted a Royal Charter to the Girl Guides Association; there have been supplemental Charters in 1949, 1960, 1971 and changes are suggested in 1976—truly the Movement moves with the times.

Early in 1918 the title of Chief Guide was conferred on Lady Baden-Powell, her husband had been Chief Scout since the beginning of the Scout Movement. B-P had also suggested that the term "Guider" should be used instead of "officer"; this was disliked by some but gradually came into use and there were Guiders for Guides long before there were Scouters for Scouts. Brownie Captains became Brown Owls at this time too.

Some of the first Commissioners had not been enrolled as Guides and felt that they could not expect others to make the Promise unless they were dedicated in the same way. When Lady Baden-Powell enrolled some Commissioners at that first conference in Matlock in 1916, it was seen that one did not have to be a girl to become a Guide and many adults since then have joined the Movement giving much valuable service.

Now that the foundations of the national movement had been

Mrs Laurie setting the example at a Fire Drill Demonstration in 1917.

established, the local Committee in Edinburgh revised its plans for dividing the City. North, South, East and West Divisions were formed, one each in Central and Leith made six. Early Commissioners were the Misses Anderson, Anstruther, Blaikie, Cornish, Millar, Salmon, Stagg, Stewart and Wood and Mrs Kennedy. Miss Brown was still Secretary, but Mrs Laurie had resigned owing to ill-health.

Miss Lilias Dalmahoy was appointed County Commissioner in March 1918; she was an excellent person to build up the new team. A General's daughter, she expected and usually got the very best in achievement, appearance and discipline. She had boundless friendship and swept all along wth her own enthusiasm and charm—as one of her friends says:

"Only Lil could have charmed all the helpers into *paying* 2/6d entrance fee into the famous sale in 1928 and then worked us 'til we dropped!"

However, the original Committee found that they were losing touch with the girls as the new Commissioners visited the units in their divisions, the ladies felt that after doing the spade work for nine years in accordance with the 1911 Constitution "their position had become a mere sinecure." After much discussion and consultation, these ladies wrote to Miss Dalmahoy with great wisdom and offered her "their help in any way she thought they could be of service."

Local Associations or support groups were being formed elsewhere but all felt this did not entirely meet the need in a big city, so the Council of the City of Edinburgh Girl Guides came into being. Mr James Stevenson (later Lord Stevenson) was elected Chairman and the members included 13 gentlemen and 16 ladies, amongst whom were the following original members: Lady Fayrer, President; Lady Clyde and Mrs Boémé, Vice-Presidents; and Mrs Baird Laing, Lady Malcolm Smith, Mrs Mackintosh, Miss Robertson, Miss McLeod and Miss Mina Brown. Many of these ladies were presented with Thanks badges at a Council meeting 15 years later and were told that any Guide would offer to help them on seeing the badge.

The Constitution of the Council was laid down but the task of policy making was left in the hands of the Executive Committee. In 1920 the County Secretary reported that there were 83 Companies in Edinburgh with 2335 Guides and Brownies. Fifty-five Companies were attached to churches, ten in boarding schools, three in the villages of Corstorphine, Juniper Green and Slateford, and the rest in girls' clubs, Y.W.C.A., the Rubber Works or unattached. What a remarkable growth from those first Patrols meeting in gardens!

4

Brownie Guides

THE YOUNGER SISTERS of the first Scouts and Guides were not going to be left out of this exciting game, so they formed their own small groups called Rosebuds and these were officially recognised in 1914. When the Founder was asked for his ideas for a better name for these energetic little people, he remembered a story about Tommy, Betty and a Brownie; this caught the girls' imagination and "Brownies" they are to this day. This story is told to every new Brownie just as it was told to six Edinburgh Rosebuds in 1916. Many groups of Brownies met all over the City for the next two years but the first to be registered taking the number of the Guide Company, was the 2nd Edinburgh & Leith Pack at St Stephen's Church on 3rd March 1918; followed soon by the 14th, the 12th and the 4th Packs. The numbers grew quickly to 493 Brownies in 31 Packs in 1919—now, in 1976, there are 5125 Brownies in 243 Packs in the City of Edinburgh.

Each Brownie must understand the Law and Promise on which the whole Movement is based before she is enrolled (or "unrolled" as one small recruit put it!) in a Pack, and Brownie Guiders help the Brownies to grow in the understanding of their duty to God by including prayers at all meetings, often using the Brownie Guide Prayerbook. The new Brownie then becomes one of a "Six" in a Pack which should not have more than 24 Brownies, and she takes her place in the Brownie Ring. Here she sings the Brownie Guide Song:

> We're Brownie Guides, we're Brownie Guides,
> we're here to lend a hand,
> To love our God and serve our Queen and help
> our homes and lands,
> We've Brownie friends—we've Brownie friends
> in North, South, East and West—
> We're joined together in our wish to try to
> do our best.

But the first song sung by Edinburgh Brownies was written by the father of Miss Janet Warwick, an officer of the 14th Pack, and he paid for 100 copies which were used at a presentation of badges in the Lauriston Hall on 16th March 1918.

After a Brownie made her promise she began her "Golden Bar," or Second Class tests, which could be taken one at a time. These

21

consisted of a number of skills which each Brownie had to do, such as skipping 20 times backwards, sewing on buttons in two ways and knowing the composition of the Union Flag. When a Brownie reached "Golden Hand," or First Class stage, she had to do all the tests at one time or have a record of having already done some of the clauses, such as laying and lighting a fire, first aid, semaphore, knitting and throwing a ball overarm. Only after a Brownie had passed her Golden Hand was she able to enter for proficiency badges. If she passed her Golden Hand before her eleventh birthday, she could "Fly-up" to Guides and wear her Brownie wings on her Guide uniform to show that she had been a First Class Brownie. Over the years the Brownie tests were kept up to date and at the Brownie conference in Harrogate in 1937 when the question of road safety was discussed it was suggested that Brownies should know something of the working of traffic lights which, along with Belisha beacons (now called Zebra crossings), had just been introduced. The question of firelighting came up often and finally an alternative had to be given—washing and ironing a tie—not nearly so exciting! Gradually the rather rigid system of tests was altered and Brownies were given more choice. The Golden Ladder Test was introduced to help Brownies who found the Golden Hand too difficult. This, like the Golden Bar, was tested clause by clause and helped the less confident child. Not until a conference in 1959 was a Brownie allowed to take two proficiency badges after she had passed her Golden Bar and before completing her Golden Hand.

In 1968 there was a radical change when the Eight Point Programme was adopted. The Promise became three-fold like that of the Guides and the salute three fingered; but the biggest change was in the "test work." No longer were there Golden Bars, Ladders and Hands with set standards; they were replaced by "Journeys" on which a Brownie could go at her own pace; challenges were made to suit each individual Brownie. The Journeys are called "Footpath, Road and Highway"; all have eight challenges in line with the new programme. As well as undertaking Journeys, a Brownie can take part in "Ventures" which are chosen and planned by the whole Pack. During a Pack Venture a Brownie may find she has completed one or more of the challenges for her Journey Badge. Ventures can be long or short, collecting used stamps, making and taking presents to old people and entertaining them, going to the trampoline centre, swimming, mannequin parades, coffee mornings and many, many more. Some are very successful and some are not. One Pack decided to plant crocus bulbs to give at Christmas to the local old people whom they were entertaining. These were duly left in the cupboard in the dark, but when the Brownies later looked at them hopefully, they found that a mouse had visited their cupboard and made a very good meal of their precious gifts; so other plans had to be made hastily in order not to disappoint the old people.

One Pack had a Brownie who had been to Butlin's for her summer holidays so she suggested that the Pack might have a beauty queen competition. This was done—but not in swimsuits in a church hall in November! The Brownies had to practise walking well and were judged on hair, hands, uniform and deportment by a beauty consultant and a gymnast. The later mannequin parade also had the Brownies walking tall to a Brownie accompanist, in an amazing collection of their own clothes. Music can play a part in Ventures as in the music competition when the schoolgirl judge (now a lawyer!) tactfully commended the violinists on the way they held their bows.

The 146 'A' Barclay Bruntsfield Pack enjoyed a Venture that brought them nationwide publicity. They entered "Our Tollcross" for the Youth Competition to mark Architectural Heritage Year. For this the Brownies went out into their neighbourhood, interviewed people and produced enough drawings and comment to fill eight pages of brown wrapping paper which they made into a scrapbook. The judges who awarded a Special Commendation Prize gave the following comments: "This highly amusing presentation was, at the same time, thoroughly informative and educational. It was produced with all the uninhibited charm of the young, and has much to tell modern society in its study of a residential area. In particular, the children, who were between 7 and 10 years old, held traffic surveys during the day and also conducted interviews with local characters. Altogether a delightful and instructive entry."

When this report was read to the Brownies, they received it openmouthed. They did not realise they had been drawing and writing a tiny piece of history!

This was not all, however. Twelve Brownies from the Pack were invited to the Assembly Rooms on 12th February 1976, along with the other prize-winners and various civic representatives, to meet H.R.H. Princess Alexandra and to receive their awards from her. A Brownie presented the bouquet to the Princess and everybody was entertained to a three-course lunch, finishing with a very large helping of chocolate gâteau and ice-cream.

In the Eight Point Programme a Brownie was allowed, for the first time, to take Interest Badges as soon as she was enrolled; this led to an increase in the number of badges taken and more and more mothers and kind friends being asked to test them. Brownies are bursting with enthusiasm to take as many badges as they can and do not necessarily understand that ambition and realism should always go together—like the Brownie who was so keen to take her Animal Lover's Badge but had not kept a pet for two years—and the other who, having observed all the exotic birds in a book, was sent back to watch the humble sparrows and blackbirds in her own back garden before coming to the test for the Discoverer's Badge.   At this age little girls are quite uninhibited and all of life is a great adventure, which makes a

Look what we did!

Badge test fun for Brownies and Testers alike.   Brownies like to be tested in every single clause and woe betide the Tester who omits a question; she will soon be reminded, or there will be complaints, as in the case of one Brownie who protested loudly that she had not been allowed to *wash* her silver toast-rack after polishing it.

What have the Brownies done at their meetings during the years?

A Brownie Guider of the 1920s and 30s, Miss Annie Duncan, said that the Brownies practised Morse, first aid, followed tracking signs made with wool on the gorse bushes, tied knots, laid the table and tied up parcels. Her Pack had a Tawny Owl from Trinidad who brought banana leaves so that the Brownies could practise tying up parcels with the leaves instead of using paper!

Another Brownie Pack made custard one evening and one was thrilled when the minister ate hers!

It was not all work, however, the Brownies enjoying picnics, visiting the Zoo and revels. The Brownies also did good turns. On each Armistice Sunday the children took gifts of fruit, sweets and cigarettes to the disabled servicemen. This was continued until 1940 at Newington House. Toys were also gathered and taken to Douglas House for convalescent children.

Handcrafts have also played a big part in the Brownie Programme. In 1951 there was a Brownie Empire Exhibition in London. Brownies made puppets dressed in uniforms of overseas Brownies and models of their homes. From the many made in Edinburgh, the model home of the 13th Pack and the puppets of the 155th Pack were sent to the London Exhibition.

In Glasgow there was a Brownie Exhibition from 26th-31st May 1952 which included handcrafts, nature, equipment and a Brownie Pack demonstration. On 31st May, Kathleen Morrison from 106th Pack (North West Division) opened the Exhibition; she also spoke at the following Scottish Annual General Meeting.

Since 1968 Edinburgh has had competitions for puppets, Easter eggs, model villages and paintings. For the 1975 World Conference in Sussex, the gifts the Brownies made, such as bookmarks, napkin rings and painted stones, were of a very high standard. More recently there was the Egg Marketing Board Competition for decorated eggs when Claire MacNaughton of Liberton Kirk Brownie Pack won the Brownie class.

Children with handicaps of all kinds have been welcomed and are able to enjoy the Brownie programme.

The first Brownie Revels recorded were on 26th May 1923, but surely the most memorable must have been the Revels to celebrate King George VI's Coronation in 1937 when 3000 Brownies went to the Zoo and had a tea party on the hill. The Packs came by train and tram, each was formed into a "chariot" encircled by red, white or blue braid with a driver to head them in the right direction. After seeing all the animals they went to the top field where the Treasurer received the gifts they had made for local charities, each Pack galloped up to him with their gift and returned to their place. The Melville Club helped with the blind Brownies that day and still remember how difficult it was to explain what a monkey looked like—let alone its antics! Afterwards there was a letter from the secretary of the Zoo to say that they had never had a visit from a better behaved organisation and that not even a tram ticket was left behind on the picnic ground.

In 1964 Portobello & Niddrie Division celebrated the Brownie Golden Jubilee by taking 400 Brownies to the Zoo. (A Pack from outside Edinburgh, to its surprise, was ushered into the queue by the Division Commissioner, apparently not content with 400 Brownies of her own!) The Brownies donated yellow rose bushes to the Zoo to celebrate the event. It was hoped that the Jubilee cake would be lowered from a helicopter to the waiting throng of Brownies on the top of the Zoo hill, but it was prevented from leaving Aberdeen because of the typhoid epidemic there. The Royal Navy, however, came to the rescue and sent the pilot in full regalia, his wife and two Brownie daughters. They presented the Division with a picture of two naval jet fighters and this is now in Headquarters.

As well as ordinary Pack meetings and Revels, there have been a number of memorable occasions for Brownies. In a Pack scrap book an unknown Brownie in 1935 writes "The Tree Planting Ceremony."

"It was a fairly good day when a Brownie, two Guides, our Brown Owl and I met at West Mayfield. We took a tram car to the Braid Hill terminus, and walked down steps into a field through which the Braid Burn flows. When we reached the field we began to look for our two cherry trees. The Company's tree and the Pack's tree were beside each other. After finding them, we went in search of Brown Owl's which was close to the burn. Then returning to our own tree we waited for the Pack to turn up. They came by the train a quarter of an hour later.

"Ten minutes later the ceremony began. First of all the guard of honour marched down in front of the platform. The Lord Provost's daughter and some members of the Town Council stood around the Lord Provost as he planted his tree, then a whistle was blown and all the trees were planted. The band struck up and the Tree Song was sung.

"After the Lord Provost had made his speech, and a bouquet had been presented to his daughter, he was presented with the Scroll by a Ranger, a Guide and a Brownie. The last event was the sending of a telegram to the King, a final three cheers, 'God Save the King' and then we went home."

A 1976 view of Brownies is given by Mrs Jane Forbes, a Brownie Guider: "Brownie Packs meet all over the City in Community and Church Halls and Schools, anywhere in fact where there is room, since a great deal of space is preferable. The girls, aged 7-10 years, meet for an hour and a half each week when they come together in the Brownie Ring, going on to play games. Part of the evening may be spent in the 'Six' homes talking about future activities and getting to know one another. During the winter months the 'old favourites' in the running around games and some playground varieties are popular. We try to cover at least two of the eight points of the programme each week and have an occasional handcrafts evening. Each year Hallowe'en and Guy Fawkes Nights are fun and much hilarity was raised when the 'wicked wizard' appeared this year clad in black cloak and fearsome mask carrying a crash helmet. An amazed Brownie declared later, 'Brown Owl, I saw the wizard going up Dalry Road on a motor bike!' We try to have a highlight each term and a Christmas Venture proved a success. After raising money at a coffee morning we set off to buy food for food parcels for local old folk. We had suggestions of everything from tinned carrots to buttons! Packing the parcels was also fun and we delivered them in time for Christmas.

"In the spring term our thoughts were largely focused on our 'Journey into Spring,' an overnight Venture to Stanemuir, where eighteen Brownies made spring charts, bookmarks and scrap books and decorated Easter eggs. Here the Brownies had their first taste of the fun of living with a number of other girls if only for a short time, a glimpse into the future of Pack Holidays, Guide Camps and Ranger adventures.

"The summer term brings outdoor activities and Brownies go to the Baths or Zoo and, of course, they have Brownie Revels. A parents' evening with the presentation of badges makes a good end to the year and a time to say 'goodbye' to those Brownies who go on up to the Guides the following autumn.

"An evening with Brownies is never dull, seldom peaceful, frequently exhausting and always different and one inevitably misses those good Sixers when they leave to become 'wee Guides' but, we hope, eventually to return as 'our Pack Leader'!"

The transition of Brownies to Guides is much more flexible now but it is still marked by a ceremony devised by the Pack—some are launched in space capsules, some compose songs, some go along the road on stilts, roller skates or pogo sticks. One Pack regularly suggests being carried up to the Company on a real stretcher—this is good practice for the Guides, but one wonders if being a Brownie has really been so exhausting! For the success of these ceremonies, the Pack Leader's help in explaining them to the Guide Company is invaluable.

Brownie Packs depend very much on their Guiders, but who are these people? They are office workers, mums, teachers, students and a whole variety of women who willingly give up not only the hour or so of meeting time each week but also much more time in thought and preparation. If 24 Brownies want to make puppets, then all the material must be made ready and plenty of needle threaders available.

To help Guiders run their Packs they have the appropriate handbooks, trainings by their District Commissioner or Trainers, and the exchange of ideas at district meetings. The Brownies, however, have had a large say in the planning of the programme so the Guiders may need help in the carrying out of a venture, *e.g.* for a music venture a tone-deaf Guider may have to ask a musical friend to come to part of a few meetings, or in the case of interest badges a nurse may come to teach first aid. Brownie Guiders are not supposed to know all the answers but should know where to find them.

From time to time Brownie Conferences have been held, the last three being in 1956 and 1959 at Wimbledon and in 1962 at Durham. Representatives from all parts of the U.K. met to discuss the proposed changes in the Brownie programme, taking into consideration the opinions of all the counties. These conferences were not all work—there was plenty of fun and fellowship. At one conference Miss Chater introduced a "Brownie's Dozen"—imagine dozens and dozens of Guiders doing "Harry McGarry" on the lawn, bringing it back to Guiders in their own counties and so on down to the Brownies themselves. Ideas for games, handcrafts, nature and all the other activities, filled notebooks, all to be brought back to Guiders at home. At Durham it fell to the Scots to entertain the company, so Andrina Wilson wrote a skit to some Gilbert and Sullivan tunes, and even the non-singers from Edinburgh were able to take part! This was just one way to show that there is a lighter side to being a Brownie Guider.

PACK HOLIDAYS

During the early 1930s Lady Balfour of Burleigh offered Pinkie House, Musselburgh, as an indoor camp, to Edinburgh Guides; as Guides did not camp indoors then it was suggested that Miss May Corson should take her Brownies there in the company of Miss Ella Dickie who had her Camper's Licence. However, it was discovered that there was a special qualification that could be taken and, on enquiring, Miss Corson found that no one in Scotland could tell her about it! But Imperial Headquarters were able to help, and sent a question paper to Edinburgh. May Corson duly qualified and the very first PACK HOLIDAY in Scotland was held. Can you imagine the fun gathering together all the beds, cups, plates, knives, forks, pots and pans and all the other things that would be needed? The rooms which Lady Balfour was giving them were empty and the Brownies and their Guiders had to improvise their home for a week. The weather was fine for the holiday so they were able to eat in the yard, which was as well since the kitchen was far away from the other rooms. The whole holiday was great fun, very near home and just the first of many Pack Holidays held by May Corson and all those she has trained and tested over the years. All the early Pack Holidays were held in empty houses, schools or village halls. Happy memories remain of the holidays at the Harvesters' Houses which were approached through an avenue of trees. The Brownies were able to make tree houses and there they had tea in the afternoons, sometimes being visited by the Countess of Dalkeith.

At Pack Holidays lots of exciting things happen. One Pack had their mascot with them, a teddy called Hamish. During rest hour one day Hamish was kidnapped; but he managed to unravel his jumper so that the Brownies would be able to follow the wool to try to rescue him. Well! . . . the Brownies were so upset about Hamish that when they met the village policeman they told him that Hamish had disappeared. The policeman joined in the hunt for Hamish and Brown Owl had some difficult explaining to do!

After using schools and halls for years, some far-sighted people decided to build special houses for Pack Holidays. Miss Andrina Wilson helped with the design of the Lady Thomson Memorial Pack Holiday House in the walled garden at Netherurd. This was opened by the Chief Guide on 1st June 1956, surrounded by Brownies from all over Scotland, including quite a number from Edinburgh.

Edinburgh's own adventure Centre, Stanemuir, was opened on 19th June 1971 by Mrs Denholm, the Scottish Chief Commissioner, with Brownies, Guides and Rangers from every division clustered round her. The first Pack Holiday in the centre was held by Miss Janette Simpson of the 9th "A" Pack (London Road Church) in July of that year. Since then, many Edinburgh Packs have had adventurous holidays in Stanemuir.

Pack Holidays are still fun whether they are held in a special house, or in a school where the Brownies have to improvise as they did over 40 years ago. Some of the improvised places give rise to such comments as, "Why did you not bring the washing machine, Brown Owl?"

Year after year we hear of Brownies choosing to have Peter Pan, Winnie the Pooh, Alice in Wonderland or Robin Hood holidays with appropriate names for the Brownies and Guiders. They have Mad Hatter's tea parties, go off to search for the North Pole or for the Lost Boys or for Dr Who!

Brownies make some presents to take home; some knit squares for blankets, and some have the excitement of lighting a real fire or peeling potatoes, or even making apple meringue pie. How wonderful it would be if every Brownie could have these magical experiences.

5

Guides

I AM A GUIDE—said with pride at all ages but felt more deeply by the girl between 10 and 16 years old who carries the name of the whole Movement. Lucky is the girl who spends those years as a Guide—having grown out of the spontaneity and enthusiasm for everything which marks the Brownie period into the formative years when she becomes more choosy. During these vital years she needs guidance especially in the permissive society of the Seventies which gives her all the choice and little direction. Guidance is needed before entering the Ranger age with its extra excitements but with added responsibilities soon thrust upon her now that the age of majority is 18 years.

Because a girl is much more free to "do her own thing," so must she give much more thought to the things she wants to do.

Because she starts in a Patrol, a family group of differing ages, who discuss their plans together, she gets used to thinking things through. Maybe what is finally decided is not just what she wants as five other girls are involved, and also, the whole Patrol must fall in with the plans made for the whole Company. This is where B-P was so wise, with the small number of 36 the Guider gets to know each Guide and in time knows the part each plays in the life of the company.

The pivot around which the Guide Movement rotates is the meeting. Every week some adults and more children spend a certain length of time with each other entirely voluntarily—they are all there just because they want to be there!

The spontaneous beginning of the Movement arose from girls meeting together to enjoy new activities out of doors. Inevitably, the early meetings had a military air because almost every family in the land had seen a loved father or brother off to the War, and the girls wanted to show that they could do their bit. Uniform was a great attraction with so many adults already wearing that of the different Services, therefore pride in their appearance, marching, signalling and first aid figured largely at Guide meetings, and service of all kinds was a major part of their programme.

Girls left school at 14 then and went straight to work in domestic service, shops, offices or factories. Their long hours were matched by their mothers', whose household chores were wearisome without the aids which the advent of electricity has brought. At the end of the day there was little to do and very little money to spare. Guide meetings provided the relaxation and exercise, the interest and the fun that these girls needed, and they flocked to join the Movement. Units of 50 girls were heard of even then!

In Units such as those in the Rubber Works and University Settlement, girls fulfilled B-P's aims in developing their own abilities in undreamt-of ways. Working all together and taking part in Shield competitions against girls with better advantages, encouraged by their Guiders to strive towards a new goal, these girls saw a wider vision and they reached out for new jobs and higher standards.

Great social changes took place between the World Wars, the General Strike and Financial Crisis affected every home. Guide meetings were a stable part of a girl's life, everyone there was committed to the same Promise and ideals, everyone "talking the same language"; so different from the changing standards all around them. Edinburgh Guiders tell many tales of the achievements of their Guides in a wide variety of activities, all kinds of crafts like leather work, basketry and embroidery were tried, Country Dancing was very popular and, then as now, teams entered in the Music Festival; the Guide Choir was thriving too. All these arts were practised at meetings as well as inspection, badge work, and "camp fire" making "Guides" a safe anchorage in a bewildering world.

All Guides had to take the same tests to achieve their 2nd Class Badge and when going on to take other badges the testers required a set standard (80% pass mark) and this meant hard sustained work during Guide meetings. Prowess in tree climbing, however, was not a requirement as one small girl discovered when she tearfully said, "I'd love to be a Girl Guide but I expect you won't have me as I can't climb a tree."

The Second World War must have affected Guide meetings considerably; many girls were evacuated and the black-out stopped the meetings until it was decided, after a slight relaxation, that girls were better employed in a meeting than hanging around the streets! Patrol Leaders took more responsibility as so many Guiders were away and Edinburgh Guiding circles were proud of the way these girls responded. "Be Prepared" has been the motto and many Guides have been surprised to find how well prepared they have been to rise to an occasion.

There must have been more Lone Guides at this period than ever before; these were Guides who lived in places where no company held meetings. Lones were the earliest off-shoot from the main Movement as many girls at the very beginning worked at Guiding by themselves with a letter a month from their Guider. In 1919 the Lone Branch was formed with Miss Victoria Bruce being responsible for the Scottish Branch. Edinburgh had a county Lone Secretary to keep in touch with Lone Guides until Miss Thomson Clay retired in 1955.

The upheaval of War changed social patterns again. Many more people had travelled about the world and were not content to return to the old grooves in 1945, family units split up and new ideas and new standards were creeping into family life. The Guide Movement gave a stable, secure meeting place for girls but young people were maturing earlier and with the Founder's ideals and aims very much in mind, the programme for the Guide Movement in the United Kingdom was reorganised.

In 1968, the new Eight-Point Programme changed the weekly meetings utterly. Instead of every girl following the same pattern of tests, the new programme was geared to the individual development of each girl towards a fuller understanding of the three-fold Guide Promise. With nearly a decade behind it, the Programme can be seen to be fulfilling its promise. Patrol and Company activities are the starting point: "If we're going to camp, we'll need to cook our dinner, so we'd better work out menus and collect recipes, and practise how to light a fire outside," or "When we go to help at the Hospital we'll have to be useful, so perhaps my auntie will teach us how to make beds properly."

So today's Guide sees Patrol and Company enterprises as opportunities for the fun of challenge, and an undertaking such as a unit Party provides the setting for ploys ranging from the designing, making and safe delivery of invitations, to discovering what kind of entertainment pensioner guests will most enjoy. One and the same activity will give to shy wee Jeannie the chance to show she is capable of welcoming guests at the door, and to older Alice the responsiblity of organising the musical items performed by her patrol.

From when she first joins the Guide unit, each girl is encouraged and helped to assess her own starting level in each of the Eight Points, and to set herself her own goals. A group of recruits, working out how to prepare for their promise by a challenge connected with "Becoming a Homemaker," will come up with answers as different as themselves: Pat, well used to cooking at home, decides that she will cook and serve the family's Sunday lunch entirely on her own, while Anne, with no background knowledge at all, will, for the first time ever, make a packet-mix cake and bring it for her Patrol to sample, and Jill will ask her Dad to teach her how to change a fuse.

With this new approach to Guiding, the Patrols have made rapid strides as self-programming groups. From merely coping with thirty minutes on their own in a weekly meeting run by the Guider, Patrols have moved enthusiastically to a point where they clamour for the whole meeting to be "Patrol Time." The Patrol-meeting in the P.L.'s house is no longer wishful thinking, but reality, and Patrols have organised successful parties, hush-ins, exploration of the Royal Mile, visits to the Commonwealth Pool, candle-making sessions, baking evenings and service projects to meet local needs.

The Guides often discovered that a completed project had covered several of the Eight Points of the Programme; for instance, one Patrol, who compiled a scrapbook of their locality found that they had even "Enjoyed the Out of Doors" in collecting material for the book! Another Patrol decided to make gifts for those in an Old People's Home and a Children's Home and found themselves happily involved in five Points of the Programme. It is true that one can no longer predict that every Guide will know how to make a bed with hospital corners, or be able to signal in Morse, or light a fire outdoors with two matches. But every Guide will, instead, be exploring and enjoying the world about her through the Eight Point Programme, learning new skills, improving standards, challenging herself to go on and to go further.

Three Guides going further.

This completely new approach was a tremendous challenge to the Guiders, who were used to the set routine of the past and found some of the new ideas rather strange. However, Guides and Guiders went adventuring together and soon the Programme was no longer "new." A Guider describes a Guide meeting in these words:

"Groups of girls of mixed ages are sitting around tables and some are chatting quietly while others are arguing loudly, all of them are planning programmes and activities to cover some of the Eight points.

"Perhaps that scene represents Guiding for you? In many cases our accommodation is limited but the enthusiastic approach of the Guides makes us oblivious to our surroundings. What is the magic of the Patrol? It is the essence of our whole programme with its relationships and group participation. Many facets of Guiding can be displayed by the patrol in action—camp, outdoor and indoor activities and service projects large and small."

A Guider often arrives for a Company meeting wondering what the evening will bring, only to be pleasantly surprised by her Guides; a Patrol project has been successful and a shy Guide has taken her first step in friendship.

Yes. There is fun, fellowship and friendship if

"We are prepared to give to all
Both great and small
All we can give."

Some Guide meetings are special! Nearly every girl will remember her enrolment meeting, with only the company and perhaps her own parents, or part of a larger meeting or else out of doors as this Guide recalls:

"I was enrolled in the 1930s when the Company was on a day hike to Cramond. As we stood in formation in the field with the Colours flying, the sun shining and the sound of the sea and the bird song around us, a horse came to the open end of the horseshoe and calmly continued munching the grass. For me this made the perfect natural background as I made my Promise."

For the Guider who enrols the girl this moment is just as important, one remembers:

"I enrolled a girl whose parents were both deaf and dumb and she had only just learned to talk; nerves and excitement made the new recruit have even greater difficulty in talking. In absolute silence everyone willed her to complete her Promise, particularly her own Patrol who, from the first, had truly taken her in as one of them. I shall never forget the look on our new Guide's face as I pinned on her Trefoil badge."

Two ten-year-old recruits in the Canary Patrol of the 202nd Company write:

"On Friday night we had a parents' evening. It was to start at 7.30 p.m. and to end at 9.30 p.m. Then the Parents began to arrive. First we started with a horseshoe Formation. Then it was our turn; we were feeling very nervous because we were getting inrolled and our own parents were there watching us. After we were inrolled some people got interest bages. One Guide got a Queen's Guide bage. Next we had our plays. First came Cinderella next The Wizard of Oz and then the Elf and the Shoemaker. Then the lights went out and we could not see a thing. Then we started to sing. After that we had something to eat and drink. When we were all full Lorna the Queens Guide cut her cake and her Father took a photograph.''

A Queen's Guide presentation is an exciting meeting when so many, who have helped and encouraged the successful Guide, share the thrill of her achievement; her Patrol and Guiders, her parents, badge testers and other friends. Having gained the highest award as a Guide, she now seeks challenges in a wider field of service.

Davidson's Mains district had a Queen's Guide, Diana Frost, who took up the challenge; she went to Uganda on a year's project for Voluntary Service Overseas before starting university studies. She worked at a school for blind children in Iganga in Uganda, and on her return showed her slides and talked about her experiences at a District Thinking Day meeting in 1968. She fired everyone with such enthusiasm that they decided to help, and they held a jumble sale and

Thinking Day, 1968.

sent £80 for the school in Iganga, through the Royal Commonwealth Society for the Blind in Edinburgh. Here is the Society's report on their gift:

"During the Christmas holidays a brick Clay Processor was built at the side of the Braille Classroom at Iganga. The School contributed to the cost of the building but the main part was bought out of the magnificent gift of £80 from the Guides and Brownies of Cramond and Davidson's Mains, Edinburgh.

"The Processer measures 12 ft. by 6 ft. and has 3 compartments for preserving and converting natural clay into modelling material for the children's use. The blind children love modelling and this equipment will enable them to do it more often than they could in the past. They will have lots of fun and also learn to make the shapes which they can 'see' with their fingers, thus aiding their understanding of the world around them. For this they will always be grateful to the Guides and Brownies in Edinburgh."

The world-wide concept of the Movement is brought right into a Guide meeting through projects like this and a girl begins to realise that she is one of a vast sisterhood of Guides. A young Edinburgh Guider, Janet Young, went as an Aide to the 22nd World Conference in Brighton, Sussex, where she saw the delegates from 93 countries working together in friendship and understanding. Throughout all their deliberations the focal point was that the Guide, one girl, whether European, American, Australasian or African, was at the centre of everything.

That one girl—offered the challenge of Guiding—is drawn into her Patrol where everyone expects her to do her best; in the modern exciting programme she accepts that self-discipline and the keeping of her Promise is all important.

The Guide Promise and Laws are the basic part of the Movement. Guiders are often seriously concerned about their application to themselves and the Guides in their care; they are sometimes faced with a bland or defiant assertion—I don't believe in God! Well, what do they do about that? Often this can happen when a girl's feelings are too private and precious to bear discussion. If there is defiance, it can be a great cry for help, from a troubled mind or spirit, that says, "Notice me!" Then the help must come first, in the guise of a direct contact and friendly concern—the rest may well follow. But there are also conscious Christians and unconscious ones; a baby cannot re-affirm the baptismal vows made for her until she is old enough to do so; she is an unconscious Christian. Till then, she is led by the example and care of her parents and friends; may not the Guiders join in, talking about their own beliefs, helping in just a little way to bring her to her own decision?

Guiders should not be too discouraged if the Guides seem to be sceptical; for the first part of the Promise, "duty to God," is passing on His love and care to those all around them. This is being a Guide.

There are suggestions from time to time of changing the words of the Promise—of making it more humanistic and leaving God out of it. Guides should remember that the Promise was given to the Movement by the Founder who was a man of deep religious conviction. He saw ''duty to God'' as the central meaning of the Scout and Guide Movement, all else stemming from this high ideal.

6

Ranger Guides

THREE WORDS STAND OUT clearly in the six decades of the story of Edinburgh Rangers: service, laughter and energy. From the earliest days of being Senior Guide Patrols in Guide companies to the present District Ranger Units, Rangers have been the "back room girls" at almost every event in the County, and have also been the vanguard on many occasions, as representatives abroad, as Colour Bearers, giving displays of skills, and instigating many ploys for others to follow.

About 1916, girls who had joined the Movement at the beginning became too old for the Guide Company and formed Senior Patrols. These groups continued until 1917 when London H.Q. thought seriously about doing something for the older girls and what they should be called. There were some wonderful suggestions, such as Pilots, Pioneers, Torchbearers, but most precious of all, Eagerhearts! As usual, Sir Robert Baden-Powell came up with the sane answer, and Rangers arrived, to continue throughout the years, forming Sea Ranger Crews, Air Ranger Flights, Red Cross Detachments and Cadet Ranger Companies. One company, called "Young Guiders Training Corps," was started in Edinburgh by Mary Sutherland in 1920, and she later started a Cadet Ranger Company in 1929 for the students at Moray House. The adoption of the name "Cadet" by some Ranger Companies is interesting. Baden-Powell said, "Why should boys have all the fun" of Cadet Corps in school and thought it a great injustice to girls that they too could not be Cadets. When Ranger Companies started up in girls' schools, Baden-Powell suggested that they should be called Cadet Ranger Corps. There the girls were taught all the things which enabled them to become leaders in the Movement when they left school, and they were helped to understand the purpose of the various tests and the ways of leadership.

Some of the earliest recorded Ranger Companies were the 4th St Serf's formed from a Senior Patrol. The 21st, with 19 girls in St David's Church, Morrison Street (this number was revived for the Trefoil School Company in 1966) and the 13th Company at St James' Episcopal Church, Leith. Then in the 1920s more Companies were registered and amongst those were the 75th St Giles' in Central District and St Margaret's as Division Rangers in West. It is interesting to find that two Edinburgh County Commissioners, one Scottish Ranger Commissioner and three County Ranger Advisers were all Rangers with the 75th Company.

While there was a Ranger syllabus by this time a great deal of initiative and imagination was required by the early Guiders to keep the interests of these older girls. Outside interests were not so numerous as they are today, but the Rangers were a happy, busy crowd doing the feminine things expected of them! Service to others, particularly hospital work, was popular, and from the "Sick Kids" in Grange to the Hospice in Abbeyhill the girls were in great demand. In April 1929, thirteen different Companies were helping in various hospitals. One must remember this entailed a great deal of work for the Guiders as there were fewer telephones then and most arrangements had to be made at meetings or, in emergencies, by calling at the homes of the Rangers, when Guiders might find themselves climbing to the top floor of Lawnmarket and High Street houses or wending their way through the maze of a housing estate.

In 1926 the 12th Voluntary Aid Detachment was formed by Miss Mina Brown; all the volunteers were members of the Guide Movement and more than 40 Guiders and Rangers met in Guide H.Q. for lectures and practical work, and sat exams yearly for Advanced Certificates. In 1927 they entered for the Rosebery Cup, open to all Edinburgh Junior Detachments and won with very high marks. A senior team under Miss Duncan won both County and Scottish events. From there they went to the finals in London and won again, and repeated the performance in 1928. This highly efficient group worked in hospital wards and Out-Patient Departments, they acted as camp nurses for Guides and gave talks and practice to the Companies. In 1939 they ran the Camp Hospital at the Rover Moot at Monzie, an International camp for 3000 boys from 42 different countries. In the war years some stayed at home to carry on as VADs and the rest joined hospitals at home and abroad. After the War this famous group was rebuilt and won the Caledonian Shield in 1948 but finally, in 1966, owing to changed ways of life, lack of leaders and few recruits, the Detachment disbanded. Just after the war, one member of this detachment was lecturing to Land Rangers on emergencies out of doors. "Take off your petticoat and tear it up for bandages," she said. There was a shriek of laughter from the girls as, brought up in war-time scarcity, few had petticoats and certainly those who did never wore them while in uniform.

In the Twenties, Rangers were venturing further afield. Ten girls went to Denbigh in Wales for a large camp. Fee for the week, plus rail fare, was seventeen shillings!

There is a stirring report from ex-members of the St James' Rangers who went to Waddow Hall, Lancashire, in 1927:

"It was raining when tents were pitched, and it continued till Thursday in the second week. The 'Scotties' camp was on high ground but those on the low ground were washed out. When the sky cleared they were told to go out, make a fire and cook a meal; all thought Captain had lost her reason! But the fires were lit—not with only one match, however—and the rain resumed in the evening!''

It is interesting to note that the medicine chest and First Aid boxes were never needed; no one was allowed to wear socks or stockings, just gym shoes. At another camp, this time in Ireland, they had to row out into the middle of the Lough to get clear water!! On the return journey they were horrified to see a herd of cows devouring towels and bathing suits left on the beach.

In 1930 Elena Lawson and Isobel Gilchrist formed the 165th Ranger Company from a small group called the Swan Patrol in the 88th Roman Catholic Guide Company. The Guiders trained with St Margaret's Rangers, and the Company flourished. Their coming-of-age anniversary was celebrated with a great supper party at which Monseigneur Chase represented the Bishop as chief guest. In 1949 they went to Belgium, and in 1950 to Rome in Holy Year. Unfortunately they disbanded on Miss Lawson's retiral in 1956 although they still have an annual get-together in November, and in Holy Year 1975 over 100 shared an evening talking of the fun and friendship of Rangering.

Other units have similar reunions when letters from around the world are read.

The pattern continued into the 30s, the larger companies flourishing and the smaller ones disappearing. A Ranger Conference in 1932 discussed "Whether Guides should continue as Rangers? Why does Rangering not appeal to the modern girl? Might it be necessary to lower the age group from 16?" History keeps repeating itself. A Cadet Ranger Company attached to the Mary Erskine School, then in Queen Street, was formed in 1933 and by 1940 there were about four Cadet Companies scattered over the city, in various Divisions.

So on to the Second World War years. Older girls joined the forces, the younger ones remaining in Rangers taking part in the wide variety of war work undertaken by Edinburgh Guides. The Companies were asked to take in more members, and girls who did not belong to any organisation were hauled in, mostly against their wills. It was an impossible task trying to instil interest and a bit of discipline into the unwilling. The idea, apparently, was to make life easier for them when they were called up to the Forces or other war work. One group, however, *was* keen on learning to march; perhaps they had heard of the fearsome Sergeant-Majors awaiting them, for they practised marching in Melville Street even when the blackout made it too dark to see. One evening they formed fours and marched up the road—suddenly the leading rank leapt in the air and with perfect discipline each succeeding one followed suit; likewise when they about-turned and passed the same spot. On returning to the light and warmth of H.Q. the leader was asked, "Jeannie, what for did ye jump up and doon?" She replied, "Oh, did ye no' see that a horse had been along before us?"

The Sea Crews had a large influx as it was hoped it was a short cut to getting into the W.R.N.S.—which, in fact, it was not; but a well-trained Sea Ranger did stand a better chance of joining the section she was most interested in.

1945 was the 25th Anniversary of the Ranger Branch and a Service was held at Windsor at which several of the Edinburgh Companies and Crews were represented.

On the upsurge of Rangering after the war, Air Rangers were started in Edinburgh by Shelagh Cuthbertson and the following is her description of this event:

"It was experimental; there was no syllabus, no uniform and nothing in P.O.R. I drew up a pre-enrolment test and the equivalent of second class—aeroplane recognition, formation of clouds, one book to be read about pioneers of flying came into it. I, as Captain, had an awful lot to learn to keep ahead of my Rangers. The Sea Scouts allowed us to use their room in Potterrow, with no heating and very little light, but we fitted up a paraffin heater and cowered round it. Uniform was another problem; we contrived through W.A.A.F. sources to get blue shirts which were smart and serviceable with our navy skirts and berets. It was a very cold winter and soon we had to find new premises, but it was a pioneer start. We were fortunate that the Royal Air Force was able to help us to pursue knowledge of the air, in fact we were actually given flights in aircraft, but this was later to be forbidden by the Air Ministry. I shall never forget our first flight over the Forth Bridge, up the East Coast and back; short but terribly exciting; from these flights we went on to learn about gliding. Our first camp was at Airth, near Donibristle, where we were shown over the Control Tower, over planes, and had lunch at the canteen. The high spot of our adventurous living was the time when two Air Rangers were given the opportunity of going on a Service Flight to Lossiemouth and back. One Ranger had a real adventure; she was offered a flight in a private plane and they had to make an emergency landing in Loch Leven, luckily near a small island. Though she was cold, wet and shaken, her Guide training came to the fore, and she sent up S.O.S. smoke signals, spotted by two boys on shore who told the police.''

In 1946 Edinburgh Air Flight was the first to have a Leading Air Ranger Certificate. Through the years they went to Gliding Camps at Balado in Fife and Dyce at Aberdeen, but all the specialised training eventually became too expensive and in the 1960s the ''flight was cancelled.'' S.R.S. Pharos became a combined Sea and Air Company. In January 1950 Air Rangers from Glasgow made a little history by flying into Turnhouse to have a meeting with the Edinburgh ''Airs.''

In 1947, rather than have a number of small units all over the City, a Cadet Company, the 1st Edinburgh, was started in Headquarters, meeting on Fridays. In this Company, girls of 16-21 years were given the opportunity to train for service as leaders in the Guide Movement. The formation of the Company fulfilled a need at that time to cater for the under-18-year-olds—the training school for Guiders would not accept trainees unless they were at least 17½ years of age. The Cadets met for some meetings as a Cadet Company; other meetings were spent with each Cadet working with a Pack or Company in her own district. At the end of about two years, a Cadet gained her Leadership Certificate, very similar to the present Young Leader's Certificate. As the girls in the Cadet Company were from all over the City, this led to an exchange of ideas. When they were learning a new game for Brownies and Guides to play, it was quite astonishing how many variations of a single theme could be found in the City.

In 1948 the Empire Ranger Week was held at Netherurd for 150

Rangers and Cadets from many countries, not only "Empire"; from Norway, Sweden, Belgium and France, they joined Scots from many places including Edinburgh. At least one French Ranger went on to camp afterwards—at St Abbs with S.R.S. Forth.

In the same year, Carsewell at Penicuik House, Midlothian, became the Ranger Campsite and was used extensively at weekends and, being near the Pentlands, it was ideal for hiking. Light-weight camping was all the rage and the smaller the tent and rucksack the better. Even toothbrushes were cut in half to fit into tiny boxes or bags. Lighter sleeping bags were becoming available and replaced the too solid blankets. St Brendan Rangers borrowed a Scout trek cart and went camping, having fun wandering the West Highlands one year, and in Ireland the following year they discovered the joys of unrationed sweeties.

The Sea Rangers spent some time on *English Rose,* the Training Ship at Poole in Dorset; they had a training muster on *Dolphin* at Leith and they visited the Home Fleet in the Forth. In fact, Edinburgh Rangers went everywhere as soon as wartime travel restrictions were lifted, even to Belgium and Jersey. From these continental links, totem, or camp names came into use which helped to get away from the "Please Captain" or "Please Miss" atmosphere and years later has led to the use of Christian names. In April 1948 combined Sea Crews bought *Water Rat,* a Captain's gig from Rosyth, and launched her on the canal. The Boat House on the canal at Ashley Terrace was presented to the Sea Rangers in 1951 and crews of Rangers and Sea Scouts spent many hours repairing it. In the 1950s Crews seemed to be very busy winning competitions or going to trainings in England and generally being urged on to greater things. "Sea Rangers ask for more adventurous boating and sailing than on the canal." It was suggested that they found an experienced trainer and shared *Foresight* and *Reliant,* two Whalers. In 1955 S.R.S. Forth and S.R.S. Reliant were first and second in the Sea Cadet Regatta at Granton.

On one occasion, Rangers from all over the city joined in a big overnight hike from Carfraemill over the Lammermuirs to Gifford— great fun was had by all. Present-day Rangers could repeat this adventure on a Friday night with the prospect of the comfort of Colstoun Cottage on Saturday and a qualification for an award in the Duke of Edinburgh's Scheme.

Challenge Hikes, Adventure weekends, Exploring weekends like this were apparently all done in perfect conditions; oddly enough there is little mention of the weather except on one famous Rover-Ranger weekend when 70 brave souls hiked over the Pentlands in appalling weather and enjoyed themselves so much that they all voted to do it *again!* A team of twenty Rangers met a more domestic challenge in the "Youth in the Kitchen" competition and "the standard of work was very high." Other activities were very varied, from the adoption of an old person in the Salvation Army Home by one group, to visits to the Fire Station by another. Rangers visited Post Rangers in their homes and in hospital and invited them to meetings when this was possible.

There was a grand bit of Rover-Ranger co-operation in 1948 when four Bonaly Rovers and four Forth Rangers went for a canoeing weekend up the canal to Ratho. A boy and a girl in each canoe, and each couple had a project to carry out on the journey on the aspects of wild life along the banks. As was inevitable, one pair searching for a wild flower tipped into the water, but extricated themselves successfully from this humiliating situation, alive though soaking. It was all really very efficiently done and tremendous fun. Rangers were asked to help at the Scout Rally that summer by running teas, a crèche and the First Aid Tent. In November Rovers and Rangers held a weekend at Hermitage of Braid and that was voted a great success too.

St Cecilia Rangers from the Royal Blind School were enrolled on 13th December 1948 and came into the Ranger ranks with a flourish. Their Captain, Ann Darroch, led them on from venture to venture in every field from singing and drama to camping and travel.

By 1950 the Senior Group had Cadets and "Land," "Sea" and "Air" Rangers; the prefix "Land" was not welcomed by many Companies as it conjured up visions of those admirable folk, the Land Army, in their very heavy working garb, during the war. However, the smart grey shirts, navy skirts, ties and berets helped them over that hurdle. The companies were adventuring into many fields and many lands: camps in Denmark, Sweden and Eire. Girl Scouts from America were welcomed and entertained in Edinburgh and an Air Ranger had a wonderful time in America.

A contingent from Scotland, led by Meta Stevenson, went to the European Ranger gathering at Berck in France in 1952. This was a truly historic international occasion, the first gathering of Rangers from Europe and many other parts of the world as well, in all 24 countries and over 1000 Rangers. Everyone enjoyed the fun and comradeship of this exciting camp but, on this occasion, there was also the opportunity of seeing the completion of a wonderful project which had been shared by all Rangers in Europe, and which would give pleasure to others long after the Rangers had returned home. For some time previously Rangers had worked hard to raise money to build and equip a Club House for young patients at Berck hospital, a centre for the treatment of tuberculosis of the bone, and at this great Ranger gathering the opening ceremony of the Club House was the climax of this truly international spirit of service to others.

The Rangers stopped in Paris on the way to Berck and after the gathering they spread out all over France in groups of about 30, five Rangers from six countries each; four days were spent at Berck, then eight days touring by bus, on the way meeting French Rangers and seeing many beautiful places and things. Finally they all enjoyed a weekend in Paris, sight-seeing and visiting the Ranger Exhibition showing studies of "women's work and working conditions." To sum up this great experience, one must quote from some of the letters written after the event.

"We were representatives of our own countries and yet a part of a much wider whole"; "We thought again about some ideas which we had previously taken for granted"; and finally from the Ranger Leader, "As I strapped up my rucksack on the last stage of the journey home I said thoughtlessly, 'So that's the end'; at once a voice said, 'We were told at the closing ceremony, this is the beginning—NOT the end'."

In Coronation year, 1953, Edinburgh Rangers ran a camp at the Trefoil campsite for other Scottish Rangers to give them the opportunity to see the Queen on her Coronation visit to Edinburgh.

The Crews were now sending representatives in all directions: to Granton with Sea Cadets where they won a Pulling Race, to Dartmouth in the South of England, and West to Gareloch. Three Crews were represented for a fortnight on an M.T.B. on the Norfolk Broads. S.R.S. Forth tried to arrange an outside ploy about once a month. They went down a coal mine, the Lady Victoria Pit at Newtongrange, and some of the Crew went right up to the coal face. They went out from Leith Docks in a tug and saw how a large Canadian grain cargo ship was brought into dock. A letter to the Admiralty at Rosyth, requesting a visit to a warship, resulted in a private visit to *H.M.S. Vengeance,* an aircraft carrier.

Despite all this activity, numbers in all companies were dropping very rapidly. New recruits were not coming from the Guide companies and again it was suggested that the age limit for entry to Ranger companies be lowered. In 1956 two well known Crews disbanded, "Foresight" and "Explorer," but Portobello and Blackhall started "Lands," and thus it went on into the '60s with only a few groups in existence. These undaunted stalwarts kept the Ranger Branch alive. The Flight had their Banner dedicated in 1960. (Its design is an Official Burgee, a gold trefoil at hoist, a trefoil appliqued on Flight Wings, the Motto in scroll on Azure fround—translated, the motto is "We seek the sky itself.") In the same year a representative from the Edinburgh Company went to the Cadet Conference in London.

In 1962 the first-ever Rover-Ranger Moot was held at Auchengillan; twenty Rangers and three Ranger Guiders were there and all these mixed activities were tremendous fun and hard work. It was suggested that Rover and Ranger Leaders might exchange places for training.

Canoeing became very popular and a number of canoes were built. In the 70s the Canoe Club was under the able instruction of Jack and Betty Cuthill, who are a good example of a Scout/Guide marriage. They go on many expeditions, to Cramond, down the Tweed, to Machrihanish in the South-West of Scotland, and wheresoever rivers run or the sea is heard. The Sea Scout Boating and Adventure Centre at Lochgoilhead became, and still is, a popular place for Rangers to train in boat work and the centre accommodates 200 Scouts and 20 Rangers.

The newest forms of organised sport coming to the fore were ski-ing, climbing and mountaineering. In 1962 the County Executive Committee bought ski-ing equipment to hire out to members of the Movement and this was looked after by St Giles' Rangers. From this beginning, Scouts and Rangers combined to run a First Aid Rescue Scheme at Glenshee each weekend, which has continued and was given official recognition in 1970.

Rangers, in "Car Wash Week," earned £100 for Ski Rescue Team.

A Ranger ski training of 15 days for three consecutive years was sponsored by Dr Autgaerden, a great friend of Lady Baden-Powell, near St Moritz in Switzerland, and the last training led to a ski tour in the Alps. A representative went from 2nd Leith Rangers to join another Scot, five English, two Swiss and two leaders. The training was very thorough, teaching them all the tricks of the trade. Carrying rucksacks and climbing was difficult, but skins on the skis helped that.

They learnt weather lore and found it most necessary in a mild winter, when avalanches are more frequent.

"Touring among the peaks of breath-taking beauty, in extremes of temperature and resourceful simplicity of existence—sleeping like sardines on shelf-bunks, melting snow for water—candles and log fires all added up to make an unforgettable experience."

1966 was a very live year. Several Cadets represented Edinburgh in London for the Cadets' 50th Birthday Celebrations; the theme was "Life is for Living" and this the Cadets did to the full! The Cadets organised and ran the Signalling Competition at Johnstonburn which many will remember with amusement and which was won by a joint team from the 58th and 76th Companies. At the Service for the 900th Anniversary of Westminster Abbey one Ranger from Edinburgh carried the Scottish Chief Commissioner's banner and another laid a wreath. More girls were realising that Rangering was fun, and some Companies restarted in Barnton, Leith, South West and South East Divisions.

In 1967 one of the Cadets was fortunate enough to gain a bursary to spend a week on the Training Ship *Golden Hinde* at Dartmouth. During the sixties, Cadets played a very full part in Senior Branch activities in Edinburgh and participated in the First Aid Scheme at Glenshee. They enjoyed many weekends together, and on one of these they learnt the hard way that a frozen chicken takes longer to cook in a hole in the ground than a fresh one!

Under the new programme in 1968 the Companies became "District" Ranger Guide Units and many more groups were registered taking their District names; these units were on the whole small; history repeated itself and only the bigger ones survived. Land, Sea and Air Rangers and Cadets lost their separate identities at this time to the great regret of many, especially the "Seas" who lost their distinctive headgear! Units may still pursue their own specialities, however. By 1970, the Cadet Company had re-registered as a Ranger Company, gradually losing its "training" bias and eventually the unit was closed. However, things have turned full circle as now there are District or Division Rangers and Young Leaders who, in taking part in the Young Leaders' Scheme, are following very much the same programme and giving service to the Guide Movement as did the Cadets.

Diamond Jubilee Year! At the Westminster service the Scottish Chief Commissioner's banner was again carried by a Ranger from Edinburgh. Rangers were in demand everywhere helping with Guide camps and other adventures. They acted as Aides at the Commonwealth Games at Meadowbank, known world wide as "the Happy Games," and wonderful service of all kinds was given at the 3rd Commonwealth Paraplegic Games which followed.

In 1971 S.R.S. Forth were given Royal Navy recognition and the following note was written by their present skipper.

> "It had long been the ambition of our skipper, Miss Molly Armstrong, for the Crew to gain Royal Navy recognition. Her enthusiasm communicated itself to the Rangers and the date of our first inspection became very important to us all. We were inspected by a W.R.N.S. Officer at our Den, then had a boating inspection in August 1971—when it was much too windy to sail, and even rowing was a strain! As a result of these inspections the Unit was awarded Royal Navy recognition and every invested Ranger became entitled to wear the recognition badge on her uniform, and the Unit to fly a special burgee. Every eighteen months we are inspected again to satisfy the Royal Navy that we are fit to retain their recognition. So far we have survived two changes of Guiders and a change of uniform to remain a Ranger Guide Unit with Royal Navy recognition."

This unit, the original St Margaret's and now 1st Pentland Division Rangers, made their own Burgee, a gold trefoil at hoist, thistle emblem and scroll with motto—"Go Forth and Conquer"—on azure background. It was dedicated on Thinking Day, 22nd February 1974.

Now read a tale of repetitive history. In 1946 the 205th Guide Company in the Grange Parish Church had far too many older girls in it, all willing to become Rangers, but not Sea Rangers which was the only senior group in South-East Division. Let Marjorie Rose, the Commissioner at that time, carry on from this point.

> "The girls were obviously full of ideas and energy and fun. I decided I'd start a company with them and any other older Guides in the division who might be interested. Accommodation was going to be difficult; we therefore decided to meet in my house. That was the start of St Brendan's. There were a number of keen campers among them, and two P.L. permit holders, ready for anything. That summer it was decided to go North-West and for the sum of £2 a head plus rail fares we set off with the trek cart via Glasgow to Inverness, and on to Achnasheen, meaning to wander and camp at will. A few miles from the start on the second day a lorry stopped and the driver asked us where we were going. We brightly replied we didn't really know. 'I'll take you to Poolewe,' he said and we went. The stories of that camp are legion and were written, but lost when the company closed. Suffice it to say that, on returning to Gareloch we were only allowed our little camp site on condition we 'would not be moving off on the Sabbath," and had therefore to hire a lorry for 10/- on the Saturday to get to Achnasheen again. Some few years

later the District Commissioner for Liberton asked me to help her train some young patrol leaders for a company at St Barnabas Church, Moredun, this being a new housing area. When the time came for registration they were given the number 205th, the Grange Parish Company having been closed. In 1976 when I went to see a new Ranger Company at Moredun, looking for facts for this book, I found it was composed of senior girls from 205th. They met in their Guider's home and their first camp when on the verge of becoming Rangers, was to the North-West and Skye wandering as we had done; but they had the simplification of the County Minibus all the way. Again the stories of this expedition have been recorded and may they be kept for posterity.''

All through the decades Rangers have given service to the community and here is an example of what today's Rangers do.

"For a number of years members of the 196th Ranger Guide Unit (Inveralmond Division) have helped to teach mentally handicapped girls from Gogarburn Hospital to swim at Dunfermline College of Physical Education. I became involved a couple of years ago when my friend pleaded with me to go down one Saturday morning because none of the Rangers who usually helped could go. I was rather loath to give up my one long lie of the week (swimming starts at 9 o'clock) and also a little apprehensive, not knowing quite how I would react, never having worked with handicapped people before. That was two years ago and I am thoroughly 'hooked' now! The girls are extremely friendly, if a little over-enthusiastic at times, some of them taking great delight in ducking the Rangers, but I have become very attached to them. It is all so worthwhile and this is why, although I have left Rangers, I still go down on Saturday mornings and am also encouraging the older Guides in my own company to come and have fun, while giving very valuable service.''

Some Guides say, "Why be a Ranger anyway?''—Round about the age of fourteen for many Guides the company set-up begins to lose interest for them. While enjoying leading their patrols, the older Guides feel the need for closer contact with their contemporaries within the Movement, and indeed the things which enthrall the ten-year-olds in their charge no longer hold any magic for the P.L. Schoolwork becomes more demanding and the time which must be given to preparation for Guide meetings if the patrol is to function in the proper manner is grudged or skimped, with detrimental results to P.L. and patrol. However the girl is loath to cut herself off from something which has been a part of her life, and is ready for a move to Rangers. In Rangers she is simply one of many, a cog in the wheel of self-government, and among girls of her own age. She is ready for the much freer approach in the Ranger Unit, the informality and the less obviously structured programme. At the same time she appreciates the wide range of activities available to her and the opening up of the world which can come from the use of outside experts and facilities.

How Does the Unit Work?—A Ranger Unit functions entirely from within itself. A small unit will make its decisions *en masse*, while a larger one may appoint a Committee with a Chairman, Secretary, Treasurer and any other office-bearers it decides are necessary to the individual unit. The Ranger Guider is there as an adult adviser, a shoulder to cry on, a brick wall to batter one's head against, a last resort when ideas fail to flow, a stepping stone between the fast-disappearing securities of childhood and the vast bewildering plain of adult society. She does not run the unit—it runs itself—and probably runs her too!

What makes Rangers Tick?—Rangers do some strange things! They get up at 4 a.m. to climb hills and watch the sunrise; they give up Saturday mornings to teach handicapped kids to swim; they go swimming at 7 a.m. before breakfast; they spend four consecutive Wednesdays running games for under-privileged children at a day centre. Why? They are vague about it, but they know one thing: they enjoy it, both the actual doing and the memories later. They find companionship, and friendship blossoms in these circumstances—going out and seeking something together, even though they may not know precisely what they are seeking.

And the Ranger Guider?—She spends a lot of time ostensibly doing nothing. The unit must function without her constant intervention and she is wrong if she is continually interfering and organising. She must sit back and let a few harmless failures happen, so that the Rangers can see how *not* to get things to work. How frustrating! Yet she enjoys being a Ranger Guider. What does she get out of it? A sense of belonging —the Rangers are quick to include their Guider in their plans and to consult her on every little point. She has a special rôle to play in their development; neither a parent nor a teacher, yet someone with a little more experience of living than the Rangers, who is willing to share that experience. She learns from the Rangers too and while broadening their horizons extends her whole vista of life. They keep her young while she helps them towards GROWING UP!

7

Extensions

LIKE THE GIRLS who joined themselves on to the Boy Scouts and astonished the Chief Scout at a Rally many years ago, the cripple and invalid young people of Edinburgh were not going to be left out of the great game of Guiding. Their courage and persistence, plus the efforts of devoted adult helpers, made this possible and in 1926 the 154th Post Guide Company was registered, followed by the 154th Post Brownie Pack and Post Ranger Company in 1929. The Post Companies and Pack were formed from girls in hospitals and their own homes, so that they could as far as possible take part in all Guide activities. A new window had been opened on their world and the bluebird of happiness was one of their first visitors.

The 135th Guide Company and Brownie Pack at the Royal Blind School, formed in 1926, were rather different as the members were all pupils, boarders and day girls, at the school and came, not only from Edinburgh, but from many parts of Scotland. Much later, the St Cecilia's Ranger Company was formed, their name signifying their love of music and the splendid musical training which was a great feature of the school. A whole book could be written about the exploits and achievements of the Blind School Company alone, which held its Golden Jubilee in 1976.

Subsequently units were formed at Princess Margaret Rose Hospital and the residential Special Schools—The Trefoil School, Donaldson's School for the Deaf, Westerlea, Challenger Lodge and the Astley Ainslie Hospital.

It is difficult, when looking back to those early days, to realise how very circumscribed were the lives of these handicapped young people, many of them cared for devotedly by their parents within the four walls of a small room. Tuberculosis was still a very severe disease and many patients spent years, often in bed on outside balconies in a sanatorium. Polio and bone diseases crippled a great number and some children spent most of their often too short lives in hospital so their activities were severely limited. Suddenly Guiding was within their reach and, with the co-operation of the hospital staff, they held Guide meetings in the wards, practised for their Guide tests and played specially adapted games. Most important of all, from the day of their enrolment, they had the thrill of wearing Guide uniform which, if not always complete, at least consisted of a tunic and tie.

The schooling of these young people was often interrupted so the interest and fun of the monthly budget (one for each patrol) with their pictures, stories and competitions, were indeed a tonic. A "Post Box" for letters, helpful articles for tests and general knowledge all cleverly illustrated, must have meant that "Budget Day" was something eagerly looked forward to! The name "Post Guide" was used to denote a Guide who received these budgets and then posted them on to the next member of the Patrol on the list. In the financial stringency of the 1930s some of the Post Rangers could not afford to post the budgets, so it was agreed in principle not to give them the money, but to pay the postage and ask them in return to knit something—perhaps one Brownie cap—each year.

From the very beginning the aim was to integrate the Post Guides and Rangers with active Guides and many were adopted by active Guide and Ranger Companies who visited them regularly, helping the Post Guiders, as they were scattered throughout Edinburgh. There were constant appeals for cars and drivers to take the Post Guiders (who were seriously overworked) to visit girls in distant parts of the city. While the adoption scheme was never completely successful, one Ranger Company visited Post Rangers in Liberton Hospital for many years.

There was a Post Division in Edinburgh and in 1933 the "Extension Section" was founded which included companies in institutions and long-term hospitals. Miss Jessie Wood was the first Post Guide Commissioner and had regular meetings for Post Guiders to keep them in touch with each other and active Guiding events. Whenever they knew there were girls in hospital who wanted to become Guides, they visited them— often to find that the Guides had done their own recruiting. One very tall Post Guide with a caliper was in bed next to a small girl stunted by her brittle bones, and the tall Guide asked the little one if she would like to join. The answer was "Yes"; she met the Post Guider that afternoon and was enrolled in due course. Those two went through Guides and Rangers together, ending up in the Post Trefoil Guild, and remained friends though they lived many miles apart. They met recently after 20 years and the grandchildren of an ex-Edinburgh Commissioner are visiting the tall one now in an old people's home. Another link in the chain!

Once again, the younger girls were determined not to be left out and a number of them approached the Guiders who were visiting in the City Hospital and asked if they could join. They formed the nucleus of the 154th Pack and were adopted by the 15th Brownie Pack, an early example of integration which developed greatly in later years.

There were soon about 90 Brownies, Guides and Rangers "on the books." The work load of the Post Guiders was fantastic; every afternoon they visited the girls in their homes, in district groups and arranged meetings in hospitals, so that the girls could get to know each other. Each Brownie received a monthly Brownie letter which *was her very own* with a message from Brown Owl, pictures, stories, etc. To a Brownie living in a tenement where the postman's knock would be a rarity, getting a letter addressed to herself must have been something quite wonderful. Many Guiders and

Rangers in different companies contributed pages for these budgets and letters. The Post Guiders obtained the names of all handicapped girls living at home from the Cripple and Invalid Aid Society and regularly visited all who wished to be Guides.

To return now to the 135th Blind School Company, they at least did not have to look for potential Guides and Brownies, and also had the advantage of meeting in their own premises with great support from the School management. The number of Guides rose quickly to between 30 and 40 and the Brownie Pack flourished with a Brown Owl who herself had been a pupil at the School. Great ingenuity was needed by the Guiders to adapt test material to hearing and touch instead of sight. For example, the Union Jack and tracking signs were taught by matches glued on to cards. Bean bags had tinkle bells attached and two completely different types of string were used to assist in learning knots. Morse presented no problems as they loved using buzzers and excelled at memory games. After 1945 the Patrol Leaders, and later the Rangers, all helped the younger Guides with their Braille and the Guider had assistance at Company meetings from Queen's Guides doing their service which was much appreciated.

The blind Guides and Rangers were great campers. Their first organised camp under Miss Thomson Clay, was in 1933 at Thankerton and they camped every year after that until the war. Although they had a hut or hall for shelter, they all slept in tents, whatever the weather, and the annual camp was the highlight of the year. They had a tremendously high standard for inspection and care of tents. "No one can roll up the brailling like the blind Guides can," said Miss Darroch, their Captain, "and their starring of the tents is perfect." Miraculously no one seemed to fall over the guy ropes, although there were guide-lines to certain places, and their uniforms were always neat. One of the great difficulties was to get enough helpers, because they had to camp in May owing to school holidays, and the nurse had the added responsibility of caring for problems to do with the girls' eyes. When the Ranger Company was formed in the 40s they were encouraged to go on expeditions (with one partially-sighted girl to assist them) to seek information about people and places in the countryside. They loved hikes, and First Aid, and they were very good country dancers. They were also great communicators and Miss Darroch recalls a hilarious meeting with the Deaf and Dumb Company when they each tried to make the other understand what was going on!

There was tremendous talent amongst all the handicapped girls and these gifts might never have been developed otherwise. Handcraft of a very high standard has been one of their great contributions to the Guide Movement. They took part in the 1928 Handcraft Exhibition to raise money to buy the Edinburgh Headquarters and to everyone's delight, the Poster Competition advertising the Sale was won by Netta Mathieson, a

Post Guide in the Longmore Hospital. The Scottish Extension's handcraft stall is still a feature at every Scottish Commissioners' Conference.

The handicapped Guides and Rangers were now aspiring to the higher Guide Awards and there must have been great excitement in the Longmore Hospital on 16th June 1929 when the Chief Guide presented First Class and All Round Cords to Cissie McGuire and Mary Holm, who were the first of the 154th Company to gain these awards. Tests for these mauve First Class badges were specially adapted to replace those impossible for a handicapped girl to pass. On this occasion the Chief Guide asked her bearer to bring forward her standard and she then explained its meaning to the Company. A Company letter, with pages produced by Post Guiders and Guides, signed by all present, was handed over to the Chief Guide as a souvenir. No one would ever forget that day. There were more successes when Betty McLeod and Ina Hannah of the 154th Company gained their Ranger Star, the first in the Extension Branch in Scotland.

It was only a matter of time before the 154th Company started to go on holiday and eventually to camp. A Peebles Company invited a Post Guide for a week's holiday, and the Largo Rangers gave a yearly invitation to two Post Rangers for a fortnight. In 1931, five Post Guides from Edinburgh joined the Midlothian Posts at Pinkie House, Musselburgh, and this became a regular event. There was a memorable holiday in Fife when twenty Post Brownies spent a month in a specially furnished house arranged by Mrs Fleming, a friend of the Chief Guide and the previous owner of No. 33 Melville Street.

Once parents had got over their fear of their delicate or crippled children going to camp nothing stopped them, and over the years some were taken with active Guide companies or camped as an extension group. Day and weekend camps were arranged with outdoor cooking, proper programmes and Colour Ceremonial, as suitably equipped sites became available.

The 56th Company and Pack at Donaldson's School for the Deaf flourished and had many contacts with other companies. Miss Jan Mees tells a delightful tale of one camp her company shared with them in the 1930s:

"Our own Guides were astonished at the speed with which communication could be established. It was only when we went to church that an unusual procedure was followed. Pat Nicholson, who ran the Donaldson's School Guides, came with us, and her husband, the Rev. George Nicholson, took the service in Humbie Church. He spoke from the pulpit facing the congregation while Pat sat where she could be seen by her Guides and relayed it all by sign language to them. Our own lot were so fascinated watching the deft manipulation of her hands that I doubt if they took in much of the sermon!

"In connection with the Deaf and Dumb Guides also, my Brown Owl and I went through to Glasgow for some weeks to teach them

Country Dancing. They did it by counting and by sensing the vibration of the music, and they were so good at it that they won the Country Dancing Cup—a wonderful achievement and we were very proud of them."

Many years later a small group of deaf Guides from the 56th Company joined the 106th and 168th Companies in Murrayfield District and were happily integrated in their activities. Hearing Guides quickly found means of communicating with their deaf friends, who joined in every part of the programme and often outshone the rest at active games. The 56th Company has closed but some Brownies from Donaldson's School have joined the 168th Pack.

The 154th Guides and Brownies were especially lucky as Miss Mary Crawford, Extension Secretary since 1933, opened her heart and her beautiful house and garden in Colinton to the Extensions. No one who knew Fernielaw will ever forget it—it had everything: a sandpit, a swing and a see-saw (used by all ages!), a big lawn for tents, a place to make an outdoor fire and ground-floor rooms for Brownies and those unable to sleep outside, Being so near Edinburgh, day campers came and also many visitors, including the Press. Just a walk round that lovely old garden helped the campers to forget their stiff legs and crutches; there was always so much to look for and enjoy. For a Post Guide or Ranger to camp with an active company was always an enriching experience for both. One Ranger Company took two Post Rangers to their camp. One was on crutches and she broke two chasing away the horses which came up the field every evening to raid the store tent! The other, who had an artificial foot and was very crippled, used to keep the woodpile supplied with small sticks which she painstakingly gathered crawling around on hands and knees, but they both joined in camp games.

By 1935 it was realised that some Rangers and Guides could actually join active companies—a further move towards integration. Budgets continued to be sent only to those Rangers confined to house or bed. The original 154th Post Guide Company was now only for Guides unable to join active companies or attend monthly meetings. They still had budgets and a three-monthly visit from their Captain. The second Company was for Guides who were able to get about but were not strong enough to *join* an active company, so they met monthly. The numbers had grown greatly and, in addition to budgets, there were all the arrangements for testing both 1st and 2nd Class work and badges. As the examiner had usually to be brought to the entrant, transport was a terrific problem and made plans for monthly meetings very difficult.

"I always remember testing Lizzie Adamson for the Local Knowledge Badge," wrote a Guide Captain. "She was a remarkable person who had a rare disease which made her completely stiff like a tailor's dummy. She was pushed about in a special chair for many years and always took part in Guide events (including the Tree Planting Ceremony at the Braid-burn Valley, where she signed the book on behalf of the 154th Rangers). She passed the World Citizen Badge and obtained her Ranger Star. Later, when she was confined to bed, she wrote to all her Guide friends, by means of a mirror and an arrangement of wires to hold pad and pencil, as she could not bend her arms. She also learnt Braille to help the blind Guides. She had a great sense of humour and to visit her in hospital was an enriching experience.''

Every Conference and Rally had its group of Extensions and representatives were sent to take part in discussions. It was a 154th Brownie who asked Princess Mary to open the famous ''Wet Rally'' and presented her with the programme.

With all their training in handcrafts, it was not surprising that the 154th Company won the Embroidery Cup in 1936, their work being the best all-round level, 73%. This work was put to a good purpose as they were determined to raise their own company funds and every year small sales were held to achieve this. Even when the members reached the Trefoil Guild, the yearly sales remained a regular feature.

Over the years, regular Broadcast Services were arranged for the Extension Branch and in 1937 one was taken by Dr Whitley, the Minister at St Giles, the Guiders made sure that every Extension member had a wireless set (often lent for the occasion) so that they could listen to the service. That year the Duke and Duchess of Gloucester visited Edinburgh to receive the Freedom of the City and one girl represented the 154th Company at the ceremony. Ever since the Munich crisis in 1938, the Extension Guiders had been concerned as to what would happen to the handicapped young people in the event of war and, with great foresight, a group of Guiders volunteered to staff a hostel if the need arose. This offer was accepted by the Education Department in 1939 and everything was planned. This inspiration was to result in the Trefoil School. Its beginning at St Abbs, the unforgettable years at Cowdenknowes, near Earlston, the move to Polkemmet and finally to Kirklands in 1957, are all recorded by Mary Crawford in *The Story of the Trefoil School*.

The war had a profound effect on the Extension Branch. The Blind School was evacuated, most of the Post Guiders were either at Cowden-knowes or directed into war work The 154th Companies and Pack had always been good at producing their own Guiders, and one bedridden Guider carried on the budgets during the war. Attempts were made to keep in touch with those left in Edinburgh, but there were great difficulties; the postage on the budgets became so heavy that it was cheaper to send them by tram!

When the war was over, things picked up again. There were fewer Post Brownies, but there were still children in Southfield Hospital, the Astley Ainslie and Loanhead Hospital. The 182nd Company at Princess

Margaret Rose Hospital was re-registered. The Blind Guides started their yearly camps again, this time at Sprouston, where the villagers took them to their hearts. A 21st birthday reunion of 154th members took place at Fernielaw, when Miss Crawford paid tribute to the way in which Post Guiding in Edinburgh had survived the war years, saying that it compared very favourably with other counties in Scotland. Ranger meetings were now held at 8 Churchhill, a convenient house with no steps anywhere with a large billiard room which would hold beds and an attractive garden. Thinking Day meetings were held there and at Mrs Roth's house in Hope Terrace, and along with Fernielaw and Cowdenknowes became a place of fun and adventure. It was now obvious that those who had been Guides and Rangers in the old days had to move on; it is a remarkable tribute to the Extensions that the Post Trefoil Guild was the first T.G., registered in Edinburgh in 1947.

In 1948 Mary Crawford received a Medal of Merit and Marjory Noble a Certificate of Merit for their work with the Extensions.

One of the most meaningful parts of company life has been the Colour Ceremonial, so it was an inspired idea for the St Giles Rangers in 1948 to present a Union Jack to the 154th Post Guide Company who had no Colours. The flag had originally been made by the Rangers for the Guides at Cossipore, India, where Miss Alexa Scott, St Giles' own missionary, was the Captain. When India gained her independence the flag was returned to Scotland, so a small piece of history now belonged to the Company.

No one who has worked with handicapped young people can fail to realise the many cases of heroic courage in the face of pain and helplessness which must have made "A Guide smiles and sings under all difficulties" a very testing law to keep. Unfortunately, it is never possible for all to be officially recognised, but in the early '50s three girls were awarded Badges of Fortitude. It was a red letter day for the 182nd Company at Princess Margaret Rose Hospital when Robina Dickson was presented with the Badge of Fortitude, their first one. This was followed in 1967 by the award of the Star of Merit for fortitude to Alison Stewart during lengthy orthopaedic treatment. Alison was a Brownie in the 15th Pack but belonged to the 182nd while in hospital.

One of the many remarkable stories in the history of the 154th Company is that of Margaret Potts who spent most of her life in an iron lung at the City Hospital following poliomyelitis. With the co-operation of doctors, nurses and Guiders, she overcame tremendous difficulties in passing her Guide tests. It was a great day when Lady Colville, Scottish Chief Commissioner, presented her with the Badge of Fortitude; a year later Lady Colville returned to present her with the Blue First Class Badge—truly a great achievement! Another brave girl, Joyce Gunn of the 154th Company and a pupil at the Trefoil School, was also awarded a Badge of Fortitude.

A different award—the Gilt Cross— was gained by Emily Nash, a Guider handicapped through polio. A young man appeared at the door of her flat; he had been cleaning his fish tank; it slipped and he severed an artery in his arm on the broken glass, but Emily managed to apply a tourniquet and thus saved his life.

The 135th Company were very proud when Sandra Wilson became the first-ever Queen's Guide in an Extension Company; since then some of the difficulties Sandra encountered have been modified. In the ten years to 1974 ten more girls in the Blind School Company have gained this award. Another first-ever for the 135th was the presentation of the "Oak Leaf" to Anne Darroch, the Guider, in recognition of her service, especially with visually handicapped Guides.

In Baden-Powell Centenary Year of 1957 there was an enchanting idea —every Guide was asked to place a lighted candle in their window and many "Extensions" showed their loyalty to the Movement by doing this.

Many also went to a Scottish International Extension Camp at the Trefoil School Site; one girl went to the Extension Camp at Beaconsfield from which campers visited the World Camp at Windsor. When the Queen visited the World Camp, Sheena Tully of Portobello and Niddrie Division presented her with a Sampler—embroidered by two Edinburgh "Extensions"—that surely set the seal on their high standard of handcraft. Mrs Murray, the County Extension Secretary, attended Norway's International Camp, meeting Extension Guiders from all over the world. The really great moment came when Miss Mary Kennedy took all the Post Guides and Rangers to the Scottish International Camp at Blair Atholl, and there they met the Chief Guide!

The pioneers of travel in the Extension Section were the 135th Ranger Company who travelled to Switzerland in 1953, every penny, £28 per head, being raised by the girls—no grants were available in those days. Their Guider was often asked, "Why are you taking blind girls abroad?" The answer has come from all the girls in the Extension section who have made countless journeys since, and with easier air travel the whole world has opened up for them.

The value of these overseas contacts can be illustrated by a service which the Extension Branch were able to give the Tourist Board. The Board published a *Guide to Edinburgh for the Disabled* after much research on the part of the Extension Guide and Ranger Companies. This idea emanated from a similar *Guide to Copenhagen* which some of the Extension Guides had been given on a visit to that city several years previously.

In 1958 Guides and Rangers of the 154th shared adventures with the Glasgow Posts; the two Guide Companies spent a weekend at the Brownie House at Netherurd, while the Rangers went to Lorne, the Northern Ireland Training Centre. The Brownie Packs in the two cities soon followed their older sisters' example and enjoyed Pack Holidays together.

A new Brownie Pack was formed at Challenger Lodge Children's Home that year and continued to provide Brownie fun and work until the Home closed in 1974. Later, a combined Company and Pack was started at the Astley Ainslie Hospital, following the tradition of forming units wherever there was a need.

Edinburgh's "Camp of the Flame" was held at Blair Atholl in 1968 in Olympics year and followed this theme. Who could have imagined in the 1920s when it all started, that the Extension Section would have their own sub-camp, named Rome, in a large International Camp? The girls felt very much a part of the whole camp, everybody was introduced to at least one new activity. One member of "Rome" came third in the Archery Competition and everybody triumphed in some small way.

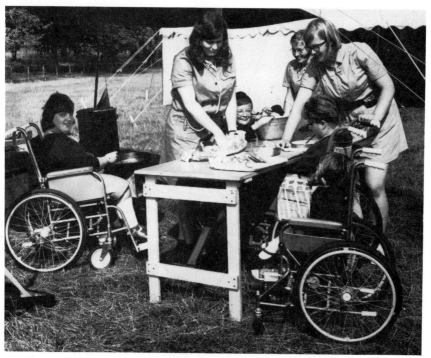

Cooking for ourselves.

In Diamond Jubilee Year the Extension Branch shared in their division celebrations and several attended the County Service in the Usher Hall; these girls will cherish the memory of the array of Colours and the vast sea of Guides in blue. Most Extension units are quite small and, through problems of mobility, tend towards isolation, so the opportunity to be part of a really big gathering is greatly appreciated.

The 49th Company (Westerlea School for Spastics) was started in 1957 and were without a Guider for a time in the sixties, so the girls formed a

Patrol within the 106th Company at Murrayfield Church nearby. On re-forming with a new team of Guiders and Unit Helpers, the Company ventured forth to camp at Vogrie, the Midlothian Centre, and have returned there for more fun each year since.

In 1972 the Company entered for the Commonwealth Headquarters Extension Competition and won it. To receive the Cup, the whole Company attended a Queen's Guide Certificate presentation in the Guide Hall. Lady Primrose, the County President, said in her opening remarks:

"The last time I had anything to do with a Guide Cup I was a Brownie taking one home to clean. As I was about to get off the bus it lurched and the cup slipped out of my hands and under the wheel."

At these words the Cup rolled off the table on to the floor! After much hilarity there was a sigh of relief when Lady Ford, Scottish Chief Commissioner, presented it for safe keeping for one year to the 49th Company.

This poem was written by the 49th Edinburgh Company who won the Guide Cup in the H.Q. Extension Competition:

Shall we? Shan't we? Answer yes!
How do we do it? Anyone's guess.
Scrap-book, model or a "tape"?
The first one. That's what we will make.
Traditional form or an original one?
A cut out Trefoil, soon was done.
We made it small and then it grew,
With cardboard, lots of scraps and glue.
Cuttings here and snippets there
(Even glue in Frances' hair).
The laws were discussed, what did they mean?
Magazines, cards, what could we glean?
Soon 10 Laws we had illustrated
(Many an evening we felt frustrated!!!)
In time the Promise was completed
We were not to be defeated.
The cover was made with string and "gold."
Into a scrap-book it did fold.
A photo on the front we stuck
And sent to London for "Good Luck."
After a while to our great surprise,
We heard the news—we'd won the prize
In 1929 to Glasgow it came
The North never again to know the fame
Till we received in '72
Our Cup from Lady Ford at E.H.Q.

In 1974 the Guider took a spastic girl with a Guide helper from the School and led a party of ten from Scotland and England to the Danish Camp at Hvalfsund. They were treated just like all the other campers and had a strenuous and enjoyable fortnight.

Two more members of the 135th Company took off, this time they were Guiders going to Iran to attend a conference on Leisure, Sport and

The happy cup winners with Lady Primrose and Lady Ford.

Culture for Disabled Youth and their Friends. A very different country and many different cultures all added up to make this a fascinating, if exhausting, adventure.

Meantime, those at home enjoyed Brownie, Guide and Ranger meetings. The wonderful summertime tea parties in Mrs Murray's garden at Gifford were eagerly looked forward to, as were other outings by car and coach. Many companies invited "Posts" to their own parties, thus getting to know one another better.

New recreations were opening up for the handicapped; the most recent is Riding for the Disabled. Mrs More Nisbet, a Vice-President of South East Local Association, was a pioneer in this field. She built an indoor school at The Drum, Gilmerton, so the children can learn in dry conditions, but they also ride in the grounds. The Guide Movement has not taken this up specifically but children attend from Westerlea and Graysmill Schools, where Guide units exist. Riding is also taught at Gogarburn Hospital and Guides from Corstorphine Hill District go there to help the children. An ex-Edinburgh Patrol Leader is now an Area Instructor in Northamptonshire.

The 154th Pack and Company closed down in 1974, the girls joined units nearer their homes or in Special Schools and the Handicapped

Trefoil Guild and the 154th Post Rangers ceased to meet as separate units, and their members linked up with their nearest Trefoil Guild whose friendship has enabled them to keep their links with Guiding. In July 1976 the Trefoil School closed. An Edinburgh "old girl" writes:

"I was at Cowdenknowes for four years, it gave me a great opportunity to mix with disabled Guides and Scouts, Brownies and Cubs who had different disabilities from my own. I especially liked the weekend patrol hikes and the extra movement I got. I learnt so much as I was taught every day, instead of having a teacher only twice a week when I was at home."

As the school closed, so did the 21st Edinburgh Guide Company, sending eight girls away to make friendly contact with Guides in their own home areas or in their new schools. The final meeting will be memorable for one girl at least. Agnes Colley received the Duke of Edinburgh's Bronze Award. She was the second girl to achieve this Award as a member of the 21st Company and all were glad to have such a happy "finale" to the Company's long and busy life.

Following the general trend towards "integration," there has been an ever-increasing number of handicapped children within ordinary units, although there are still some flourishing Extension Units, usually attached to Special Schools. These units provide opportunities for full participation in the Eight-point programme at levels and speeds best suited to the individual girls, and all the Extension units play a full part in their various districts and divisions, and indeed in the County.

8

Local Associations and Trefoil Guilds

THE LOCAL ASSOCIATION is a body of people called into being by the Commissioner to help her in relationships with Local Authorities, educational bodies, parents and the general public; and to provide financial and other support for the Movement in the locality. It has no responsibility for the running of Units.

In the words, "I am part of all that I have met" lie the aim of this fine body of women for, although members may not necessarily have been Girl Guides, they are firmly with them in all that they do.

This is the story of two typical Local Associations in Edinburgh, the first one being in South-East Division. Parents of Guides and Brownies and other interested members of the public were invited to a meeting when the purpose of a Local Association was explained. Guides provided refreshments to show what they could do and suitably impressed enough volunteers who formed a committee, one of whom was press-ganged into becoming the Secretary. At the first meeting on 1st April 1947, the committee drew up a rough constitution which was later formalised by a District Commissioner who was also a lawyer. At the A.G.M. Mrs Morison Miller, J.P. and Town councillor, was elected President; Mrs Shelagh Cuthbertson, Division Commissioner, was the Chairman and Mrs Henderson the Secretary.

The first task was providing tea for the Guide Division Seven-a-side Hockey teams and there were generous offers of coupons for rationed foods. In those days of rationing no one had butter or margarine to spare, so the committee asked the local Ministry of Food for a permit for extra rations to feed 70 people! The next mention of Hockey Sevens was in 1949 when the committee agreed to provide the buns, but the Guides paid for the lemonade—a fair compromise!

From their earliest days the South-East Local Association has helped at county events, such as the Christmas Market in 1947, and also kept in touch with other Local Associations in the city for mutual help and the exchange of ideas.

The Scottish Local Associations' Conference held in Edinburgh, was the highlight of 1948 and delegates came from all over Scotland. The Chief Guide addressed the conference and although she had toured Scotland, attending as many as five meetings in a day, she inspired her hearers with her abounding energy and enthusiasm.

In the division the Local Association members worked hard at fund-raising to benefit the Packs and Companies and helped them in numerous practical ways; they made camp overalls, sewing innumerable buttonholes, Brownie bags and other items of equipment; they coached Guides and Brownies for badges and acted as testers; they provided refreshments when required and always sought to have close personal contact with the children.

When the Trefoil School moved into its new home at Kirklands the committee decided to raise money and furnish one of the dormitories. Mrs Henderson's enthusiasm spurred on the members to great efforts and eventually all was complete with bedside tables, beds, linen, curtains and even a gay picture on the wall. The committee visited the school to see the finished dormitory and agreed that "their room" looked lovely. They asked that it should be called Blackford, a strange peep into the future when their own division was to be re-named Blackford Hill.

The Local Association gave the division a World Flag which was handed over to a Colour Party at the A.G.M. Subsequently they raised funds to help pay for the Division Banner. Members regularly attended Thinking Day Services and at one of these, a red letter day for the whole division, the Banner was dedicated and the World Flag handed on to the Rangers.

Acting on the suggestion of a District Commissioner, the Division and Local Association arranged that their funds should be merged. They agreed that this joint fund would be used for division secretarial expenses, donations or loans to new Packs and Companies, and a uniform fund; also an annual contribution of £2 was given to the County fund for new units, and an annual birthday present sent to the Trefoil School. The Local Association continued their fund-raising and presented a lightweight tent and a "Manikin" for demonstrating mouth-to-mouth breathing to the division and also donated £100 to the Stanemuir Adventure Centre. They have given funds and practical help to the 135th Company and Pack (Royal Blind School) especially when these Brownies attended the opening of the Brownie House at Netherurd.

The second Local Association in this story was formed in Portobello and Niddrie Division in 1963 and it also has given considerable financial and practical support to the division. Two shops, selling second-hand goods, opened in 1967 and 1970, were very successful and enabled the Association to give annual grants for expenses to Commissioners and money to new units, as well as a great deal of camping and other equipment for general use in the division, and it also paid for the metal badge for every Queen's Guide. Members of the Association have been generous in giving hospitality to overseas visitors and, typically, they gave a donation to an Edinburgh Guider with the 1st Company, chosen to represent the Guide Movement at a U.N.E.S.C.O. Cultural Conference in India, even though she was not a member of the division.

Many Guides and Rangers helped at Meadowbank Stadium during the

Commonwealth Paraplegic Games in 1970 and became involved in the concept of sports for the disabled. So the Association, "being a part of all that I have met," gave a sum of £150 to the Games on their behalf.

In 1947 all Badge testers, many of whom were Local Association members, were invited by the division to a mammoth tea party as a "Thank you," so the Association returned the compliment by asking every Guider to a fork supper.

One interesting feature runs right through the history of this Association. Even at its inauguration they argued that mothers support organisations for their sons, so why are fathers so seldom seen supporting their daughters? Whether as a result of this opinion or not, the first Treasurer and the second President were men, and there is still a devoted male member providing a link with outside organisations such as the Rotary.

These two Local Associations, alike, yet differing in so many ways, show that many parts make a whole. Other Associations in the city, Corstorphine, Davidson's Mains, Hailes and Murrayfield, which are now closed, have similar stories to tell. When Davidson's Mains disbanded, the members gave £200 to the Stanemuir Adventure Centre and £40 to Johnstounburn. In 1975, because of boundary changes, two more Local Associations, Currie and Balerno and South Queensferry, were welcomed into Edinburgh Guiding.

All Edinburgh's Local Associations have been a vital part of Guiding, often relieving the active Guiders of some worry or a task needing to be done, releasing her to work with the girls. Their interest and enthusiasm are shared by members throughout the United Kingdom.

Perhaps they were perfectly described by the Chief Commissioner, Mrs Walker, at the Local Association, Trefoil Guild and Supporters' Committee Conference in London in 1976 when she thanked them all "for being such indispensable friends."

"I am part of all that I have met." If this be true of Local Associations, how much more can it be said of TREFOIL GUILDS, who have indeed been part of the Guide Movement, and are continuing as un-uniformed, but well informed members.

The Girl Guides Association founded the Trefoil Guild to provide an organisation for all enrolled members who, on ceasing to be actively connected with Guiding, wish to remain in the Movement. Members agree:

(a) To keep alive the spirit of the Guide Promise and Law;
(b) To carry that spirit into the community in which they live and work;
(c) To give support to Guiding.

The very first Trefoil Guild in Edinburgh was the Post Guild (now the Handicapped) which was registered in December 1947, followed in 1948 by Duke Street. The County Guild was formed by Miss Dalmahoy in 1949 for those who could only meet once or twice a year, but liked to keep contact through the Guild. Some half dozen more Guilds sprang up in the fifties—from Companies, Districts or Divisions. There were many ways of recruiting, and this was one member's experience:

"The telephone rang in my house one evening, and the speaker told me she had been asked to start a Trefoil Guild. She had consented, and was now anxious that as many of her old Guiders as possible would join her to establish the Guild on a sound footing. My reaction was, 'Thank you very much, but I am really much too old to sit on the floor.' She laughed, 'My dear, I couldn't sit down on the floor if I tried.' In the end I promised to think it over. I did, and I have never regretted it."

And that was how South-West began in 1952.

Portobello and Niddrie Guild came into being in 1956 after a preliminary meeting with Miss Marjorie Noble, who was County Trefoil Guild Recorder at that time. These Guilds, together with St Giles' and St Serfs' in 1953, Newhaven in 1958, Port of Leith in 1960 and West, who closed down but came alive again in 1975, have given, and continue to give, a wide variety of service.

In Jubilee Year 1960, there was a Scottish Conference in Edinburgh. The local Guilds acted as hostesses and gave hospitality. On the evening of 2nd April, there was "Community Singing and Light Relief." The latter was a parody of the old Guide song, *Guides on the King's Highway,* and the Guilds gave a spirited impersonation of themselves as they sang! There was a housewife in mobcap and apron singing, "Who goes there?" . . . "The Trefoil Guild." The words of the first of five verses were:

> We were the Guides on the King's Highway
> and it's that Jubilee which we keep today.
> We're the old Girls' Branch, with initials T.G.
> Though *we* only started in '43,
> there's Mums and Grans and there's Aunties too—
> (As though we hadn't enough to do),
> Jubilee, don't forget, Birthday Teas, Jubilee!

Chorus:
> Up Guilds, Trefoils, 'tis no time for sleeping,
> Though we may be growing old, our minds are fresh and free.
> Look wide, think well, memories still keeping,
> Be a friend to all the world, this year of Jubilee.

So, fun and games with the Trefoils, but lots of hard work as well. Marjorie Noble gave a report on her visit to Windsor World Camp, representing Edinburgh Guilds.

"It was a thrilling experience; we worked very hard staffing the Coffee

Bar for the Camp, but it was all worthwhile when we met the Chief Guide.''

The Trefoil Guilds manned the Snack Bars at ''Spotlight on Guiding'' in 1964, and also the Rest Centre. Fifty-two people joined the Guilds as a result of this.

Throughout the years, the Guilds have helped to stock Guide Headquarters with crockery and kitchen utensils. They have given donations towards the Guide Hall, the Adventure Centre at Stanemuir, the Guide Orchestra, a training fund for new Guiders, a subscription to the Handicapped Section of Guides, The Guild of Service, and to Christian Aid. In all, £600 has been raised, usually at the popular annual Coffee Evening, for these and other purposes.

Presentation of the Trefoil Guild seat at the entrance to the City Hospital in 1970.

One of these ''other purposes'' was to entertain members from Belfast Trefoil Guilds and Local Associations to a lunch at 33 Melville Street. These visitors were staying at Netherurd for a restful weekend in 1970. They spent the Saturday morning shopping in Edinburgh and after lunch they went to North Berwick for tea, given by East Lothian Guild, and then back to Netherurd for the evening. If not exactly restful, it is hoped that the Belfast members were refreshed by their visit.

Many 21st birthdays have been celebrated, but South-West Guild's party was unique in one respect. They enjoyed a dinner in the Braid Hills Hotel as the guests of one of their own members, for the joy and friendship she had received through Guiding.

Each year, on or about 24th October, Guilds celebrate Fellowship Day as Guides hold their Thinking Day. In Edinburgh, Guilds take turns to act as hostesses to the other Guilds, and arrange the meeting with an international theme and invite guests and speakers. Business affairs start the meeting, the County Commissioner keeps the members up to date on Guide activities and, after the guest speaker, there is tea, when old friends may exchange news.

Individual Guilds hold their own meetings once a month, having guest speakers and visiting places of interest in Edinburgh and elsewhere, and one Guild has an annual outing to an Edinburgh theatre.

All Guild members have helped at Guide events, and as regular badge testers within their divisions. Frequently the Chairman of the County Trefoil Guilds has been asked at the Executive Committee meeting for help, perhaps with running a crèche for babies and toddlers at the regular coffee morning trainings held in Guide Headquarters; or to serve soup and, later, tea at trainings held in the Guide Hall for Commissioners, Trainers and Guiders, often from all over Scotland. They must derive some pleasure at using the well thought out equipment in the little kitchen, which they themselves provided. Whenever they see the need, Trefoil Guild members can be relied upon to be there.

In case one may be inclined to think that life in the Trefoil Guild is only given to serious service, listen to this tale.

"Miss Enid Nicholson, then Scottish Adviser, suggested a Sports Circle. This was at St Andrews, and what could be more appropriate—Golf for Trefoils! Over a midnight 'cuppa' Lady Langham, Mrs Lowson and Mrs Paterson went a step further. Why not have games with England, Ulster and Wales? London was approached, they approved, we were off!"

Edinburgh and East Area have a flourishing Golf club—members from Edinburgh, Peebles and East Lothian have four meetings a year and play for the Durham Spoon, presented after the first International match played at St Andrews in 1969 by Miss Gibson, one of the opposing players. They also have a Hole-and-Hole Competition for a cup presented by Mr and Mrs Michelsen. The season is rounded off with a social Annual Meeting, usually more hilarious than businesslike!

Edinburgh can be very proud of the part they have played in building up the Trefoil Guilds. Since 1952, the Guild in Scotland has been run by four "Edinburgh Guides," Miss Ella Maxwell, Miss Meta Stevenson, Miss Enid Nicholson and Mrs Gloria Lowson. Although known as Recorder, then Adviser and now Chairman, the responsibility has been the same. All four have distinguished themselves in many branches of Guiding, and it is no wonder Trefoil Guilds have flourished with such leaders.

Meta Stevenson writes:

"During my five years as Recorder the thing I should perhaps stress was the growing importance of the A.G.M. which was held in different towns each year—one in Motherwell was a highlight, when the Chief Guide was our Guest of Honour. I remember reporting that our membership was 1999, and asking for one more member!! My last effort was the planning of a residential weekend Conference (incorporating the A.G.M.) at St Andrews. Such weekends are now regular events and an important part of T.G. in Scotland.''

Enid Nicholson says:

"The final outstanding project was the collecting of funds for the fire escape at Netherurd, which was done through sheer hard work and self-sacrifice by all.''

Gloria Lowson has carried her membership for Edinburgh out into the wider world of International Fellowship. She says:

"I was chosen as one of two Trefoil delegates representing Great Britain to attend the 9th General Assembly of the International Fellow-ship of Former Scouts and Guides in Australia—half round the world and back in 25 days. With Guild members from 14 countries, we spent 15 days travelling and sight-seeing, having discussions as we travelled, broadening our outlook and finding out how the other half of the world lived. After that, how could I give up—I wanted to pass on to Guild members all that I had gained—and through service, show my appreciation of the trust that had been put in me.''

Mrs Lowson continues to do this, and is still reaching out to wider horizons, as she has just been appointed a council Member of the above Fellowship of Former Scouts and Guides. To quote once more:

"All started from a little note handed to me by one of my Guide daughters many years ago: 'A meeting is being held at ——— with a view to starting a Trefoil Guild'.''

Daughter, Mother—Trefoil Guild, Guide, are part of the whole, and will go forth to the future with ever-widening vision.

9

Badges and Training

GENERAL BADEN-POWELL first used a badge system in the training of young soldiers in the 5th Dragoon Guards. Baden-Powell did not agree with the method of "licking these young men into shape through drill, drill and more drill," so he devised attractive methods of giving each man a personal pride in his own progress. Through developing his own qualifications and abilities a man will contribute more to society, thereby benefitting both himself and his fellows. This vast experience gained in India and Africa, plus his genuine interest in youth, was put to good use when B-P devised the Boy Scout Badge system and, later, one for the Girl Guides.

B-P's method was to encourage all-round efficiency through the 2nd Class and 1st Class badges; the tests for these, set out in 1910, cover observation and tracking, exercise and expeditions, First Aid and life saving, fire lighting and cooking, thrift, recruiting, tying knots, knowing the points of the compass, the composition of the Union Jack, the Scout or Guide Laws and being able to read and write.

Variety came in the second group of badges given for proficiency in service subjects and hobbies, their large number being intended to ensure that every boy and girl, however limited in ability, might find some badge to stimulate them to better achievement and to become personally enthused in subjects that appealed to them. The standard for gaining a badge was the

"amount of effort exercised by the individual . . . through cheery self-development from within, not formal instruction from without. This brings all on to a footing of equal possibility."

These are B-P's own words but his ideas were interpreted differently at times and rather rigid examination style tests became fashionable between the Wars and until 1968 when the new Programme was introduced to bring back many of the Founder's intentions.

Many women in Edinburgh today (and millions in the world) must owe their present skill and interest in a hobby, or even their careers, to the moment when a Guider or Patrol Leader said to her, "Which badge will you take next?"

The first badge a Guide earned was the Trefoil or Promise Badge, its three leaves representing the Threefold Promise she made at her enrolment ceremony when, having passed the Tenderfoot Test and wearing her uniform for the first time, she received the badge from her Guider and was welcomed into her Patrol, the Company and the Movement. Then she went on to work for her 2nd Class Badge covering very basic Guiding skills, and not until she had gained this badge could she go on to take the Proficiency badges with their great choice of subjects.

Many testers were needed for these badges and members of the early committee tested some and recruited their friends to do others as the subjects increased. (There will be many a wry smile amongst those readers who remember this time-honoured way of bringing new blood into the Movement!) Those first badges were signs of the times—artist, needle-woman, naturalist, minstrel, interpreter, sick nurse and cook represented feminine pursuits; ambulance, signalling and the outdoor badges were for the pioneers; whilst the popular cyclist and horsemanship badges showed prowess in the only individual methods of transport of the day.

Testers met to discuss their problems, then as now, and in 1915 put forward some down-to-earth ideas:

Laundress Badge: "Wash some red flannel" would be more practical (and pioneering) than "Starch a boiled shirt."

Sick Nurse Badge: "Smallpox seems a very severe disease for girls of 12 to nurse and should be excluded from the list!"

Swimmer's Badge: "As it is difficult to get girls into the baths wearing long skirts and boots, could they be allowed to swim double the distance in their costumes." This badge was included in the 1st Class test but many girls lived in places without baths or pools and couldn't learn. Alternatives to swimming were asked for and suggestions made to overcome this difficulty.

New badges were suggested—Ju-Jitsu, Knitter, Printer, Textile Worker, Handyman, and a request for Esperanto recurred in the 1950s!

Criticisms and ideas have gone from testers through Scottish to Imperial (now Commonwealth) Headquarters through the years, and testers might be surprised at the number of alterations made as a result. Communications do break down but on the whole the tests are up-dated in a sensible way. Innumerable testers have willingly and voluntarily given their time and skills for Edinburgh Guides, meeting many small girls nervously embarking on new ventures and they are glad to see a younger generation interested in their own specialities.

Surely one of the "originals" is Mrs Margaret Pearson, who writes at the age of 102 years in March 1976:

"When examiners in First Aid, Nursing, etc., were difficult to find because of the 1914/18 War, the Red Cross got V.A.D.s to take on the work; there were 8-12 of us and we used schools in different localities to examine 100 or so Guides in an evening. When we were not required any longer we were each given a Silver Thanks Badge at a little ceremony in St John's Church, Princes Street. I kept on for a time with the Post Guides and remember examining a Guide with T.B. in the City Hospital; we sat in a wooden verandah, the front all open to the snow then falling—outdoor treatment in those days! I was born too soon to be a Guide myself and can only boast of being a Vice-President (of Midlothian), but my interest in Guides has never failed.''

Right from the start Guides were keen to learn and their Captains helped and trained them. The 1st Midlothian Company gained the earliest 1st Class Badges in October 1910 and in the Badge census of 1914 there were 126 Proficiency, 17 2nd Class, 6 1st Class badges and 4 All Round Cords. For these, a Guide needed her 1st Class and seven other badges, including an outdoor one not done for her 1st Class. Gold Cords were gained by two Patrol Leaders in 1922 and one in 1927; these were very rare and were awarded to two more girls in the 1930s and five in the 1940s. In order to help their Guides with badges, the Guiders went to trainings where they also became involved with practicalities as one of them remembers:

"I was keen to help the Guides with their Vet's Badge so we attended the "Dick Vet" where we were set to bandage a horse—not a small pony—a huge Clydesdale which towered above us and took miles of bandage round its middle; we had to use step ladders for "over and under." A similar enthusiasm for badges took us to a Baby Home where willing nurses taught us how to bath and change babies—How slippery wet babies are—we were terrified of letting them fall.''

Acting has always been a popular activity and Rangers enjoy taking Group Badges, so many years ago the 7th Ranger Company entered for the Player's Badge. Eight of the girls took part in two short plays; one was Shakespearean (compulsory) and the other was *Six who pass while the lentils boil!* A rather fierce tester failed their first effort, maybe because one player's hose were descending in the final scene! More experience in make-up and firmer stitches in the costumes ensured a "Pass" at the next attempt.

Many organisations and kind people have helped to train Guides and Brownies, in particular the Red Cross, St Andrew's Ambulance Brigade, the Fire Service and the Police. Year after year, classes are held for Guides, giving knowledge to the girls which they may use later in life. The excellent liaison of the Police with Guides taking the Cyclist's Badge, resulted in some Guide cyclists leading the parade in a Safety First Demonstration. The Scottish Beekeepers' Association agreed to examine Guides for their Bee Master's Certificate for 2/6d instead of 5/- as Scottish Headquarters paid an annual subscription. Country Dance Societies gave dancing classes, and staff at the Outlook Tower offered to give talks on the Royal Mile.

One early Guide recalls:

"About 1913 we acquired a small piece of land next to Glenogle Baths and began an allotment. A lady—Miss White— came from one of the colleges of gardening to give us lectures on Wednesday evenings and on Saturdays; and in summer, we dug and sowed and finally reaped. We grew vegetables chiefly but a few roses also. I still remember Miss White's lectures on pruning and grafting."

Atholl Crescent Domestic Science College staff very kindly tested for many badges but one of them protested when a Guide arrived to take Cook's Badge and had never cooked anything in her life! The staff also suggested that baking pastry or cakes should be taken out of the test as so many girls had no ovens at home in which to practise—this was in the 1920s. One Ranger did make pastry at Atholl Crescent but used cornflour by mistake! The kind tester whisked away the resulting heavy slab, and when more suet had been chopped (no "Atora" then) and the steak and kidney pie was baked, the Ranger was congratulated on her light pastry.

The Rotary Club stimulated an interest in badges when they asked Girl Guides to take part in a Handcraft Exhibition in Waverley Market in October 1956; it was opened by the Lord Provost and lasted a week. Badge work was the theme for the Guides' display, and classes were held for months previously to teach new skills embracing all from Artist, Basketmaker and Camper to Needlewoman, Toymaker and Woodman. Colours were hoisted and lowered each evening, demonstrations and exhibitions were given by divisions and stewards were armed with "Policy, Organisation and Rules" to answer any questions.

Many Guides were reluctant to work for what is now the Commonwealth Badge because they felt it required a tremendous amount of academic research and the ability to write well; moreover, they dreaded the test itself. All too often this was the last badge a Guide needed to gain her Queen's Guide award, and in an attempt to change this situation, Commonwealth Headquarters altered the syllabus in 1973 in the Second Edition of the *Guide Handbook* so that Guides not only had a much wider choice, but could demonstrate their interest and knowledge of the Commonwealth in a variety of ways, many not needing academic skills. The Guide Friendship badge was also introduced at this time to encourage girls to make new friends and widen their interest in Guiding Overseas. Edinburgh Guides are very fortunate in having the Commonwealth Institute in the city where the staff welcome the girls, giving them leaflets and encouraging them to use the library for their research. On the day of the Commonwealth test many girls have been agreeably surprised to meet overseas testers, sometimes in national costume, who are only too willing to talk about their homelands. They take a great interest in the Guides and their projects for the badge as so often they are themselves studying in Edinburgh.

Badge secretaries were appointed in divisions and districts in the 1930s (actually they were called Examination Secretaries and there is mention of an "80% pass mark being required"—not quite what B-P meant!). They worked nearly as hard as the girls, finding testers for so many subjects, arranging a suitable place and time for the test, and telling the Guider who informed her Guides. Sadly, some Guides were (and still are) guilty of great discourtesy by not arriving for a test and failing to apologise—they went on the "black list" and were not allowed to take a badge for some months. (However, in 1975, about 6000 badges were gained, so most girls are in the right place at the right time and most of them remember to say "Thank You.")

1968—a year of change—a new look to Guiding—a new *Handbook*— a new programme—new badges—new age groups. The eight points in the programme, all leading out from the Promise, gave more scope for adventure, skills and service to be explored, and enjoyed by Guides who were now able to join at 10 years old, leaving by their 16th birthday, but they could become Rangers at 14 years.

The Guide Laws were re-written to be better understood by the modern girl, the 2nd and 1st Class Badges disappeared, the Tenderfoot Test was replaced by the Eight-point challenge and when the Guide is enrolled she is now allowed to take at once the newly-named Interest Badges, of which there are 70. A new Eight-point badge is awarded annually by the Guider in consultation with the Patrol Leaders' Council, the name now given to the Court of Honour, to show that the Guide has progressed and developed during the year; this could be through new experiences and new challenges accepted, without the Guide taking any badges.

The Queen's Guide Badge syllabus and the design of the Badge were altered in the new programme; Queen Elizabeth (now the Queen Mother) gave permission for this award in 1945, the insignia for which was to be Her Majesty's crown surmounting the First Class Badge. A special test was drawn up, aimed at producing the best type of all-round person, who can be relied upon to live up to the ideals bequeathed to us by Baden-Powell and to the honour of wearing a Royal Badge. The prospect of gaining this award has spurred many Guides into taking badges they would never have attempted otherwise and they have enjoyed this stretching experience.

The tradition in the Guide Movement of giving service was reinforced by the introduction of the new Service Flash. To earn this badge a Guide has to give sustained and regular service for at least three months, such as teaching in Sunday School, being a Pack Leader with her local Brownie

Pack or helping each week in a hospital or children's home. Alternatively, if she cannot undertake regular weekly service because of homework or other commitments, she can give a minimum of 40 hours' service, consisting of various tasks undertaken for different people at different times. A record is kept by the Guide and in either instance the service given must be approved by the District Commissioner. Often a Guide finds that working for her Service Flash is the beginning of a deeper interest in the particular field she chooses, and is a challenge to her resourcefulness in finding where there is a need which she can fill. Most Guides love to help and even the younger ones are able to earn this badge by doing jobs which are within their capabilities. They find a great deal of pleasure and satisfaction in doing something for others and often carry on with the service long after the minimum requirements of the Service Flash have been met.

As Edinburgh has such large numbers of Guides certain badge tests have always been arranged by the County Badge Secretary, particularly for badges such as First Aid, Emergency Helper and Firefighter where classes have to be arranged for the Guides before they are competent to take the tests. The County Badge Secretary also acted, and still does, as co-ordinator, giving advice and moral support to Guiders and Badge Secretaries; the most unlikely request to find a tester for any badge in the Programme was no problem to her!

Regionalisation in 1975 meant that country areas and two more divisions were added to the County; with travel becoming lengthy and fares rising regularly, it was decided that as many badges as possible should be tested in divisions and districts, cutting down on the "County" ones.

In 1972 a new badge entry form was adopted by the County, based on one which Portbello and Niddrie Division had been using successfully for a number of years. This aimed to cut down the paper work for Badge Secretaries and also to reduce the possibility of girls taking badge tests for which they were not fully prepared, by including provision for the signature of a parent as well as that of the Guider when a test was requested. This has been particularly helpful in making sure that parents of Brownies are completely in the picture and do not have to rely on a vague, "Mummy, Brown Owl said . . . !" but it is equally applicable to Guides. If Guides get a lot of enjoyment and personal satisfaction working for and achieving a badge, so do the testers sometimes have fun from the actual tests.

For instance, at a Toymaker's Badge test an eleven-year-old Guide brought a woolly ball which was slightly damp and smelling strongly of disinfectant. She explained, "My awfu' wee brother threw it in the bucket when me mum was washing the floor!" Another Guide interpreted only too literally the clause "Dress a doll" and BOUGHT dolls' clothes and put them on a doll at the test.

Some very odd replies have been heard at the Emergency Helper

Badge tests—"What would you do if you were lost in a wood?" brought the prompt reply, "Look for a bus!"

There are times, too, when the Guide is blissfully unaware that perhaps her efforts are not being wholly appreciated. One tester, frustrated by the extreme slowness of a Guide taking half an hour to iron one blouse for her Laundress Badge test, was completely taken aback by the Guide's remark, "It must be a great help to you to have us Guides giving you a hand."

TRAINING

"I'm doing my Book Lover Badge, Brown Owl."

"Our Patrol wants to take the Outdoor Cooking Pennant—What do we do?"

"Let's visit Hillend Ski Slope and then try for our Skier Interest Certificate."

Brownies, Guiders and Rangers are gaining more and more interesting and exciting badges and certificates each year. This increases the need for instruction and training to cover such a wide range of topics. The girls are helped to acquire their skills and knowledge by their Guiders and by various "Outside Experts." Do the girls wonder how their Guiders themselves have learnt skills to pass on to them? Just as the girl asks the question—so does the adult:

Training? What for? Who goes?
Why should I go? When? Where?
For how long? Who does it? Who benefits?

Training has, from the very beginning of Guiding, been seen as an essential and serious part of the Movement, but it has to be enjoyable—a lesson learnt through fun is a lesson well learnt!—could this almost be a Guide proverb?

The first recorded training for Guiders in Edinburgh was in 1916 when Lady Fayrer gave a course on "The Duties of a Guide Officer." The following year, 1917, in July, the first training in Scotland was held for a week in a house near the Braid Hills. This help for Guiders was organised by the County Commissioner for Edinburgh, Mrs Laurie, and by Miss Buchan Hepburn, who was County Commissioner for East Lothian. The trainings covered a wide range of topics, including a Fire Drill Demonstration—and Mrs Laurie herself jumped from a first-floor window into a blanket held by the "rescuing " Guiders.

In 1919, the second Training School was held at Liberton and was organised by Miss Agnes Maynard, one of the first trainers appointed. A pattern was emerging, and during the 1920s the Guiders' Training School for new Guiders was held annually, on one night a week throughout the winter. The trainings were organised on the Patrol System—promising

Guiders acting as "Patrol Leaders" and other Guiders acting as her "Patrol." One rather novel suggestion was made by Central Division in 1922 that Guiders might benefit by exchanging units for one evening! In 1926, Miss Nicoll, the Examination Secretary, went to St Colm's Women's Missionary Training College once a week for six weeks to "do Guiding" with the students. This is the kind of training which helped the fun and excitement of Guiding to spread so quickly in distant lands.

The early Guiders saw leadership potential in their Patrol Leaders as they matured and, to train them, Ranger Cadet Companies were started in 1916. These girls of 16-21 years were taught all manner of things that would eventually enable then to become Officers or Guiders in the Movement. Throughout the years a number of Cadet Companies existed in Edinburgh and the girls followed a training schedule in Leadership very similar to the present-day Young Leaders' Scheme.

Guides in Edinburgh who had gained their First Class Badge also realised their responsibility for "keeping up a high standard of Guide ideals and work in their County" and formed the First Class Guides' Club. They met together at least three times a year for lectures and discussions on Guide Training and any other subjects which interested them. As far back as March 1924, they had a talk on the "Romance of Edinburgh." During the summers, the club, with the help of a licensed Guider, organised camps for Guides from companies which otherwise would not have had the chance to enjoy this adventure in Guiding. Club members also served as "dogs-bodies" at numerous County functions. From the First Class Club emerged the Melville Club, formed so that "members of the First Class Club on becoming Guiders might not only continue the work begun in the First Class Club, but also, by further service, extend its ideals of fellowship and of a high standard of Guiding in the County." The Melville Club also held at least three meetings a year, enjoyed social get-togethers and helped at numerous events.

Pre-warrant training courses for new Brownie and Guide Guiders continued at Edinburgh Headquarters throughout the Second World War years. The Guiders were required to attend the course for one evening a week for eight to ten weeks and sometimes the venues were varied—including the grounds of Daniel Stewart's College. (Can you imagine the present pupils' reactions to such a scene as Guiders being instructed in Drill or Signalling or First Aid Practice!) Guiding at this time must have made a real impact on the public, for Edinburgh also staged a display of "blitz-cooking" in Princes Street Gardens and in Melville Street.

At the end of the war, Netherurd House was opened as the Scottish Training Centre and Edinburgh Guiders were, and still are, encouraged to take advantage of the trainings and conferences there. At the beginning of 1946, Miss Margaret Torrance, an Edinburgh Trainer, was appointed Secretary to Netherurd and has been Guider-in-Charge there since 1948.

In 1946, a new qualification for trainers, the Training Certificate, was introduced. The Headquarters Instructors remained as specialists in their own field but the certificate was reviewed and endorsed annually within the County. Through the years many Guiders with a flair for helping adults have gained this certificate and been able to inspire and instil confidence into both new and experienced Guiders and Commissioners in the City. Some of these have followed on to take the Training Diploma and have trained throughout the United Kingdom and beyond.

Miss Andrina Wilson, a Brownie Trainer, and Miss Chris Lumsden, a Guide Trainer, trained Guiders during the war years and afterwards, both in Edinburgh and throughout Scotland. They both acted, at different times, as Chairman of the Edinburgh Training Committee and both gave service overseas—Chris Lumsden went as a trainer to Nigeria and Andrina Wilson, cutting short her term of office as Brownie Adviser for Scotland, undertook two years' Girl Guide Training in Malaya.

Miss Greta Collyns, an Edinburgh Guide Trainer, was appointed as the Scottish Training Adviser in 1953, serving until the end of 1958 when she went on tour to the Far East and Hong Kong. One of the great innovations which Miss Collyns introduced during her time as Training Adviser was the Mobile Training Scheme in 1954. This involved trainers travelling to the outlying parts of Scotland with a Mobile Training

Caravan. She also worked a great deal outside Scotland, at Commonwealth Headquarters, and in all parts of the world—Europe, the Americas, the Far East and Africa—training leaders and helping them to build up their own training teams. Her final appointment was General Secretary for Scotland from 1962 until 1967.

Miss Rina Marshall, a Camp Trainer, gave considerable training help in Singapore and on her return became County Cadet Captain.

Miss Sheila Thomson was the first full-time salaried trainer in Scotland and later became Overseas Training Adviser, C.H.Q., and then was the trainer for the Pacific area.

The following trainers have served in full-time Scottish appointments:

Miss Evelyn Blackie, in 1967, served for a year as the Trainer with the Mobile Training Van (and now in 1976 has been appointed Brownie Consultant).

Miss Betty Robertson, an Edinburgh Brownie Trainer, worked at Scottish Guide Headquarters from 1971 to 1973 as Trainer for Development.

At present, two other Edinburgh trainers are in the Scottish team: Miss Molly Armstrong, a Ranger Trainer, is now Boating Adviser for Scotland, and Miss Winnie Hogg is Assistant to the Training Adviser and is responsible for arranging the Training Van tours. Many more names will come to mind as Guiders remember the Trainings they attended.

During the 1950s the Guiders' Training School continued providing an eight- or nine-week course for new Guiders, culminating in a residential weekend. Several innovations were introduced in the late 50s:

—the provision of pre-warrant trainings for married Guiders in the mornings with a crêche for young children, staffed by members of the Trefoil Guilds and Local Associations;
—trainings at Craiglockhart Roman Catholic Training College for nuns and lay students, including several from Africa;
—experienced Guiders attended advanced trainings on a number of topics.

There was a marked increase in the trainings planned for Guiders at District and Division levels and this trend continues today.

Do any Guides go to trainings? Yes, indeed—many Edinburgh Patrol Leaders have attended, and enjoyed, the regular trainings held for them at Netherurd. Some divisions have held most useful Day Conferences for their Patrol Leaders in Edinburgh Headquarters, when the whole house has been a hive of activity.

In 1968, when the Eight-Point Programme for Guiding was introduced, even more emphasis was placed on training at District level, involving the whole District team. The Commissioner and her Guiders helped each other, although trainers were available to give assistance if needed.

On Saturday, 22nd November 1969, Edinburgh held its first Day

Training in St George's School for all Guiders and Commissioners. Over 300 Guiders attended and made the venture such a success that it was repeated in March 1971 when about 350 Guiders attended.

Guiders had been asked six months previously to give their ideas of subjects to be covered during the day; outside experts dealt with some of these and trainers from other Counties helped the Edinburgh Training Committee. The training sessions of approximately three-quarters of an hour, for small groups, went on all day using every part of the school. The science laboratory was an excellent place to hold the splendid hand-craft session where all could "have a go." On both occasions, St George's School was most generously lent to us, and the Local Associations of Portobello and Niddrie and South-East Divisions provided lunches and endless cups of coffee and tea. Yet another pattern was being established for, in October 1975, even more Commissioners, Guiders and Young Leaders invaded James Gillespie's School for another exhausting but very profitable Day Training. During the day, Guiders from the areas of Harlaw, Turnhouse and Inveralmond, recently included in the County, were welcomed into Edinburgh Guiding.

The success of the Day Trainings and countless other trainings in Edinburgh is due to their planning and organisation by a sub-committee of the County Executive—the Training Committee. The make-up of this committee has changed much over the years but during that time countless people from different sections of Guiding in every Division have given their time, energy and knowledge to ensure that Guiders and Young Leaders receive the help they require or request.

In 1971, the District Study Paper Scheme was inaugurated and this helped to strengthen the District teams by providing them with written material on Brownie, Guide or Ranger topics to be used in conjunction with the appropriate Handbooks. The ensuing discussions which arose helped to solve problems by sharing experiences and knowledge and enjoying a sense of caring. "Fireside Trainings" at that time, and now, proved to be a great success.

In January 1973, a qualification for Guiders was introduced—the Adult Leader's Certificate. In the past a Guider was required to work with a unit for at least three months and to attend a course of pre-warrant training before her Commissioner considered issuing her with a warrant. Now, an adult who wishes to become a Guider is appointed to a District in the first place and undertakes a period of training to gain the certificate prior to being warranted to a unit. It is anticipated that the Adult Leader's Certificate may take up to, but not longer than, one year to complete. The Guider works towards this by herself and calls for additional help as she needs it, but throughout, she discusses her own progress with her Commissioner and is given help and encouragement during her first year as a new Guider. The need for trained leadership has always been realised by the Guide Movement and the high standard achieved is acknowledged by other youth organisations who accept the Adult Leader's Certificate as a qualification in trained youth leadership. The Edinburgh Training Committee organises a number of interesting and varied trainings each year and opportunities do arise for Guiders to attend residential training courses in Scotland and beyond. The South-East of Scotland Training Association also provide Leadership Courses for people working in various fields of youth work and there is usually one Edinburgh Guider at least on the annual course.

At the same time as the Adult Leader's Certificate was introduced, the Young Leaders' Scheme was started for girls between 16 and 18 who wish to train for leadership in Brownie Packs and Guide Companies. The Scheme is under the direction of the County Leadership Adviser, though many divisions have representatives who promote the Young Leaders' Scheme in their division; they gather together the girls who are doing it to compare notes and ideas and help them gain their certificates. The training plan is very similar to the Leadership Certificates previously taken by Ranger Cadets. The girls are also challenged to become personally involved in activities with people of their own age while they work with Packs and Companies. Their youth and enthusiasm quickly establishes good relationships with the children in their units, enabling them to put into practice the training they are receiving.

This has given a brief outline of trainings in Edinburgh, but many opportunities have arisen for Guides, Rangers, Young Leaders, Guiders and Commissioners to attend Trainings and Conferences anywhere in the United Kingdom and abroad. Recently Guiders and a Commissioner have been to Waddow, Durham, Coventry and Sheffield for trainings and conferences, with subjects ranging from the Eight-Point Programme, the Promise and Law, to camping and outdoor activities.

There is one conference which has been attended by Edinburgh Commissioners ever since the first one at Perth in 1918. This is the Scottish Commissioners' Conference, held sometimes in hotels, but in recent years in University buildings. These well-organised conferences provide Commissioners from all over Scotland with the chance to exchange ideas, discuss policy changes, launch new programmes, study papers or new training certificates, and to hear speakers from kindred organisations. A good number of District and Division Commissioners from Edinburgh attend and many friendships are made between islanders and city-dwellers, highlanders and countrywomen, all talking about the same thing—Guiding.

At times the talking has to stop and the Guide signal for silence is the admiration of all who encounter its use, particularly male guest speakers —or hall porters.

It was during lunch at a Conference in Dunblane Hydro in 1971 that the hall porter came into the dining room, looked helplessly round at the sea of blue-clad figures and said to Audrey James, the Scottish Secretary, sitting at a nearby table, "There is a telephone call for one of your ladies but how do I find her?" She at once stood up and raised her right hand, on seeing it her neighbours did likewise and STOPPED TALKING, and in seconds over 400 tongues fell silent. The poor man was himself speechless at the effect of one raised hand but managed to pass on his message! This signal was increasingly used by the Guide Movement in World War II when whistles were blown only by Air Raid Wardens in times of danger and not for signalling commands to children!

It has been used to still the hubbub at many trainings and readers will have happy memories of the innumerable trainers from Edinburgh and outside who have so willingly given their time and energy to help Guiding to flourish in Edinburgh. So much friendship, inspiration, confidence and fun has ensured that it is the girls who benefit most from the training courses that their leaders attend—after all, it was "the girls who began it."

THE DUKE OF EDINBURGH'S AWARD SCHEME

H.R.H. the Duke of Edinburgh introduced his Award Scheme in 1956. It offers young people a challenge in personal endeavour and achievement.

There are three separate Awards in which young people take part, starting with the Bronze Award at 14 years, the Silver at 15 and the Gold at 16; the upper age limit for all Awards is their 25th birthday. They do not need to progress from one Award to another, but may start the appropriate Award according to their age.

The scheme is not just another organisation; young people do not belong to it. It is operated on their behalf through schools, colleges, youth organisations, industry, the Police and the Armed Forces, or they may "go it alone."

The Girl Guide Movement has included the Award Scheme in its own programme and it is an "Operating Authority." One member of the Scottish Girl Guides' Executive Committee is the co-ordinator for Scotland; Guide Counties in Scotland have an Award Scheme Adviser and most Divisions in Edinburgh have one too. She encourages the girls and puts them in touch with those who will guide them through the interests, projects, courses or expeditions which they undertake.

As the Guide Badge system, so the Award Scheme has helped to bridge the generation gap, and older people have been delighted to find young folk who are keenly interested in their own life-long hobby or skill. The goodwill generated through working together is a very heartening experience. Young people are encouraged to develop existing interests and to find fresh opportunities for fun, excitement and satisfaction in their leisure time.

There are five Sections in the Scheme:

SERVICE
EXPEDITION
INTEREST
DESIGN FOR LIVING
PHYSICAL ACTIVITY.

Four sections must be done for each Award, candidates choosing between Design for Living or Physical Activity. For a Gold a girl has the additional choice between going on an expedition or working as a resident helper for some worthwhile project; also she must spend at least five days at a residential course mixing with others not previously known to her.

A girl can start her Award Scheme in one place and complete it elsewhere. Girls have come from the North and West of Scotland, England, Northern Ireland and India to continue their Award in Edinburgh, and *vice versa*. Edinburgh Guides have taken part in the different sections accepting the challenge in many ways, and 28 have gained Gold Awards.

In the *Service* Section they have helped in homes for children, old people and the mentally and physically handicapped; and in hospital canteens and shops, with Sunday Schools, as Pack Leaders and Assistant Guiders. A trainee nurse joined the Conservation Corps and, on her off-duty weekends, bicycled from Edinburgh to Doune to work with a group cleaning rubbish from ditches. Some Rangers at the Trefoil School for the handicapped made Picture/Word Cards for the Y.W.C.A. International Centre to help with teaching English to immigrants. Girls have worked for and, where applicable, gained National Certificates in Child care, First Aid, Life-saving, Police Service, Care of Animals and many others.

Expedition: Basic training for light-weight camping is part of Guiding, but for an Award girls must plan their routes and have worthwhile purposes for their expeditions. They have visited castles and places of interest in the Islands and on the mainland, studying flowers, wild life and weather signs. Groups have stayed in hostels, caravans and barns as well as in tents; usually they have walked, but some have been on bicycles or in wheelchairs.

Worthwhile Projects: Girls who have chosen this alternative have helped at camps for under-privileged and for handicapped children, also at the School for Training Guide Dogs for the Blind in Forfar, working alongside the permanent staff. They found this most interesting and worthwhile; one girl spent some time blindfolded so that she could feel what it was like to be guided by a trained dog.

Interest: From a choice of about 400 interests, Edinburgh Guides have sampled at least 60, encouraged and helped by adults with their specialist knowledge. In addition to the usual hobbies, girls have studied geology, philately, heraldry, pewter work, cacti growing, librarianship, meteorology and playing the organ. When an Adviser was taking an overseas Guider round the Museum of Antiquities, she found that one of the custodians would be willing to help a "Gold" candidate with her project of "Lighting through the Ages." Both found this fascinating and the girl later gave her collection of candlesticks to be sold for charity. A rock climber was assessed for an award in Turkey while there on an educational cruise. Some of the handcrafts made by Guide candidates were on display in the Award Scheme Caravan at the Royal Highland Show in 1974.

Design for Living: Courses in the art of make-up and hair styling, with a fashion show for the assessment, are very popular. (Will boys be wanting to join now that they have the choice between this section and a Physical Activity?)

Handicapped Ranger Guides at the Trefoil School furnished and decorated a model bedroom all to scale. A "Gold" candidate studied Special Housing in Edinburgh and did the required project while at college in England. Another chose "Extending Frontiers" and was able to combine this with a *Residential Qualification* at "Our Cabana" in Mexico. Girls have also been to courses at Adventure Centres, Carberry Tower and Netherurd.

The ultimate goal is the presentation of the Gold Award Certificates by the Duke of Edinburgh himself at Holyroodhouse. This takes place once a year and afterwards all Scottish Girl Guide winners of the Gold Award in recent years have been invited to tea at Edinburgh Guide Headquarters in Melville Street, along with their parents and leaders. Girls from all over Scotland are interested in each other's path to their "Golds" and in their common interest of Guiding.

Now that more Guiders holding Gold Awards are working with Units in Edinburgh, many more Guides are being encouraged to take up the Duke's challenge.

The first Edinburgh Guide to achieve her Gold Award was Patsy Miller in 1961. She writes:

"I was a Ranger in the 75th Company and embarked on the Scheme lightheartedly; it was all fun and life was hectic. Our residential weekend at Netherurd with other youth groups helped us all to appreciate the value of each other's programmes.

"The exhibition of all our hobbies and collections at the George Square Infants' Department gave me a salutary lesson on the high standard that the Award Scheme could demand and get. I was so aware that I had not really reached it that I was amazed when the Duke actually spoke to me about my postcard collection . . . perhaps he spoke to us all that day!

"Now I am living in Belgium. Two of my daughters are Brownies and I have made the fatal promise to re-train as a Guider—it could easily have been as an Award Scheme Adviser—I'm lucky—I've had a taste of both.''

10

Property—Heritable, Rentable and Moveable

GIRL GUIDE UNITS in Edinburgh usually meet in schools or in church or village halls and have not built Guide huts especially for meeting places as many Scout troops do. This has relieved Guiders of the responsibility of the upkeep, security and other worries which arise through owning a property. A locked cupboard in school or hall is usually sufficient to hold equipment needed for meetings. Tents and camp equipment may require more space but these are becoming more and more a District or Division concern and, with help from Local Associations and parents' Support Groups, are probably kept in an attic or garage.

Administration at County level, on the other hand, needed a permanent office, rooms for meetings and storage facilities even in the early days; later, an ever-increasing range of activities demanded the addition of more properties, both static and mobile. This chapter tells the tale of forethought and wise investment through the years to ensure that the right accommodation was available to meet the needs of a growing Movement with a wide-ranging programme.

EDINBURGH GIRL GUIDE HEADQUARTERS—33 MELVILLE STREET

Melville Street was just a drawing on an architect's board when the Battle of Waterloo ended the Napoleonic Wars in 1815; Edinburgh's New Town had grown little during those 23 years of war and there were still green fields and wooded slopes west of Charlotte Square. However, James Gillespie Graham had drawn his plan, Robert Brown had designed the elegant house elevations, and building began on land owned by gentlemen whose names are reflected in those of the streets and crescents all round. William Street, however, was named after the monarch of the time—William IV.

Melville Street was to be the principal feature of this plan and Sir Francis Walker of Coates had his own family house built in the centre facing Stafford Street and he owned the feu of "No. 33," which was built by John Nicol in 1825.

The house was first bought by William Bonar on 7th November 1825 for £2100; three more families occupied it over 104 years, and the widow of James Alexander Fleming sold it on 22nd May 1929 for £2,900 to the Trustees of the City of Edinburgh Girl Guides—Miss Dalmahoy, Miss

Wallace Williamson, Miss M. Brown, Miss J. Wood and Miss M. Wood. Much later—on 10th August 1948—the Trusteeship was vested in the offices of the County Commissioner, the County Secretary and Assistant County Secretary (Finance) and remains so now. It was at this time that Mr Ivor Guild became legal adviser to the County and his advice has been invaluable.

The house was already well known in Guide circles as Mrs Fleming had been a good friend for years; she had stored goods in the cellars of "33" for the many jumble sales which were held—to raise funds—to buy materials—to make up into useful and pretty things for the great Handcraft Sale in the Assembly Rooms which raised the price of the property. After she moved to Fife she became a fairy godmother to the Post Brownies, who still talk about her, having them to stay in Upper Largo for a month each summer, and she sent fruit, flowers and vegetables to the hospitals in which some were patients.

The main structure of this already friendly house is little changed since 1825 and has fortunately retained the original railings and balcony when so many were removed in World War II to be turned into guns. However, the cesspits under the roadway fortunately have been removed to make way for main drainage. One modern amenity was actually built into these new houses in 1825 and that was piped water, as the formation of a Water Company in 1819 at last ensured a fairly reliable water supply for the city whose population had often been "thirsty and unwashed" in the past, when they depended on water carts. Even so, the Laundress Badge had to be cancelled once due to a water shortage in 1959! Inside, many of the original adornments have been preserved, such as the lovely plasterwork on the ceiling, the marble mantlepieces, wallpaper, brass fingerplates on natural wood doors and the polished wood banister which carries one's gaze up to the graceful cupola.

Miss Dalmahoy's ten-year-old dream having come true and with the problems of home ownership to be faced, Miss Jessie Wood formed the first House Committee, who were immensely cheered in their task by the gifts that came in to furnish the new house. Some were in kind but many were small sums of money raised by units all over the City. Everyone had a hand in beautifying their new home, and this at a time when they were also helping to raise money to build Imperial Headquarters in London.

One gift, her photograph, was from Lady Baden-Powell, who must have been the very first visitor in June when she was warmly welcomed and shown round by all the Commissioners, and Miss Brown and Miss Nicoll. The Chief Guide said, "I am immensely pleased with your Head-quarters and do not know another like it—a great achievement raising the money by a Sale for its purchase."

Heartened by all this goodwill, the House Committee started work; much had to be done to make the rooms suitable for Guide use and the re-decoration was undertaken by many members of the Movement. D.I.Y.

was the motto even then, and rules and charges for booking the rooms available to Guides were drawn up. Such was the demand, no Company could book a room for more than two nights a month or more than two weeks ahead! There was a charge for the use of the kettle—6d for companies, 2/6d for districts and divisions! It was decided to advertise all the rooms on the top floor to let, to give a steady income towards the upkeep. Most important, it was essential to find a caretaker willing, not only to look after the fabric of the house, but to welcome the invasion of girls and Guiders in the evenings and at weekends for occasions as varied as large conferences and trainings or one small Guide taking a badge test.

Flitting

From the beginning, House Committees, aided by the County Secretaries and the caretakers, have dealt with all eventualities with amazing resilience. Experts have generously given valuable advice, tradesmen have been remarkably good to the Girl Guides, some exceptionally so, when rendering their bills. Of course, mishaps are legion but disasters have been rare and everyone seems to have taken in their stride such things as the next door chimney coming through the roof, dry rot and burst tanks and pipes.

In the War they coped with blacking out and blast proofing the windows, saw to the building of the huge cupboards in Room 2 to take "cigs and chocs" for the Mobile Canteens—30 years later the Scouts removed those cupboards to B-P House to store Gang Show costumes, and Room 2 became the Guide Office.

Fire precautions are kept up to date and security was tightened after a typewriter was stolen in the '30s; purses, the centenary clock in Room 1 and mail were taken in the '60s, so all doors unfortunately have to be kept locked. "Pirates" used the car park and now chain and padlock keep them out.

Regular maintenance and redecoration is an on-going concern of the House Committee who ensure a welcome to this friendly house by having gay window boxes, and flowers all the year round in the entrance hall.

Tenants have varied from a piano teacher whose pupils' discords annoyed the others to a family who lived happily on the top floor during the War; and more recently there has been a Social Security Office and a theatrical costume designer. All get a friendly welcome and the rent they pay is a vital contribution to the funds.

The caretaker engaged in 1929 was the first of ten kindly women who have served generations of Edinburgh Girl Guides with firmness and good humour. They have lived in the basement flat with their families and have become involved in all that happens at "33." Many readers will remember them with appreciation for the help given so readily.

Many children have grown up in No. 33 and it is good to hear of 21st birthday parties and wedding receptions taking place. All these families gave so much of themselves in looking after the Guide house which was their home. Remember, too, the husbands who have done endless jobs which have saved either further damage or more expense.

The present caretaker, Mrs Bradley, adds this to the story:

"On entering '33' for the first time I took a good look around, liked what I saw and hoped I could stay. I had come as a candidate for the job of caretaker. That was September 1971 and here I am, five years later, firmly established downstairs. This lovely old building is Guide H.Q. to most people, but to me and my family it means 'home.' Much has happened since we came. It has been painted outside and in, all the old 15 and 5 amp plugs changed to 13 amp, the plumbing has given cause for alarm, the roof has leaked, the gas supply has been converted to North Sea Gas, windows have been broken and door locks have jammed. The Hall, too, has not stood still; the walls have been painted, the floor sanded and re-varnished, the gents' 'loo' transformed into an attractive kitchen and the emergency lights have failed on testing, luckily not in an emergency! However, we can proudly boast that the building was never out of use whilst work was being done.

"We have made friends with Guides from other parts of Scotland and England who have dropped in for the night and slept in the Hall or Room 1. We have shared a pizza pie made by American girls who were sleeping in Room 1 and who entertained us, unintentionally, half the night with guitar music. All visitors are met and greeted properly, but occasionally time-tables break down and people arrive too early or too late. One such occasion was when a bus-load of Guides, homeward bound from the World Camp, arrived two hours early! Fortunately it was a lovely summer evening and they were glad to stretch their legs after being cooped up in the bus all day and to have juice and crisps.

"However, most of my time is devoted to our own Edinburgh Guides. Preparing a room for a badge test or a First Aid lecture, or helping prepare the Hall for a Queen's Guide Badge presentation or the A.G.M. No task is too large or too small and each one is important to me. Each year something new happens and life at H.Q. is never dull. It has echoed to the sound of bagpipes, electric guitars, ballet music, the voices of Girl Guides singing and, on one occasion, a Brass Band from Amsterdam. People come and go and changes are made, but this grand old building remains secure. It has a character of its own and caring for it is a very real pleasure."

BUILDING THE GUIDE HALL
by Kathleen Bell, Chairman of the House Committee

"It was with much trepidation but great excitement that the House Committee and I first gazed upon the plans for our new Hall in 1963. Looking at the back garden, with large ash tree and mews garage, we wondered—could it possibly become the reality of the artist's impression?

"When the tenders had been accepted we held weekly meetings with representatives of all the trades and firms involved, and in time all the building materials of all types and textures were chosen. Great care went into our choice—we toured timber yards in Leith Docks to study wood for floor and panelling; we visited glass store sheds and looked at many doors and windows around the city before choosing the glazing; the heating and lighting systems meant visits to houses which were forward examples of our electrician's work. In fact, every handle, knob, light fitting, tile, toilet fitting, etc., was chosen by one or more of our Committee. Honour must be paid in a very large way to Jean Pattulo, our Secretary, as she never accepted anything which she did not consider the best obtainable and she coped magnificently with the massive correspondence involved.

"As building the Hall adjoining the back of No. 33 meant altering the area flat, our caretaker, Mrs Thompson, and her family were flitted temporarily to the top flat—fortunately the lease of one of our tenants had expired. Mrs Thompson's devotion and tolerance during this difficult period will be remembered by us all.

"When work began on the foundations an ancient stone arch was found but no date could be ascribed to it and soon the Hall covered it. The next decision was about colour schemes and curtains.

"A great disappointment to the House Committee was that no kitchen was planned in the original layout; but later the regulations about toilet facilities were eased and a kitchen was made and most generously equipped by the Trefoil Guilds.

"At last all work was completed and, although no formal opening was planned, a party was held for the Council, the Executive, the Architect and those others most involved. Later, every Division had a party for as many Guides and Brownies as possible to come and see their own new Hall.

"The ash tree was now only a memory and my Committee are proud to have been part of this worthwhile addition to our Headquarters and to know that past, present and future Guides have benefited and will continue to do so from all our efforts."

GIFFORD COTTAGE AND JOHNSTOUNBURN

On a bleak morning in January 1962 the telephone rang at E.H.Q.

"This is the Y.W.C.A. We have a cottage near Gifford which we do not use in winter. There is another one next door which is vacant. Would the Guides consider sharing the use and expense of the two cottages with us?" Mrs Keppie, County Commissioner, takes up the story:

"A cottage? *Indoor* camping? (This was long before Adventure Centres came in and before the value of residential experience was recognised—except, of course, by B-P). Would the Guides come to prefer indoor to canvas camping? Would we get soft? But think of the adventures we might have!—and the residential trainings!

"The offer was accepted and the cottage was an instant success; bookings were very heavy and many Guide companies, Ranger units, districts and other groups had fun and adventure in the lovely surrounding country.

"In September 1963, the Y.W.C.A. gave up their share of the tenancy, and Edinburgh County took over the lease of both cottages. This made it possible to have joint Rover/Ranger weekends.

"Soon the estate needed the cottages and we were warned that the lease would expire at Whitsun 1964. The experiment had proved an enormous success, so much so that it was decided to start searching immediately for alternative accommodation. However, it was not easy to find the ideal Indoor Centre. Eventually, when we had been searching for eighteen months, without success, it was suggested that until we found what we were looking for we should use caravans—one to sleep in and one to eat and live in. By December, two suitable caravans had been selected but not actually bought, and a list drawn up of landowners in the Lothians and Borders known to be kindly disposed to Guides who might be willing to accommodate the caravans on their estates.

"Letters to them were posted early in January and several encouraging replies were received. One of these was from Mrs Elworthy, the owner of Johnstounburn, who said that she would be very pleased to have the caravans there, but before we decided on this, she had a suggestion to make and could we come and see her? On 20th January, Mrs Aglen and I went to Johnstounburn and Mrs Elworthy showed us the stable loft which was to become our much loved Adventure Centre.   We were enchanted with everything—the accommodation, the beautiful grounds with the little lake for canoeing, the accessibility from Edinburgh—and most of all, the warmth of the invitation; Mrs Elworthy actually *welcomed* the thought of so many children enjoying her property and was very anxious that we should agree. As Betty Cunningham, she had been the first Captain of 75th Company, so Edinburgh Guides were well known to her.   On 1st February, the Executive Committee accepted the proposal and tremendous activity went on each weekend to get the Centre ready for use in the spring.   Queen's Guide candidates went down with helpers and scrubbed and polished; Rangers wielded paint brushes and Dads wielded hammers; beds and equipment were assembled and two canoes were bought from the Campers' Club. Eileen Alexander did a tremendous job co-ordinating the work as well as being 'O.C. Painting.'

"Early in May, the 198th Company had the honour of being the first adventurers and spent a wonderfully happy weekend—the first of many for their Captain, Miss Elsie Easson.

"There was so much to see and do: exploring, firelighting, orienteering, rounders; birds, trees and flowers to recognise; and natural material abounded for handcrafts in the winter evenings—and, of course, no self-respecting adventurer failed to make the rope descent from the loft window to the ground 15 feet below.

"There were some glorious summer weekends, but it could be very cold in winter—and winter was just as fully booked as summer. Canoeing was quite tough in winter but no one thought of *not* having their turn! The snow often lay quite deep on the moors, too—the 193rd Patrol Leaders had a splendid adventure crossing from Kirktonhill to Soutra Aisle via the old Roman road in mist and snow.

"Mrs Elworthy very kindly gave us the disused tennis court and adjoining strip of grass for our own use, and this was an ideal site for Patrol camps.   There were Division and District weekends, trainings for P.L.s and Guiders, Advanced weekends; there were Brownie Revels and pack outings; even the Trefoil Guild had parties.

"We enjoyed Johnstounburn for ten happy years, and Mrs Elworthy will always be remembered with much gratitude by those who had the privilege of visiting this much loved Adventure Centre."

STANEMUIR

In April 1968, the County Commissioner and North Division Commissioner were spending a working weekend at Dumbarton "fitting out" the

C.C.'s yacht *Trefoil*. On Saturday afternoon they exchanged their paint-stained boiler suits for immaculate summer uniform and set off for the Glasgow County Camp Site on the shores of Loch Lomond, for the official opening of their new Brownie House. What a happy occasion! And what a wonderful place for Pack Holidays—lucky Glasgow Brownies! The two visitors from Edinburgh were very impressed and not a little envious.

The idea that Edinburgh should have its own Brownie House was introduced at the next Executive Committee meeting. With many country schools closing and Pack Holiday accommodation increasingly difficult to find, the momentous decision was taken to start planning our own House and there began the hardest part of the whole project—the search for a site. Many areas were suggested, many landowners approached and many sites visited, but it was not until March 1970 that the site near Carnwath was agreed upon. It belonged to Major McDonald Lockhart, a generous and far-sighted landowner, who was willing to sell us an acre for the building surrounded by four acres of heather-clad rough ground, all for a very nominal sum.

Throughout the two years of searching, the Brownie Trainers, Pack Holiday Permit Holders and our architect drew up plans for our ideal Brownie House; estimates were obtained and a fund-raising campaign began. When the plans were altered to include use of the house by all age groups and all the year round, the name was changed to the "Guide Adventure Centre" and this increased our chance of being awarded a capital grant. After one setback the Scottish Education Department and Edinburgh Corporation agreed to finance the project 50% and 25% respectively, leaving us to find 25%. Each division was set the target of £250, helped by publicity from a specially-designed brochure. A wonderful anonymous gift of £2000 came to us—surely from someone who *knew* the value of Pack Holidays and residential weekends—and the response from all sides was tremendous.

A small committee under Toni Lawson Hall met regularly to thrash out plans for equipment, furniture and decoration. Much thought was also given to the future care of the building and a system of visitors was evolved.

One snowy day in January 1971 the foundations were laid; the building quickly took shape and in April the committee held their meeting "on site" in the drying room huddled round a paraffin heater. Gradually they worked their way through problems of insurance, special lock requirements, refuse disposal, fuel storage, fire precautions, prevention of frozen pipes, etc., etc., and were glad of the constant and kindly support from the neighbours near the gate, Mr and Mrs Veitch, who keep a kindly eye on this latest bit of property.

Meanwhile the committee sewed all the curtains, sorted and checked equipment and cleaned until late on 18th June, ready for the opening ceremony the next day.

Opening Day was a happy occasion; Mrs Denholm, the Scottish Chief Commissioner, performed the ceremony, the house was blessed by the local Minister, and all ages from all the Divisions were represented in a vast one-day camp in the grounds, and *everybody* inspected the house. The pre-warrant trainees stayed overnight and —tragedy—one who wished to take a bath found that there was no plug! This was rectified before the house committee enjoyed *their* celebration stay the following weekend. Some experienced difficulty in climbing into top bunks and this convinced them that bunk-ladders were needed—but in the main, the house was felt to be what had been intended—a place for all ages of the Movement to share time, thoughts and activities throughout the year, and for many years to come.

The joy of having this wonderful Centre built so that Brownies, Guides, Rangers, Guiders and the handicapped could enjoy the game of Guiding in a more challenging and exciting way, gives the Stanemuir committee members and visitors who regularly check the centre particular pleasure in doing their job. The routine inspections and the chores of the annual autumn-clean can (almost!) seem fun when they think of the pride the children have in their "very own house."

Happily, all users of Stanemuir have obviously enjoyed their visits, and while the children love the fun of illicit midnight feasts in their bunk-beds snuggled under the "Downies," the Guiders appreciate the excellently-planned facilities, particularly the well-equipped kitchen. They were, perhaps, not so enthusiastic in 1975 when the enormously increased fuel costs forced the committee into having pre-payment electricity meters installed for heating and cooking.

The Centre can be enjoyed by Extension Guides and Brownies too, as it was carefully planned with ramps, adaptable doors and toilet facilities suitable for wheel-chair users. It was, however, unlikely that anyone visualised the use of the Centre by boys, but one troop of Scouts staying in mid-December voted Stanemuir to be in the Hilton Hotel category. Parties of boys and girls from Lothian Region Primary schools have stayed at Stanemuir during term time, when the house would otherwise have been unused. They have found this a highly successful venture and it is perhaps appropriate that in this way appreciation can be shown of the debt owed to the local authority for the generous financial help given to Edinburgh Guiding.

COLSTOUN OLD MILL COTTAGE

Lady Broun Lindsay offered Bruntsfield District in South-West Division the use of this cottage on her estate near Gifford many years ago. In the late 1960s the District team felt that they were no longer able to make full use of this delightful cottage, nor could they maintain it properly. With the owner's permission, the Old Cottage became a County responsibility and, in particular, the Outdoor Activities Adviser took it under her wing. Mrs Pat Donald, her family, friends, many acquaintances and 1st Leith R.G.U., became involved in making the cottage and adjoining paddock into a blissful retreat for 12 Guides, Rangers or Guiders in the heart of East Lothian.

Having accepted the challenge of the potholes and ruts in the estate road, the unit arrives either on foot, having bussed to Gifford, two miles away, or by car and van to the door. Foam mattresses are rolled out in the two upstairs rooms—sleeping bags laid on them and beds are ready in a trice. Although the cottage is intended to give only basic shelter, the comforts of a modern electric cooker and light, a flush toilet—even a bath—and a wood-burning stove in the sitting-room, which can heat the water too, means that all the country pursuits outside can be and are enjoyed to the full.

Ranger units—those back-room girls—have spent many happy weekends painting, mending and refurbishing; also, with the help of East Lothian Venture Scouts, they spent years digging treasure, including a five-barred gate and a huge iron pot, out of the paddock; they levelled it, estate workers rotivated the ground, and the great day came for sowing the grass seed in April 1975.

No roller could be found, so a team of Guiding wives and willing husbands did the deed—first the husbands in line abreast tramped side-ways across the field, marched forward one step and returned again—and again—in front of their line the wives raked level the lumps and clods, and pulled out the last of the weeds—next the sower went forth and scattered the seed evenly and carefully—once more the tramping husbands and raking wives covered the field which seemed to get bigger and bigger as limbs became weary. Great satisfaction was felt on looking over the gate in true country style at a job well done and even more so when the grass grew in spite of the drought; it was a great moment the following year when a patrol of Dumfriesshire Guides pitched their tent on the new grass.

Many Edinburgh Guides remember this lovely peaceful place and realise how lucky they are to have it on their doorstep.

THE GUIDE MINIBUS

Edinburgh Guides took to the road and bought their first minibus in 1966. It was replaced in 1972. Both have been 12-seaters and have been used and appreciated by numerous units and branches in the Movement.

This mobile piece of property has to be cared for and housed; Mrs Butters has dealt with maintenance for years—this is sometimes a problem due to the varied styles of different drivers. Parking facilities have been equally varied, from "Inveralmond" to the Edinburgh University O.T.C. premises and now "Tor." Once more the County is so fortunate in its friends.

An Official Drivers' List is drawn up from those Guiders and other adults who pass the police test required before being allowed to drive the minibus. A telephone call to one of them from Mrs Jean Murray, the booking secretary, must often be the prelude to many adventures with Brownies, Guides and Rangers.

Mrs Keppie, County Commissioner, helps Rangers to pack the Minibus for its first expedition.

The blue Minibus with gold Trefoil on its side has become a familiar sight all over Scotland; its roof rack may be loaded with tent poles and equipment for the camp at the end of the journey, or on most winter weekends there will be skis up aloft and eager Guides and Rangers inside, heading for Glenshee and a day's ski-ing. More sedately, it has cruised round Edinburgh, the Lothians, the Borders and the Trossachs taking international visitors on sightseeing tours. But let the Minibus "speak" for itself (or should it be herself) in letters "written" to the County Commissioner and the Editor of this book about two very different journeys undertaken by Edinburgh Guides and Rangers.

(Four Guiders, one Young Leader and seven Guides from Moredun District went over the sea to the Isle of Skye.)

"Ninth and Final Day, 12 July 1975.

"Dear Mrs Wilkie,
    "All the Guides have now had a turn at writing letters home, so now I think it's only fair for me—the thirteenth member of the party—to write to you.

"There I was sitting quietly in Tor in your care, when suddenly these Guides came and hijacked me. I suspected something was in the air when I made that trip out to Trefoil last Saturday. I was expecting an easy Sunday run, but instead they loaded me up (even the little roof-rack) with camping gear, and piled themselves on top, and rode back to Moredun in me.

"Do you know, they've been doing it all this week too! Since Friday, 4th, there's only been one day when I wasn't taken somewhere, and more often than not I was staggering along with all their luggage (as well as them).

"And it's not just that I've been dragged around everywhere (734 miles in fact!) but *where* I've been, along single-track roads a lot of the time, with passing-bays to pull into so that other cars could come by, and wild country with mountains and bogs, and civilisation miles away. I did think of breaking down just to show them who was in charge, but changed my mind when I saw how desolate it was—so far from home!

"And anyway, I suppose I really did quite get to like them after a while. True they took me for granted, and made me work hard, but they did remember to give me rests occasionally. And some of the places we went were wonderful. I suppose they dropped a lot of crumbs in me in the second part of the week when the weather turned wet, but they did give me drinks of petrol too. You could say that they were never quiet (except when they were asleep) but they taught me a lot of new songs, and now when I'm spending quiet weekdays at Tor, I shall be able to sing 'From out the battered elm tree,' and 'Hurry back home' and 'Over the sea to Skye' to amuse myself. Or even 'The sun has got his hat on.'

"When we went over to Skye last week, we crossed by the long route from Mallaig to Armadale, but today it was the short trip from Kyleakin to Kyle of Lochalsh—and I enjoyed it much better as I wasn't squeezed in so tight, or sunk to lower-deck level. We sang all the sad going-away songs as we drove on to the ferry.

"Back on the mainland, it was a big change to see full-sized roads again, and so we romped along, through lovely loch and mountain scenery, back towards Fort William. When we got to the Ballachulish ferry we joined the queue, and the ferry, when we got on it, made me quite dizzy with all the swinging round, but once on dry land again, they headed me on, so what else could I do?

"Mid-afternoon I thought we'd arrived at a camp site, when food and gas cooker and Guides all left me, but it was only a picnic halt, and on we went again.

"And, in fact, we came right home, soon after six o'clock. Then did they jump out and put me back at Tor? Far from it! I had to go right to Margot's house, where they pitched their still-wet tents in her back garden to dry—all nine of them. Then to Moredun, where at long last they all piled out. In almost no time the roof-rack was emptied, the inside was cleared, and they all melted away to their own homes. In procession with Hilary's car, we drove down to Beetle's house, where more bits were unloaded, and I was treated to a much-needed spring-clean. Feeling very smart, I was driven back to Tor, with Hilary's Mum escorting me all the way to take the driver back, and so now I'm back at my usual home—till the next group of Guides comes along to take me away with them.

"My springs are gradually relaxing, and I'm feeling more rested now, but what a trip it was! I think it was the furthest I've ever been—certainly it's a week I'll remember for a very long time.

"Despite the luggage and the crowding
    . . . and the crispbread crumbs and the gunge
    . . . and the narrow roads and the rough tracks
    . . . and the hard work and the midges
    . . . and the Guides and their songs . . .

—or maybe *because* of them. It might even be interesting to hear what they're thinking of doing next; some of them will be Rangers soon, they tell me, and they might get up to anything!

"So a very tired goodnight from me, before I get the rest I think I've earned.

"I had a lovely time, now I can think back over it. So goodnight, and lots of love,
             from CSC 526L.

P.S.—I wonder if that Scout minibus that lives in the garage next-door has adventures like me? He might like to hear about all I've been doing with the Moredun Guides. . . . Could you perhaps introduce us some time?"

(Rangers visited C.H.Q. to plan their Diamond Jubilee.)

                                              "30th March 1976.
"Dear Editor,
    "Whenever I heard someone travelling in me recently talking about your book on Edinburgh Guiding, I felt I really had to write and tell you what took place at the beginning of March 1976. I'm sure the Rangers won't mind me telling the story—probably quite glad really as they're all such busy people.

    "Towards the end of every week I wonder if I'm going to be taken out for any adventures at the weekend or simply left to think about past trips, and the first week in March was no exception. I was pleased when I was picked up and driven to Melville Street. Where was I going, I wondered.

    "There were eleven of them altogether: nine Rangers, and two Guiders, who took it in turns to point me in the right direction.

    "We headed south-west out of Edinburgh. Ah, I thought, Netherurd;

but no, we went right on, through Biggar and further. A mystery tour? The Rangers were in high spirits, singing loudly and more or less tunefully, and I hummed along down the A74. At about a quarter to nine I was brought to a halt in a car park somewhere near Carlisle and they all departed muttering something about coffee and beefburgers; I had to be content with a cold wind and conversation with a teddy-bear one of the Rangers had thoughtfully left to keep me company. Not till they straggled back did I get my refreshments at the filling station. Such selfishness!

"We bowled along again; and on and on. By now there was peace from inside, as all but the three in the front were sleeping. Somewhere near Birmingham I was becoming exceedingly tired—never before had I been so far south—and my beloved Scotland was becoming a mere memory.

"Then about 4 a.m. I couldn't believe my headlamps; after going round several roundabouts twice, we drew into—wait for it—Heathrow Airport! Help! Beware of low-flying minibuses! However, they left me where I could watch the planes and took themselves off for a couple of hours to freshen up in the *overseas* arrival lounge.

"Then they took me for breakfast on the M4 and cleaned me up. We now pointed towards London and I managed a squint out of my sidelights as they took me on a conducted tour of Harrods, St James's Park and Buckingham Palace. They started talking about parking me, and seemed to be having some difficulty, so I chose a garage for them and charmed the owner into giving me space in his forecourt for the day. Parking in London is no problem if you know how to go about it!

"I settled down in the garage and prepared to chat up the cars coming in for a snack. Suddenly I heard the patter of feet and was rudely hauled out of my haven, and before I knew where I was, I was in Buckingham Palace Road, stopped on a yellow line with my hazard warning lights flashing, and they were disgorging themselves and most of their luggage. Rapid *au revoirs* of "Six o'clock at the shop," and I took off again at a rate of knots in the direction of my friendly garage, passing several neat and tidy groups of Rangers on the way. What a contrast to the Edinburgh contingent! (I've got a funny feeling, though, that the luggage contained carefully packed uniforms!)

"What happened the rest of the day I'll have to tell you from what I gathered in conversation later. While I sat in my garage the party had split up into two, the Guiders amusing themselves by going sight-seeing, and the Rangers reshaping the future of Rangering.

"Apparently 1977 is the Diamond Jubilee of Rangers and a meeting (called a Think-In, I think) was held for about 300 Rangers from all over the U.K. to say how they would like to celebrate it; they divided into discussion groups for most of the day and talked about nation-wide camps, visitors from overseas (do they all use that lounge at

Heathrow), service projects and slogans. It will be a busy year and the Scottish representatives tried to point out the merits of holding a camp in or near Scotland rather than the South of England. Personally I can see no comparison!

"Having got so many Rangers to London the crafty H.Q. staff (is that what the C stands for?) wanted everybody to discuss what the next lot of Guides coming into Rangers should be doing during the next few years. If the other 291 Rangers had as many ideas as my nine they'll be a lucky lot of lassies, and busy ones too—don't tell them, but Rangers make everything sound such FUN. There was some chat about Ravens and a little bird twittered that the Scout minibus and I might be going out together some time—coo!

"I had another sightseeing trip that evening. They took me round Piccadilly, Trafalgar Square, crossed me over the Thames by as many bridges as they could find, then to crown it all they got me lost. One-way systems I'm used to—the Edinburgh variety anyway—but honestly! It must have taken an hour to do what would have taken them ten minutes on foot—not that that would have been much use for me. Every time the one with the map gave an instruction there was a 'No Entry' or 'No Turn' sign. Eventually they succeeded in getting me to Covent Garden where they were spending the night in a church hall.

"I gathered they had a comfortable night. I didn't. I was rudely awakened in the wee sma' 'oors by snow. Snow! I ask you! It never snows in Central London! And I couldn't even put on my heater to keep poor Teddy warm. The Rangers piled back inside me when daylight came, and we set off, heading for home. They stopped fairly frequently for refreshments all round; apart from all the chat the journey north was fairly uneventful. I learned a few new songs, and made the interesting discovery that videophones have obviously been installed in West Linton. At least I inferred so from the way the Rangers gave directions to parents about where to meet them in Edinburgh—hands waving all the time.

"And so to bed. They brushed me out, fed me and tucked me up in Tor, where I spent half the night telling the garden scarecrow all about it. Only I don't think he believed me!

"Let me have a copy of the book when it's finished, please. I'll keep it in my glovebox for the odd spare moment.

Yours,

CSC 526L.

P.S.—When's the next Ranger Think-In in London? Let me know in plenty of time and I'll arrange to have a burst tyre, or something. Please. . . !

P.P.S.—I've just heard that there will be a Ranger Camp in Scotland in '77—so glad my lot made themselves heard. It's to be at Fordell Firs—super place—didn't you and I go there together once?"

11

Rallies, Events and Competitions

"I PROMISE TO DO MY BEST"—the first phrase of the Promise spoken at the most important event of all as each recruit commits herself to Guiding. An event which has been repeated thousands of times in Edinburgh and from which all other events in this story have their beginnings.

The Guides in 1913 at one of the earliest rallies certainly did their best when Miss Baden-Powell, B-P's sister, reported, "A fine turn-out of girls and they looked very smart indeed." For the next few years the Guides paraded annually at rallies held in different parts of the city, such as the grounds of the Royal Infirmary, Queen Street Gardens and Heriot's School grounds. They demonstrated their skills at first aid and signalling, once competing for Savings Certificates, and always gave displays of marching and Colour ceremonial. At the rally held in Queen Street Gardens in 1916 the first County Banner was dedicated.

It was customary for a well-known civic or military dignitary to inspect the Guides at the rallies and when Lt. Col. Arthur Rose inspected the girls during the First World War he said, "I could not have believed that girls could have stood so steadily at attention." Not every occasion went so smoothly, however. A Guide at the 1922 rally said, "We practised a welcome in semaphore, but unfortunately did not know until the last minute that there was a change of Inspector, but we just signalled the original message, hoping no-one could read semaphore."

Guides at St Bride's School, the first school company in the city, showed similar resource in 1917 when their company was inspected by the County Commissioner. Uniforms were difficult to buy so the unfortunate boarders had to make their own, and on the fateful day their stitches were not in time and safety pins had to take the strain of seams!

Another school company paraded with their mascot, a fox-terrier called Bobby, who stood in front of the Guides all lined up in impeccable order. When the inspecting officer, Lt. General Sir Frank Davies, stopped to inspect the Guides, Bobby turned his back and sat staring stolidly in the opposite direction.

Gradually the military flavour of the rallies changed and in 1924 the Guides enjoyed a Signalling race, and in 1926 actually marched past the saluting base without their Guiders!

By 1930 the rallies became more informal and although they still retained the high standard of marching and ceremonial, the programmes had a more light-hearted approach. Divisions chose and sang their own songs for the march past; at one, "North" chose "Cock of the North" for their song tune. On one occasion 700 Guides, who had to be at least five feet tall, executed a Maze March, while the smaller Guides danced a musical "Drive" wearing gym tunics and black stockings with coloured ribbons for reins. The whole rally was controlled by whistle and flag signals and these had to be learned thoroughly beforehand. The Guides were complimented on their splendid performance despite the fact that it was very hot, which no doubt accounted for the instruction—"Each company must bring a water-bottle and smelling salts!"

The weather at the 1937 rally went to the other extreme and the rain forced the organisers of a rally for all Youth Organisations to change the venue from outdoors to the Forrest Road Drill Hall where there was room only for Patrol Leaders and Seconds. The Lord and Lady Provost received gifts from the Guides which represented their "Good Turn" to celebrate Coronation Year. One thousand, seven hundred and two gifts were ceremoniously placed in red, white and blue baskets, the ones in the red and blue baskets for infants and old people, and those in the white for Sunday School Missions in Canada. The gifts for Canada were sent to two Edinburgh Commissioners, enthusiastic supporters of the Missions, who gave them to Scottish settlers in remote parts of the country living in very primitive conditions.

Formal rallies were not the only occasions on which Brownies and Guides met together. Brownies held their own Flower Service in St Mary's Cathedral and invited 30 Canadian Guides to join them and entertained their visitors to tea afterwards. In 1935, the Silver Jubilee of King George V and Queen Mary, the Guide Movement chose an imaginative way to celebrate the occasion by presenting 400 flowering cherry trees to be planted in Braidburn Valley, a pleasant park on the south side of the city. A crowd of over 5000 watched as the Lord Provost received a cheque for the trees from a 1st Class Guide and, followed by colour parties carrying the Union Flag and County Banner, planted the first tree. Immediately, Guides and Brownies planted their trees, one for each Company and Pack, and rounded off the proceedings by singing the "Tree Song." The Lone Guides presented a seat for the park, and every springtime the glorious blossom is a reminder of this happy occasion.

Two years later, on 9th May, Guides and Brownies from all over the city streamed along Lothian Road on their way to services at St Cuthbert's Church for the Brownies and the Usher Hall for the Guides. 5000 Guides filled the Usher Hall where a new World Flag was dedicated; about 3000 Brownies saw three Division Banners dedicated at their service and *Brownies* were chosen as escorts, an unusual honour!

Some Edinburgh Guiders attended a very different service in 1951. Instead of the vast crowds of girls in a large city church or the even larger Usher Hall, there was a group of adult members of the Movement in the beautiful drawing-room at Netherurd, the Scottish Training Centre. They were there for the dedication of a Communion Table, Lectern and Prayer-desk presented to Netherurd by Edinburgh for use at the Sunday services held in the house.

There was great excitement in 1953, the Coronation Year of Queen Elizabeth II, when every girl and adult was challenged to do a Good Turn by rendering some small service to the community. The County raised money to plant cherry trees in the Meadows and for plants in a flower-bed in the Canongate and, as Miss Inches, the County Commissioner, said, "Companies, Packs and individuals have worked and planned and saved to give a tribute of love and service in honour of the Coronation of our Queen. For years to come there will be reminders in the city—in churches and schools, in old folk's and children's homes—of this great event." Edinburgh Guides celebrated the Coronation in great style with a rally at Dreghorn at which there was a magnificent display of massed Colours and appropriate ceremony, and General Barber took the salute. Fun, however, was the order of the day; there were sideshows, competitions, displays of outdoor skills, assault courses, bridge building and, to end the day, a camp fire at Bonaly with a pageant with the Commonwealth as its theme. Representatives from each Division brought gifts to the camp fire, placing them in baskets: butter from New Zealand, oranges from South Africa, rice from India, apples from Canada and so on. These gifts were later handed to old people's homes and children's homes. Each Division also handed over in a sealed envelope details of a good turn already done, and one of these was eventually sent to the Queen.

If Coronation year was exciting B-P's Centenary year in 1957 was even more so! Every girl shared in the various activities to celebrate the centenary and many carried out good turns in their own and other people's homes in response to the Founder's last message to "build happy homes." On Thinking Day, Guides and Rangers from every Division climbed the hills of Edinburgh very early and hoisted the World Flag demonstrating their loyalty for all the city to see. South-West Division Guides and Rangers climbed Allermuir at dawn, quite a feat on a frosty February morning; Portobello and Niddrie Guides climbed Arthur's Seat and there sent off "Good Turn" balloons spreading the Guide message of friendship far and wide, and with an added bonus for the finders who were able to claim a good turn from the sender!

Rangers, Guides and Brownies joined with others all over the country in lighting Candles of Friendship in their homes, and a group of 70 Rangers ended Thinking Day with a barbecue at the Trefoil Campsite—a few hardy girls camping overnight in the huts! Services of Thanksgiving were held all over the city on 24th February and Scouts and Guides shared a special service at the High Kirk of St Giles attended by the Lord Provost and other distinguished citizens.

Fourteen representatives from the County went to the National Service in Westminster Abbey. Later in the year Guides again joined the Scouts in combined activities for a week in June. Each evening they gave displays and entertainments in Princes Street Gardens and at the end of the week had an impressive finale at a camp fire on Calton Hill, which was lit by a torch carried by runners from the Gardens.

At the beginning of "Scout and Guide Week" the Guides staged a spectacular County Rally at Stenhouse Stadium which opened with an impressive March Past, when the salute was taken by the Chief Commissioner, Miss Anstice Gibbs. Rangers gave splendid displays of First Aid and Rescue, and Guides demonstrated tent pitching, cycling and a musical drive and also introduced a lighthearted look at the early days of Guiding. In reply to greetings from the Chief Guide the Guides released hundreds of pigeons carrying their messages. The whole afternoon was exciting for performers and spectators alike. As the County Drama Adviser said later, "I had seen an entertainment that was in every way first class. Above all, it was real; the performers were doing something they understood and loved. They were Guides and proud of it." The organisers had many hectic moments and certainly had never visualised themselves in the rôle of "Seven maids with seven mops" when, because the stadium had not been in use, they had to scrub every single seat before the rally!

Birthdays have always been one of the best reasons for having a party and Ranger, Guide and Brownie units, Districts and Divisions celebrated Jubilee Year in 1960 with all kinds of parties and celebrations. Often they shared their fun and festivities with others—children, old people, lonely ones and those in hospital. Everyone joined in a Thanksgiving Service in St Cuthbert's Church and in a Camp Fire on Calton Hill when the County President, the Duchess of Hamilton and Brandon, was the guest of honour. The Lord Provost and Magistrates gave a garden party at Lauriston Castle for members of the Movement in Edinburgh and Midlothian. About a thousand Guiders, representatives from the Trefoil Guilds, Local Associations, the Council and many others enjoyed this generous gesture.

Edinburgh Guides were greatly honoured in 1962 when they were asked to provide a Guard of Honour for His Grace the Lord High Commissioner and his party, on their arrival at the General Assembly of the Church of Scotland. The High Commissioner complimented 32 Queen's Guides from Edinburgh and 10 Guides and Rangers from Perthshire on their smart appearance. A little later, in June, 100 past and present Queen's Guides kept up this high standard when they attended the Commonwealth Youth Service in the city.

In the sixties there were great changes in Guiding, starting in 1964 when "Spotlight on Guiding" surprised and enlightened the general public. The following story of Edinburgh "Spotlight" has a special meaning for all those who took part and throws the spotlight on the *raison d'être* of Guiding—fun for oneself through working with others to give service.

"Spotlight on Guiding was a nationwide public relations exercise, focussed on a week in March 1964, aimed at replacing the general public's image of Guiding 'as a Movement of marching, signalling and knot-tying do-gooders' with the up-to-date reality. Every County in the United Kingdom was invited to play the spotlight in their own way, be it large or small. The County of Edinburgh decided to make it a searchlight!

"We decided to hold a week-long Exhibition in the Waverley Market. We reasoned that the Edinburgh public was accustomed to visiting exhibitions there, and once inside we would really show them modern Guiding!

"A 'Spotlight' Committee was set up with Mrs Kathleen Simson Hall as Chairman, and throughout the summer of 1963 we worked hard to get the project off the ground. Our architect designed a very imaginative layout complete with a mountain ski-run, a camp site, a mini-loch and beside it a patrol camp site. There were to be 27 stands, all actively demonstrating Brownie, Guide and Ranger activities; for instance— Funfair—Brownie Handcraft—Golden Ladder—Brownie Glade—Pack Holiday House—The Studio—Spotlight Bakery—B-P House—International—Extensions—Challenge and Achievement (Guide Tests). A workshop was set up at H.Q. to paint cork letters specially made for the stands, which were simple raised platforms; atmosphere and effect would be achieved by good lighting. Each stand would have to be continuously manned and provided with materials for eight nights.

"There was also to be an auditorium seating 200 and here, each evening, the Exhibition would be opened by a V.I.P. guest, and we would present an hour's light entertainment—aptly christened 'A Spot of Light Relief.'

"We were determined to involve as many of our 10,000 personnel as possible; the organisation was quite complex, but we had a good system of communication and the eight divisions worked wonders in allocating their rotas. During the Christmas holidays auditions and rehearsals were held for 'A Spot of Light Relief' and the Rangers practised ski-ing and first aid—for an 'accident' would be staged on the mountain each night.

"At last, two days before 'Spotlight' opened, we were allowed into the Market. What a vast, empty, gloomy cavern—and COLD! (The heating system had broken down.) Could we really put over the fun of Guiding, establish a warm, happy atmosphere in this place? But the stands started sprouting up, the market echoed with the cheerful clang of hammers, the electricians put up hundreds of *spotlights* in strategic places, squads of Rangers dashed around with paint pots, other helpers draped miles of coloured muslin round the base of the platforms. The camp site took shape; 400 square yards of real turf were laid; real trees 20 feet high grew up overnight; the mountain miraculously appeared (scaffolding covered with canvas realistically painted to resemble snow, rocks and grass) and winding down it the ski slope! Artificial ski slopes were a rarity then. Several Commissioners and Trainers were initiated into the mysteries of working the coloured spotlights so that each evening the sunlight on the camp sites and mountains would give way to a beautiful sunset as the Guides sang 'Taps.' Indeed, all the lighting effects were tremendous and—almost—made everyone forget how cold it was; for the heating remained firmly OFF and we had snow, frost and freezing temperatures throughout the week of the Exhibition.

"The bitter weather and the fact that we were unable to have a 'Royal' visit understandably affected the attendance of approximately 20,000. Guides from all over Scotland came in large numbers, but the exhibition failed to attract the general public to the extent the committee had hoped. This, in turn, affected the Bakery, the Snack Bar and other money-making stands. The final deficit, even after a wonderful donation of £1000, was £491. However, if 'Spotlight' was not a financial success, it was a happy, exciting and memorable project in every other way.

"On Saturday, 14th March, the Lord Provost formally opened 'Spotlight on Guiding,' and each evening hundreds of Brownies, Guides, Rangers and Guiders played their part, demonstrating test and badge work, Pack and Company meetings, handcrafts, road safety, international Guiding and a host of other activities. They pitched tents and cooked meals while Rovers and Rangers demonstrated ski-ing, canoeing, climbing and pioneering. On the Sunday evening, hundreds of Guides and visitors gathered at the camp site for a 'Guides Own'—a short service of thanksgiving and re-dedication.

"There were some traumatic moments every night; the production team for the entertainment never knew up till ten minutes before opening time what cast they would have available for the show, but it opened punctually, full of sparkle and talent. A few minutes before the scheduled official opening the auditorium was almost deserted (everyone was still dispersed around the myriad activities)—but when the V.I.P. 'Opener' stepped on to the platform, every seat was occupied.

"But these moments were all part of the fun. The whole week was indeed full of challenge and achievement, of colour and action, of friends meeting, of commitments fulfilled. That all went (more or less!) according to plan, was a tribute to the enormous administrative task so ably undertaken by the Guiders in the County during the year of preparation.

"And every evening when we came together for a short Epilogue, a quiet time at the end of a busy day, we remembered our Guide promise of duty to God and friendship to all, a promise we shared with millions of Guides all over the world."

The changes foreshadowed by "Spotlight" became effective in 1968 when Edinburgh launched the New Programme with enthusiasm. Brownies, Guides, Rangers and adult members of the Movement gathered in the Usher Hall for an inter-denominational service, and were inspired by the address given by the Rev. Dr. Leonard Small to meet the new venture with zest and courage. After the reading of the Guide Law the whole congregation renewed the Promise together, row upon row of blue and brown uniformed girls with a background of massed Colours—an unforgettable moment! The next day divisions and districts started distributing the attractive new handbooks, celebrating this milestone of Guiding history in every way imaginable, and with the maximum amount of publicity. The County arranged an attractive display of modern Guiding, featuring the new handbooks, in a shop window in the city centre.

It seemed no time at all after this excitement before Diamond Jubilee Year arrived and everyone, from Brownies to the County Commissioner, were involved in celebrations, in National or County events or in their own divisions. Once more, everyone gathered in the Usher Hall to renew the Promise at a most impressive service, afterwards walking to Princes Street Gardens, where a seat was presented to the city on behalf of the County. Fulfilling the Jubilee Year's theme of "Three Cheers—for a person, a place and yourself," North-West Division also presented a seat —to Edinburgh Zoo and had a very happy time themselves at the handing-over ceremony in April.

Back to the Usher Hall in June, when many talented girls from all sections held a very enjoyable Folk Fest. Some of them performed again, heavily disguised as natives of distant lands, when Guide companies competed in a Commonwealth Challenge for the Victory Shield at Dreghorn on 20th June. Each company dressed in national costume, dressed a doll, cooked dishes of their chosen country and finally performed an appropriate song or dance. The day ended with a campfire after the competitors had exhausted themselves on a strenuous assault course and at a handball tournament!

Thankfully, such hectic physical exertion was not asked of the adults when they enjoyed a Dinner-Dance in the Assembly Rooms in October. Husbands and boy-friends joined in this very happy evening and some were amazed to see the age range from Ranger to Trefoil Guild enjoying themselves as one.

During the year, representatives from the County went to all the National celebrations, the services at Westminster Abbey and Cathedral, the Royal Reception at Whitehall, the Wembley Spectacle and the Garden Party at Buckingham Palace. One of the two young Guiders who went to the Garden Party said, "As the Queen left she stopped in front of our group and asked us where we came from. She also remarked that there were quite a lot of us at the Palace that day!"

Not only Guiding events were being celebrated in Edinburgh in 1970. The 3rd Commonwealth Paraplegic Games took place from 26th July to 1st August, and fulfilling the challenge, "Cheer a person and a place," over 70 Guides, Rangers and Guiders spent long hours selling programmes at the Games and doing strenuous domestic chores at the "Games Village" at Turnhouse. As the Activities Adviser commented, "Edinburgh Guiding was on show and they did us proud!"

Edinburgh Guiding was again "on show" in 1973 when they joined in the *Evening News* Centenary procession in the city in May. The Guide float depicted "Guiding from 1910" and on this very windy day the "modern" Guides wearing camp overalls, shorts and cagoules envied their "old-fashioned" counterparts snugly wrapped in long serge skirts, thick stockings and boots!

In June, however, they had the opportunity to warm up at the County Athletics Shield Competition at Meadowbank Stadium. Even if not competing, they were probably rushing around as members of the enormous and efficient team of "back room" girls and adults who, under the direction of Mrs Pat Donald, the County Activities Adviser, made this event such a resounding success. About one tenth of the girls in the County took part in the varied programme and many competitors, especially the Brownies, were thrilled to run on the very track used by famous athletes, and to see their names in lights on the scoreboard! An exciting afternoon ended with a "Guides' Own Service" and a simple ceremony at which three trees were planted outside the stadium as a lasting reminder of a great day.

1974 was the Brownies' Diamond Jubilee Year and how they enjoyed it!

Lady Ballantrae, wife of the Lord High Commissioner, and Mrs Wilkie, County Commissioner, helping Brownies to plant the heaths.

They had district and division Revels with "Rosebuds," "Anniversaries" and "Brownies of other Lands" as themes. They did special good turns in their Packs, with "knit-ins," "hush-ins," concerts, and one Pack raised £52 with a sponsored "dig" which went towards donating a seat to the local hospital. In May they had their own service at St Cuthbert's Church and afterwards swarmed joyfully to Princes Street Gardens where chosen Brownies from each division planted heaths in the Gardens. One spectator was heard to say, "I never knew there were so many Brownies in Scotland, let alone Edinburgh."

With similar enthusiasm, the Brownies in May 1976 competed with the Guides and Rangers in the finals for the County Swimming Shield.

After the division heats, held in various swimming pools and involving much organisation in districts and units, the successful competitors converged on the Commonwealth Pool. Again a superb "back-up team" of stewards and recorders, helped by the experts from the Scottish Amateur Swimming Association, ensured that the lengthy programme went smoothly. Rows of uniformed Guides and Brownies with parents and friends, cheering on their teams, filling the entire spectators' accommodation, made an unforgettable sight and sound! The manager of the pool, who must be used to big numbers, afterwards congratulated the County on the efficiency of the organisation and said he had not believed it possible to deal with such large numbers at a swimming gala—a feather in her cap for the Activities Adviser!

Competing for trophies has made the events more exciting and Edinburgh Guides have had this pleasure for many years. In November 1918, immediately after the end of the First World War, Miss Jessie Wood presented a shield, to be known as the Victory Shield, for annual competition among Guide companies. At that time Brownies were eligible to compete as well as Guides, and at first there were always prolonged company inspections by members of the Council who marked attendance, punctuality and appearance as well as knowledge of knots, First Aid, nature and similar skills. Very often the final of the competition was a surprise test including seeing how the patrol system worked! In these early days the same companies tended to win year after year. Over the years the format of the competitions has changed—in 1969 a challenge was set for Patrols, and in 1975 the Shield was awarded to the company which produced the best selection of gifts for the delegates to the World Conference in Sussex that summer.

In March 1921, Mr Duncan of York Road, Trinity, gave the St Andrew's Shield for athletics, and Mr Archer, also of Trinity, gave the St Margaret's Shield for swimming. The events were to be played off in divisions, the winning team in each division to be in the finals at the rally in June. This was changed in 1924 when it was decided that the shields should be competed for biennially in the year when there was no rally. As techniques have altered and standards improved, so have the athletics and swimming competitions changed in character.

Mr James Stevenson, the Chairman of Council in the 1920s donated

Signalling Flags for competition in morse and semaphore. His interest in Guides began when he helped a Guider to instruct her Guides how to signal in Heriot Row Gardens. Like the shields the flags were given sometimes to a company, sometimes to a division. Few units now learn how to signal and these flags have not been awarded for some time.

Miss Esme Dalmahoy, the sister of Edinburgh's first County Commissioner, gave an Embroidery Cup for yearly competition to encourage the Guides to take an interest in her special talent. Over the years there were few entries for this cup, so in 1952 Edinburgh offered it to the Scottish Rangers for competition.

Many of the events in this chapter are about achievements in one or other aspects of Guiding, but one regular County event which encompasses the whole programme takes place at Headquarters when the Countess of Rosebery presents Queen's Guide Certificates to girls who have gained the highest award in the Guide section. The girls, their parents and Guiders enjoy a happy evening, often hearing Guides, Rangers or Guiders describe their visits abroad. Here is the Guide, who was welcomed into the world family of Guiding at her enrolment, now celebrating, with her own family around her, the achievement of an award based on the ideals of B-P entitling her to wear the Royal Badge.

12

Organisation Between the Wars

THE YEARS OF PEACE between 1918 and 1939 brought the consolidation and the rapid expansion of the Girl Guide Movement in Edinburgh and around the world. The tradition of good organisation for which the Guides are well known was built on the excellent foundations laid by the first local committees. The decentralisation of the administration into County areas throughout Britain was almost completed by 1920, each County Commissioner adapting the flexible system according to the needs of her own town or county or island community.

The County Commissioner was, and still is, solely responsible for the appointment of all Division and District Commissioners who in turn found Guiders for the Companies and Packs; all these posts require different attributes and different training so the recruiting of adults to enable more girls to enjoy Guiding was, and is, always in the forefront of the County Commissioner's mind. She was also responsible for appointing the County Secretary to work closely with her throughout her term of office.

In Edinburgh, Miss Lilias Dalmahoy was County Commissioner for 20 years and she was indeed fortunate that Miss Mina Brown was willing "to accept the great changes of 1918" and remain as Secretary and continue to serve Guiding so loyally. With their co-operation and advice, the new teams were being built up. The Division Commissioners formed districts, usually three, four and sometimes five, with a Commissioner responsible for 10-15 Companies and Packs in each district. The Captains' meetings ceased to be at County level and they met in their divisions (though they requested an annual "get-together" to exchange ideas and enjoy an evening with all their contemporaries). The early companies had grown up very independently so the new Commissioners needed all their tact to persuade some captains to conform to new ideas and to weld their divisions and districts into a Guide family.

The family was the basis of the Patrol system—the Founder wisely set the number in a patrol at six and the smallest recruit grew up with girls of differing ages, with help and advice from those older than herself to start with, which she in turn passed on—along with the traditions that all good Patrols acquire through the years. A Guide Patrol differed from a school class where a girl was always in her own age group and from home where a parent was in charge; and the Guider too was different from teacher and mother—more like an older cousin, which they very often were in the early days. Many other organisations have adopted B-P's good plan but don't always acknowledge it as his!

The Patrol system was well established by 1918 but Company numbers often surpassed B-P's objective of 36 for Guide Companies and 24 for Brownie Packs. B-P wrote in *The Scouter:*

". . . from experience no man who is not a superman can give real individual character training to more than 32 boys—I found in my own case that 16 were enough for me and I have allowed for other Scout-masters being twice as capable—hence the 32 limit!"

He evidently thought that Guiders could manage four more! Many of the Companies were 40 or 50 strong and in danger of becoming "just a youth club" unless more leaders came forward. A number of Guiders left after the War as their circumstances changed and often a whole new team was needed for a unit, as ideally each should have three Guiders! Lilias Dalmahoy soon gathered around her a dedicated team following her own high standards; many were women whose brothers, husbands or fiancés were killed in the War and they joined the Guide family, devoting themselves to many generations of girls for years to come. Their reward must surely be in the happy memories one hears on all sides and the (now elderly) voices saying, "Oh—we had the most wonderful Captain." These Guiders committed themselves through the Promise they made—of duty to God, to country and to others before self—this is at the heart of Guiding, and with the ten Guide Laws for direction, made their units different from the youth club next door. The other factor in that difference was the self-government through Brownie Pow-Wow, Court of Honour or Patrol Leaders' Council and Ranger Council, each girl having some responsibility for the well-being and success of the group around her, however small.

As co-operation and discussion took place within the units it followed that the Guiders conferred in their Districts with ideas and suggestions flowing through their Commissioners to Divisions and thence to the Executive Committee. The chain of communication in Guiding is not just one way, but with every link strong and taut, it follows the pathway from *County Commissioner to the smallest Guide and Brownie and back again.*

Lilias Dalmahoy's first task after building up her team was to find somewhere to provide a central point for meetings and where all Guides and Brownies could assemble and get to know each other outwith their own units. Mrs Hamilton Bruce had furnished a room in 5 Queen Street for earlier meetings (and the table around which the first committee met is still in use at H.Q. today), but larger premises were required. In 1920 Scottish Girl Guides bought No. 12 Melville Street and let the drawing-room flat to Edinburgh and Leith for their first headquarters.

The first test of the new organisation must have been the Rally which was inspected by Princess Mary in July 1920. A practice parade was held in the grounds of Donaldson's School when James Stevenson, the Chairman of the Council, assisted in marshalling the girls into order and advised on the military aspects; he remembered "that the practice took longer than he—or the girls' parents—expected but the Parade was a great success. How satisfactory to see 'Edinburgh and Leith' assembled as a unit."

The 4th Brownie Pack marching past Princess Mary.

In November 1918 the Victory Shield had been presented by Miss Jessie Wood—the first Division Commissioner to be appointed—and when the athletic and Swimming Shields followed later, the competitions for these set the pattern for annual events for decades to come, along with rallies and camps. All these are written of elsewhere.

Such a variety of activities added to traditional Guiding required an expanding team. Training schools for Guiders were already held regularly and a training committee and adviser were appointed. A Camp adviser, Examination secretary, Ranger adviser and International adviser came next as these aspects broadened and secretaries were appointed for Lone and Post Guides and for Extension Guides, as handicapped Guides were called. Edinburgh held a leading place in the development of this branch. The special relationship which had developed through the early years with Edinburgh Corporation was confirmed when the Lord Provost agreed to become Honorary President in 1920 and his successors have followed his example ever since.

All this work was done entirely voluntarily and very little mention is made of the office work involved, but the handwritten minute books end in 1925 with the advent of a typewriter—perhaps of "1910 vintage"—as the replacement of such a one was requested in the 1950s!

1929 was the year when Miss Dalmahoy's dream of a real home for Edinburgh Guides came true with the purchase of, and move into, 33 Melville Street—her vision and energy in pursuing it gave the County this lasting memorial to her.

Finance was ever a problem to be faced and overcome, especially during the crisis in the early '30s which delayed the celebrations of the Coming-of-Age of the Girl Guides' Association by a year. In October 1932 a Scottish Commissioners' Conference was held in Edinburgh; the Chief Guide attended it but she also joined the Edinburgh Guiders at their 21st Birthday party at which Mina Brown was asked to cut the cake. Watched by all, she found in the first slice (careful planning!) a Gold Promise Badge—her own "coming-of-age" gift from all her many friends in Guiding and a "thank you" for 21 years of service to the County.

How fitting that the party was for the Guiders—the real V.I.P.s of the Movement! They were the ones in contact with the girls, they really knew the needs of youth, they gave far, far more than the "one evening a week" which was the visible part of Guiding; much time was needed to prepare for that meeting and more time for events, camps and holidays. However, many Guiders served on the various committees which ran the County business; they spent precious evenings in Headquarters representing their Divisions on Training, Camp, Competition or Events committees. They brought the up-to-date point of view direct from the smallest recruit to the County Commissioner via these committees. Their out-going participation in County administration through the years, together with the Division Commissioners who form the majority on the Executive Committee, have kept Edinburgh Guiding vital and on the move.

In 1935 Lady Constance Blackburn agreed to become President, taking over from Lady Maud Warrender. As the number of girls increased the City was divided again making eight divisions in 1935; new and younger Commissioners were being appointed. Then Miss Thomson Clay, the Camp Adviser, suggested that all advisers should be on the policy-making body and the County Committee was started. The Executive Committee met at 2.30 p.m., then the advisers joined them at 3.30 after a cup of tea (and, we believe, some delicious home-made cakes) and the County Committee finished off the business. How busy these years must have been! A minute states, "Guiding seems to be absorbing more and more time," followed later by another, 'August is declared a holiday month from Guiding."

King George VI's Coronation Year of 1937 was a busy one. Consider just two events organised in Edinburgh. The first was when 5000 Scottish Guides were amongst the huge rally of Youth Organisations at Murrayfield in front of Their Majesties; 1000 of those were Edinburgh girls who

performed a bell tent pitching and striking competition between the eight
Divisions which is still spoken of with awe 40 years later. Then 3000 Edinburgh Brownies celebrated by visiting the Zoo; divide that by 24 and realise
how many Guiders were involved, or divide by the two or three children
in one's own family and realise how hard each Guider worked!

But what a wonderful finale that year was for Lilias Dalmahoy and
for Mina Brown who retired in that winter. Both asked that they should
not be given any personal presents. In this they followed Lady Baden-
Powell's example; she asked not to be given gifts when on her travels; she
preferred to have contributions towards the Guide houses round the World
or to the various funds connected with the Movement. However, a grateful
Girl Guide Association presented its highest award—the Silver Fish—to
Lilias Dalmahoy and she was asked to be a Vice-President of the Edinburgh Girl Guides' Council.

Miss Dalmahoy, County Commissioner, greets Princess Mary and Lord Provost outside
St Giles, with a 1st Class Guide Guard of Honour on Armistice Day, 1937.

A friend said years later: ''Miss Dalmahoy built up Edinburgh Guiding
from 25 Companies and Packs to over 400 and blazed a trail in many forms

of Guide service . . . she gave herself with all her energy and infectious enthusiasm to the development of the Movement. With great personal integrity and love of beauty she saw clearly the value of high standards . . . above all she cared for the individual . . . and each felt that she was their friend. By her shining faith and her sound judgement she was able to put first things first and she built Edinburgh Guiding on things of the spirit. . . her charm and gaiety gave to Guiding the happy setting which it should always have.''

The following letter, written by the Chief Guide (on her wonderfully expressive typewriter), after receiving the honour of Dame Grand Cross of the British Empire, indirectly pays a warm tribute to Lilias Dalmahoy.

> Pax Hill
> Bentley
> Hampshire

June 27th 1932

Dear Lil

Thanks ever so much for your dear kind letter congratulating me on the G.B.E.—which is YOURS REALLY! It belongs to EVERY Guide, though I just hold it for you!

People have been so wondefrful about it,and of course I am terribly happy that it has landed upon me at this moment too ,as it DOES make a nice special extra thrill to the Coming of Age year.

I have just got back from the Veteran's Camp ,and it was so nice seeing Miss Hotchkis and so many ''Scotties'' thers !

Forgive this short note , but I have got rather a lot to write at the moment .

Lots of love and my warm thanks for your delightfu l note

Yours in haste

OLAVE

It must have been a formidable task to follow so well loved a personality but Miss Verona Wallace Williamson took up the challenge. She had begun the Brownie Pack at St Giles, been first a District then a Division Commissioner and was an excellent choice to lead the County through the difficult years ahead. Along with Miss M. A. Turnbull as Secretary, this much younger County Commissioner gathered a younger team around her, helped by the ''ten-year rule'' brought in by Imperial H.Q. in 1938. Allowing four years for the rule to become fully effective, all future appointments of Commissioners would be for five years, with possible renewal for three years, then for two years, and a lapse of three years must occur before re-appointment in the same capacity. This excellent rule meant that no one stayed in an appointment for life, "new blood" and "fresh minds" were brought in but "experience" was not lost as new appointments were available.

The Executive and County Committees continued but Verona Wallace Williamson instituted a Court of Honour with the Division Commissioners only, to discuss their problems, get their advice and exchange ideas. A Finance Committee was set up with Miss E. Tod as Secretary and they met twice a year. A new Roneo machine was bought and a County news sheet sent out to each pack and company through division and district channels to help in giving accurate information. In spite of this, throughout the years there always has been someone who hasn't heard of a Training date, an exciting Camp Fire or the latest International invitation, but even Guides, Patrol Leaders, Guiders and Commissioners are only human!

Can the Chief Scout ever have approved the title of Examination Secretaries? In 1938 they became Badge Secretaries.

War clouds were gathering over Europe and the Munich Crisis sounded the alarm bell for many women who, with sinking hearts, turned once more to prepare for War. Since 1936 Guiders and Rangers had been allowed to attend Air Raid Precaution lectures in uniform. Guides everywhere turned out to assemble and distribute gas masks, and to help evacuate children and babies in 1938: thankfully this was to be just a rehearsal but the Executive Committee were alerted for future action.

However, in May 1939, Girl Guides went on show all over the country during "Guide Week"; Edinburgh opened its Headquarters with an exhibition, every day different companies and packs held demonstration meetings, and on Sunday, 7th May, there was a service in St Giles. The Guide Council held their Annual Meeting in St John's Church Hall asking every District and Division Commissioner to come in uniform, bringing with them four non-Guide friends; 14 new Guiders were recruited as a result. McVittie's displayed a cake with a camp scene on it in their window. Surely many Edinburgh folk knew more about Girl Guides after that week.

All the usual activities continued, badges were tested, camps attended, meetings held throughout the summer; but Hitler's troops marched into Poland and on 3rd September 1939 Great Britain was at war with Germany. Guiding still continued with fewer and fewer doing more and more—out of 40 Commissioners on the register 23 were on "temporary leave of absence" and a similar proportion of Guiders were away too. How did the small band of women do all the wonderful things written about in the chapter on "Guiding in Wartime"? Somehow they coped, bringing some cheer into the dreariness of war and the Guide spirit lifted many heavy hearts in those days.

13

Guiding in Wartime and
Guide International Service

LEND A HAND—Be Prepared—Service and the Good Turn—these familiar words have been the inspiration for countless actions and activities from the early days of Guiding in Edinburgh and Midlothian and, with the coming of the Great War in 1914, members of the Movement became involved in many forms of service, such as flag selling, knitting comforts for the troops and crews of minesweepers, messenger duties, collecting books and bottles for salvage, fruit picking and even running a sphagnum-moss-picking camp at West Linton.

Several activities were undertaken in company with the Y.W.C.A. or with the Red Cross and over the years these good relationships have continued to their mutual advantage.

War Service Badges were awarded for 100 hours' War work—the first three being gained by the Captain and two Guides of the 1st Company, and although there are no details of the work which they undertook, there is a typical story of twin Guides who were determined to gain the coveted badge. They were in a school Company and keen to do their share of war work so they offered to help with cleaning sphagnum-moss which was used for wound dressings. It was dull and tedious work and no doubt 100 hours of it was a daunting prospect. Then, joy of joys, they were given the job of driving a pony and cart from the dreary cleaning room to the storage house. They piled the sacks on the cart and set off as proud of their war work as any General! Also, a Guide of the 7th Company remembers:

"We went every Saturday morning in 1917 to run messages between the depot in Lauriston Place and the Red Cross Stall in the Princes Street Arcade where home-made marmalade was sold for the war effort. We visited the junk shops to collect empty jam jars which we wheeled about in an empty pram. Not very glamorous, but we felt we were helping to win the war—nothing else would have persuaded us to wheel an old pram filled with dirty jam jars." In May 1918 there were 698 Guides and 211 Brownies in Edinburgh, a modest number to carry out all the work which they had been asked to undertake.

In 1916 after an air raid a Guide of the 6th Company went to one of the damaged parts of the city and offered her services. The same spontaneous reaction come from a Patrol Leader in 1939 on the outbreak

of the Second World War—"I have called up my patrol: what can we
do to help?"

This 'phone message, received by a Guider in the early days of the war
in 1939, was typical of the spirit with which the Guides still left in Edinburgh after the evacuation faced the situation. It came as a challenge and
an appeal; somehow Guiding must carry on and find some means whereby
its younger members could answer the call of war service.

During the first days of the Evacuation, over 100 Guiders and Rangers
escorted parties of mothers and children to safer parts of the country,
spending anything from a night to ten weeks away from their homes.
One 16-year-old Guide looked after a party of nine, smoothing away
very real difficulties between host, staff and families, with great success.

A little band of twelve, who had discussed the problem of the evacuation of housebound handicapped children with the Education Department,
volunteered for full-time work with these children and achieved their
aim in a way that far surpassed their expectations. Instead of merely acting
as helpers, they were sent on 4th September-the day after war was declared—
to take over an empty house in St Abbs. Nothing daunted, they proceeded
and, with the help of camp equipment and other borrowed furniture, were
ready to receive the first crippled children the *next day*. They carried on
for ten weeks, then moved to Cowdenknowes, near Earlston. Here, with
equipment supplied by the Education Authority, they established and ran
a properly constituted school until the end of the war. This work so proved
its value that medical and educational experts supported whole-heartedly the
idea that it should continue on a permanent basis, and to those pioneers
we owe the Trefoil School, a School for physically handicapped children,
approved by the Scottish Education Department. The staff worked on a
voluntary basis for the *whole war*, help being provided during holidays and
weekends off-duty by many Guiders and Rangers. Read more in *History
of the Trefoil School* by Mary Crawford.

The first of many messenger services was formed early in September
1939 and did good work for the Regional Civil Defence Office where,
at first, Rangers and Cadets operated a full-time service. Guides also
acted as messengers in emergency offices at the City Chambers, the
Petroleum Office, the W.V.S. and for a first-aid post. The Guiders'
V.A.D. started a surgical-dressing work party, giving out work; and a
wool depot was also started. Salvage of all sorts was soon being collected,
and the first big collection of books for the Church of Scotland Huts
was made using a trek cart borrowed from the Scouts, and trek cart
parties were regularly called out. A register of volunteers was kept at
Headquarters so that the many requests for help could be met quickly,
and the object was never to refuse anything, however strange the request!

In November, the former County Commissioner, Miss Dalmahoy,
asked for help from Guiders and Guides in the staffing of the Randolph

Canteen, Randolph Place. As the Canteen gave an all-day service, it was not possible for Guiders to staff it completely, so they formed the two evening shifts and many of them continued this work for the duration of the war, while on Saturdays, Sundays, and in the holidays, Guides washed dishes and peeled potatoes.

From January 1940, a rota of Guiders and Rangers, working a seven-day week, staffed a Mobile Canteen which served searchlight and other army units near the city and in the surrounding country until the end of the war. The driver's first problem was to find these units! All road signs were removed on the outbreak of war and many Guiders were thankful that they had learnt map-reading as Guides—in spite of that, there are many stories of the van going round in circles before locating a well-camouflaged gun site! The Guides also had their part in this work; every evening for six years they met the returning van and washed the dishes—no throw-away plastic in those days! The Canteen was run for the Church of Scotland, who made Edinburgh Guide Headquarters a sub-store so that the vans could be replenished each day. Very big cupboards were built in Room 2 to stock the chocolate, cigarettes and other supplies. By July, the work had so much increased that a second van was necessary. Guiders and Guides from various companies provided Christmas presents for the Army Units and this practice was kept up in some form every subsequent Christmas of the war. The outstanding events in the Canteens' career were the five days and nights when they served the troops embarking for Norway at Leith Docks, and the three days spent in Clydebank after the blitz. Doris Morison Inches tells the story of the first day.

"The usual routine of stocking up the Canteen and making ready for a round of visits was interrupted by a telephone call from the Church of Scotland Headquarters telling us to take the Canteen through to Clydebank and to carry as much water and tea as we could manage. This was an emergency! We realised then that we were wanted to help out after a raid as, when we had been on duty through-out the night during an alert in Edinburgh, we had seen the reflections of fires away in the West.

"I remember that we had hardly been in bed before this day began! We left for Clydebank about 11 a.m. literally swimming in tea. There had been some holes in the van where the sides met the floor, and we had had mouse trouble, so these had just been stopped up; now we found the tea that slopped over couldn't get out!

"The first impact was on going through Glasgow: we were stopped at a bombed house where rescue workers were digging in the garden: we supplied tea and then went on our way to Clydebank.

"We reported at the Town Hall which itself had been bombed. Officials there were trying to cope with many bombed-out people. We were told to go up Kilbowie Road and there we served teas until supplies ran out. We needed water to make more tea and were offered some by a man who said he 'was pumping it out of a sewer'!! We got it from the Army instead and made fresh supplies which, in addition to being drunk, were used to heat a baby's bottle and to fill an old lady's hot-water bottle, as we had no separate water supply! We went down one street which was blazing on each side and saw an A.R.P. Warden sitting at a table in the middle of the road doing his job—we remembered that we had been amused during our own training when we had been told that this was the action to take when the Post had been destroyed. There were some pathetic shattered houses and flames were coming from the top of gas pipes sticking up in the air. One road we avoided had a large notice board up saying 'Unexploded Bomb.'

"On looking back, I seem to recall that we were left on our own to get on with the job once we had been told where to go, and this gave us confidence and the feeling that we were doing something real and necessary.

"We went on working until it got dark and our supplies were finished. People were no longer coming to us as they needed to get into the Shelters. We decided to go home and on the way, looking back, we saw that another raid had started. I believe the 'Guide' mobile van was the first civilian one on the job in Clydebank."

A book was written about all the Church of Scotland Huts and Canteens called *A Badge to be Proud of,* by Lewis Cameron.

Often the work was very arduous, but it was abundantly appreciated, and a very happy comradeship grew over the years which was evident in March 1946 when a party was held, attended by men from the Units served and representatives from the garage, the dairy, the bakers' shops, the Church of Scotland Huts Committee and the Guiders, Rangers and Guides who had taken part in the work.

Throughout the war years the whole County worked hard to contribute to the various Guide appeals, following the Guide practice of earning what they gave.

In 1940—for the Air Ambulances and Lifeboat—£465 13s 8d.
In 1941—when Edinburgh Guides decided to donate a Mobile Canteen
          to the Church of Scotland—£632 16s 6d.

This provided one of the lighter moments of wartime as the Chief Guide came to hand over the Canteen to Dr Warr, c.v.o., the Dean of the Thistle, who received it on behalf of the Church of Scotland.

In her own inimitable way the Chief Guide stood on the steps of St Giles and beckoned to the Guides to come closer, and they swarmed forward in a happy throng—a Ranger, Guide and Brownie came forward with the key which the Brownie handed to the Chief Guide—she then unlocked the door of the Canteen and invited Dr Warr to step inside—there were the smiling faces of yet another Ranger, Guide and Brownie all ready to serve the troops! Dr Warr said that he had never been so touched in all his life of receiving gifts as on this occasion.

The Chief Guide and Miss Wallace Williamson, County Commissioner, at St Giles in 1941.

In 1942—for the Baden-Powell Memorial—this money was to be invested in War Savings—£1822 0s 11d.

In 1944—for the Guide International Service for Relief Abroad —£807 1s 3d.

Saving and collecting and make-and-mend became a way of life— perhaps stimulated by the Guides helping to distribute Ration Books. Jam jars, sold for ½d a jar, helped funds considerably and collections of rose hips, a valuable source of Vitamin C, also earned hard cash. Cotton reels, in those days made of precious wood, were also collected in great quantities.

The needs of young people outside the youth organisations were especially great in wartime so an effort was made to help by opening a club for boys and girls in Guide Headquarters for two winters. This paved the way for a more ambitious scheme in a very needy neighbourhood which met with immediate success in the "Square Centre," Granton. More of this later.

Camping had always had a prominent place in the Guides' programme and this training and experience was put to good use in 1941 when the first Scottish berry-picking camps were held; and these continued each summer, attended by many Guides. Rangers and Cadets also worked in forestry and harvesting camps.

In 1941 blitz cooking was added to Guide duties, and each Company gave demonstrations of how to set up a fireplace built of bricks and to cook in the open—even in Princes Street Gardens. They had the necessary materials ready and suitable sites noted, so that if heavy bombing made it necessary they would be able to help householders in this way.

All through the war, Guides and Rangers gave regular help at various hospitals. The Officers' Hostel had a bed-making squad on Sunday mornings and help was also given at the Y.W.C.A. Hostel. Other Canteens had Guide helpers and a shift of Guiders worked in the Princes Street Canteen throughout the war.

Each Christmas Guides and Rangers took gifts and sang carols in the Castle and other hospitals. There was also a choir of Rangers and Guides who practised together for several evenings before going on a round of visits to hospitals and canteens.

For many years Guides had collected moss for the Earl Haig Poppy Factory in Edinburgh, and this was continued with renewed vigour to provide supplies for medical purposes as well as for the factory. Herb-picking was another activity requiring great care in separating the varieties.

Some companies took the "Dig for Victory" Challenge really seriously and on two occasions at Headquarters there were commendable shows of vegetables.

Guiding emerged from the war period tried and not found wanting. As in the First World War, many members qualified for, and were proud to wear, the War Service Badge, reinstated in 1940 in recognition of 100 hours of voluntary service.

THE GUIDE INTERNATIONAL SERVICE IS AN ENTHRALLING STORY

Like Guiding itself, the suggestion first came from the girls themselves. Amongst the many letters sent to Headquarters early in 1940, a twelve-year-old Guide wrote, "Shouldn't we start saving so as to send help to our friends in the occupied countries?" By 1942, a Committee was formed which, under the name of Guide International Service, became a founder member of the Council of British Societies for Relief Abroad. A fund was opened, which by 1945 rose to £111,000. This purchased the valuable relief supplies and financed the teams who were sent abroad to countries liberated by the Allied Armies. What a challenge this was to the Guide Movement, especially to those members who were in a "reserved" occupation and unable to join the Forces. In the middle of a war here was the call—to be prepared to help when the war ended.

Volunteers, some of whom came from Edinburgh, underwent a strenuous and exhaustive training. As one Guider said:

"Training began in 1942—helping at a home for physically handicapped children, trekking many miles in all weathers with only a minimum of the protective clothing which is available today, learning to skin a rabbit, mucking out the byres, with very unco-operative cows in them, being able to have a *complete* wash in little more than a pint of hot water, organising a day at a school meals centre and trying to learn Polish and German, were just some of the things we did."

In 1944 the first team of Guiders reached Greece. There, under hazardous conditions, they fed the starving, tended the sick and distributed medical supplies and clothing, until such time as the Greek authorities were able to take over, aided by the Greek Guides, some of whom had already been working with the G.I.S. The teams wore A.T.S. Officer's uniform with the distinctive G.I.S. flash on the left sleeve; its Trefoil was an "Open Sesame" to many hearts.

By 1945 the Mobile Hospital Team and two Kitchen Canteens had reached Holland, where, within sound of the guns, they established three Hospitals to combat the threat of epidemic, and operated feeding centres until the whole country was liberated. The Dutch were then able to take over their own welfare aided by supplies from the G.I.S. and other sources.

In Germany the first task was to help clean up Concentration Camps, and to set up special Hospitals with maternity and T.B. wards for the Displaced Persons. From then on nine teams were responsible for the welfare of groups of D.P. camps. They organised feeding schemes, clothing distribution, clinics, workshops and community centres, while gradually, small numbers of D.P.s were able to return to their own countries. Volunteers spent from four months to a year with a team. Jean Stenhouse of Midlothian was with one looking after five to six thousand people in twelve D.P. camps—some task! She also helped to staff holiday camps for children, bringing life and laughter to many who had never known that freedom. Betty Ballantyne was an Edinburgh Guider who was in the third team, and was sent from Holland on to the Belsen Concentration Camp. Helen MacDonald was with the fourth team for a year. Margaret Gregory was in one of the two teams allocated to German welfare in the badly bombed Ruhr, where in nine months it was estimated that they distributed one and a half million meals to undernourished children. In another district they helped returning prisoners of war from Russia, and the many German refugees trying to reach their homes.

The Advisory Officer for all the teams in Germany was Verona Wallace Williamson, the County Commissioner for Edinburgh, who overcame the war-time difficulties of travel and disruption to add this extra task to an already demanding job. All volunteers in the G.I.S. speak little of their achievements; it is only indirectly that one hears of the invaluable and self-sacrificing work they did. (It might be mentioned here that the Sue Ryder Homes are a direct result of Sue Ryder's experience in G.I.S.) The idea had spread to Australia and New Zealand where teams of Guiders trained—some coming to Britain to do so—and were sent to Malaya when Japan surrendered, and did valuable welfare and medical relief work there.

By 1950 the G.I.S. was the only voluntary Society remaining in the British Zone of Germany, having been asked by the International Refugee Organisation to remain for one more year. Their main concern was with two sections of the Displaced Persons—the would-be migrants for whom they provided welfare at the Emigration Centre—and those D.P.s who were rejected as migrants on age or health grounds and needed much help and advice. Three training courses were arranged which enabled five hundred able-bodied men and women to qualify for jobs and many welfare schemes were initiated for the old. One scheme for training the young people involved a G.I.S. team who encouraged Guiding among the D.P. children so that they would be enthusiastic to resume Guiding when settled in their new countries. This team also contacted former German Guides and enabled a group to study methods in England before forming Girl Guide Companies once more in Germany.

One side of war-time life is worth emphasising as it affected everyone, especially growing children and mothers trying to bring up a family—this was food rationing. It is hard to imagine the ration per head per week of one egg (when available), 2 ozs. of butter, 4 ozs. of margarine, 8 ozs. of sugar and 1/8d worth of meat—that alone is cause for a hollow laugh now, yet the miracle was that there were, in fact, few hollow tummies then. Biscuits were a rare treat, "on points" like tinned meat and soup.

The Displaced families in the camps suffered too. As they were being considered for resettlement in the countries which opened their doors to limited numbers of refugees, an ailing grandparent or sick child meant rejection of the whole family. Elderly relatives would beg the rest to leave them but loyalties were strong and many refused to go unless all went. Guiders who saw these heart-breaking cases knew that a little extra food given to those most in need could make the difference between new life for all the family or a living death in the D.P. camps. They begged to be given that extra food and streams of parcels left Edinburgh through the years with food contributed by the Guides from their own meagre rations. Many a mickle makes a muckle, and in response to the special 1950 Christmas Appeal two thousand parcels were sent to the camps!

Clothing was sent too; most was usable but some needed attention, like the bundle of one thousand new lisle stockings which had slipped from the crane when being unloaded from the ship and arrived sopping wet!

Then there were one hundred pairs of un-paired boots which took hours to sort!

As a footnote—the uniformed Girl Guide Movement qualified for an issue of clothing coupons in 1949. These were distributed in Edinburgh through divisions and districts—three for each member—enough for one and a half pairs of stockings!

The fascinating story of G.I.S. is told in the Book *All Things Uncertain* by Phyllis Stewart Brown.

14

Messengers—Banners, Pigeons and Scrolls

WHY DO BANNERS convey a message?

Before the days of instant contact by radio some means of rallying the clansmen to the side of their chieftain was required. The flag or banner, carried beside the leader, was the rallying point in battle. As long as the flag flew the men were inspired to fight. The bearer played a key rôle as the "Colours" (as they are known) were the prime target; the capture of them frequently decided the fate of the battle, and they were defended to the death. (Revolutionaries nowadays try to capture the radio station before all else.)

Guides have two different Colours—one the Union Flag and the other a Company Colour or Flag, visual reminders of our country and of the loyalty due to the Queen inherent in the Guide Promise. Before Colours are paraded for the first time they are brought to church to be dedicated, and are always treated with great dignity and respect.

Traditions are rightly maintained by the Guide Movement which has retained its Union Flags, Company Colours, Division and County Banners; the ceremony of the Colours and the discipline which accompanies it is an integral part of a Guide meeting. A Guide, Ranger or Guider chosen as Colour bearer or escort realises that she is carrying out one of the highest duties towards the Queen and the Guide Movement that she can be asked to do. Colour ceremonies practised beforehand and well executed can make a lasting impression on the spectators, especially on the young, the leaders of the future.

Edinburgh Girl Guides possess many beautiful hand-embroidered banners which incorporate the local history and traditions of the divisions. In the early days embroidery was a skill much encouraged by Miss Dalmahoy, the first County Commissioner, whose sister presented an Embroidery Cup in 1935. Miss Dalmahoy was responsible along with other Guiders for embroidering the beautiful County Banner which was dedicated in 1931. On a pale blue background is the cross of St Andrew in silver, the Castle to represent the City in silver, red and black, with the Edinburgh motto, *Nisi Dominus Frustra,* and in the centre the Trefoil surrounded by a garland of Scottish wild flowers. This banner is now always carried when the County Commissioner is present at a church service or official meeting and when not in use is on show in a display case in Room 1 in

H.Q. A story is told that at the wet Rally in 1931 when the County banner was carried for the first time in public, the colour bearer was very loth to dip her flag in the mud of Stewart's Playing Fields!

The following Divisions have hand-embroidered banners which in some way depict the local history of the Division. The banner of:

Blackford Hill was designed by Miss Molly Wood and embroidered by Miss Burns and various Guiders. It is pale blue and has a town with open gates to symbolise the open country which bordered the Division and a star—"open unto the fields and to the sky." The sheaves of corn symbolise the Districts with their "fields"—Mayfield, Prestonfield. There is also a Trefoil.

Braid was also designed by Miss Molly Wood and presented by Miss Maisie Wood, the Division Commissioner. This banner has an orange background representing the Edinburgh Orange Colours and the cross of St Andrew. The oak tree, the carved acorn on the flagpole, together with the motto *Stand Steadfast,* represent the donor's name.

Dunedin was made by the Guider and Guides of an East Division Company for the then East Division (now Dunedin). There is a St Andrew's Cross and a Trefoil, the Castle to represent Edinburgh, and the heart with cross to symbolise the founding of Holyrood Abbey by King David I in 1128.

Forth was designed by Miss Molly Wood and shows the cross of St Andrew, the Trefoil and the North Star, to represent North Division as it was then. The undulating line—white on green—represents the Firth of Forth and the ship is the *Golden Hind.*

Leith was designed and painted by Miss Molly Wood and shows the cross of St Andrew, an embroidered Trefoil, and a ship with the Virgin and Child and *Persevere*, the last two being the coat of arms and motto of the Port of Leith.

Pentland was embroidered by Rangers of St Margaret's Ranger Company whose banner it originally was. The gift of the banner to the old West Division took place when the Ranger company became a combined operation unit of Sea and Air Rangers. The subsequent adaptation to the banner was carried out in a convent in Kent. The banner shows St Margaret's Chapel because originally the West Division included Edinburgh Castle and the Division Ranger Company took its name from the Chapel.

Portobello & Niddrie was also designed by Miss Molly Wood and is pennon-shaped. It has the cross of St Andrew, the Trefoil, an undulating line representing the sea coast at Portobello and a harbour and a ship.

Raeburn was originally the banner of the 22nd Edinburgh Guide Company (St Cuthbert's) and was sewn by Miss Annabel Kidston in 1951, the 25th Anniversary of the company's formation. In 1975, the company, having been closed, the banner was offered by Dr Small so that it could continue to be used and it was given to the new Raeburn Division. It shows the cross of St Andrew, the Trefoil and the pectoral cross of St Cuthbert (from the original cross in Durham Cathedral).

Turnhouse. This shows the cross of St Andrew, the Trefoil and a lantern with rays of light gleaming from it representing the lantern which hung for about two hundred years in a niche on the outside wall of Corstorphine Parish Church to guide travellers over the rough marshy ground to the east. To endow this light, the "lamp acre"—a piece of ground on the left bank of the Water of Leith at Murrayfield—was given by one of the Forrester family. The river in the banner represents the Water of Leith.

Wester Hailes is the most recent of the banners and was designed by a Guider and sewn in 1975 by a member of the Royal Society for Self Aid of Gentlewomen. It has a St Andrew's Cross, a Trefoil and the Bonnie Prince Charlie Bridge at Slateford, a notable feature in the Division.

And how is the design of a banner chosen? The story of Wester Hailes banner gives an insight into this. First there was a great deal of research into local history, and visits to the Edinburgh Room of the Central Library showed that most of the historical interest centred on the Slateford/Longstone area. Bonnie Prince Charlie figured in the stories and actually stayed in Gray's Mill overnight. In view of this the inclusion in the banner of a representation of the Bonnie Prince Charlie Bridge at Slateford was an obvious choice. Dorothy Steedman's design was submitted to the Lord Lyon for approval because there are certain heraldic rules which must be observed and any proposed design for a banner has to conform. After approval of the design it was then drawn to scale so that an estimate of the cost of the banner could be given. This proved to be approximately £100, a daunting thought, but thanks to a tremendous effort on the part of the whole Division the money was raised at a jumble sale in 1974. A year later the banner was dedicated on 14th December at a special service at Slateford/Longstone Church.

In September 1961 during the Edinburgh Festival most of these banners, along with some from other parts of Scotland, were on display in Tolbooth St John's Church. Forty banners were shown and about a thousand people saw the exhibition, which was called "At the Sign of the Golden Trefoil." These banners have all been dedicated in church when they were new; but the very first consecration of colours in Edinburgh took place on the 13th May 1916 in West Queen Street Gardens during the then Midlothian Girl Guides' Rally, when the inspecting officer was Lady Beatty. This flag, a Union Flag, was displayed for a few years in the '20s in St Giles Cathedral in the Shrine of Youth, along with the flags of other youth organisations. Every time the flag was removed for ceremonial use there was a short ceremony and a prayer was offered. In May 1937, to celebrate the Coronation of King George VI, Miss

Wallace Williamson replaced this Union Flag with a new County World Flag.

In September 1976 the Executive Committee agreed that the beautiful County banner, made in 1931, was becoming too fragile to be carried and should remain in future in the showcase in Edinburgh Headquarters. A new banner will be made.

PIGEONS! What have pigeons to do with Guides? What indeed? Did you know that pigeons were used in war to send information, that they fly more swiftly for their master when he truly loves them and cares for them like a member of the family? That the very speediest can fly at 90 miles an hour? That the message paper is as thin as thin, and is fastened in a neat roll to the carrier pigeon's leg?

When plans were being made in Edinburgh to celebrate King George v's Silver Jubilee, a Leith Commissioner had the happy inspiration that the Guides should send a message by carrier pigeon to the King. The City Authorities took up the idea enthusiastically and so, on 11th May 1935 just after the Duke and Duchess of York arrived at Murrayfield Stadium, a flight of pigeons took off with loyal messages to His Majesty from all the Youth Organisations assembled there.

Then in 1943, it was decided by Imperial Guide Headquarters to close the Baden-Powell Memorial Fund by sending pigeons from all over Britain with birthday greetings to the Chief Guide. "At that time I was in Peebles; I can well remember the great occasion when the Guides released our precious pigeons—three times round the square they flew, then away to Edinburgh with our pigeon post," wrote a Commissioner to a friend. Meanwhile, at St George's School playing fields, Miss Wallace Williamson, the County Commissioner, and her Guides were waiting for pigeons from Counties in Scotland to arrive. The lofts were at the end of the field—birds appeared in the sky, flew towards their homes, and excited Guides surged forward—equally excited pigeons flew off! This happened several times till the Guides were prevailed upon to bend their heads and stay quite still. While in this attitude of prayer, the pigeons flew into their lofts and all was well. A woman journalist turned to the County Commissioner and said, "What will you mad Guides get up to next?" The messages were sent on to London, and a Belgian Guide had the honour of releasing the pigeon with the Edinburgh message.

A happy result of this idea was that part of the Baden-Powell Memorial Fund was assigned to the upkeep of pigeons for the Services. Further uses of the Pigeon Post crop up in "our mad doings." The highlight of the South-East Brownie Revels at the Inch was the message of greetings sent to the Trefoil School when they occupied their new home at Kirklands. The baskets arrived with the pigeons—the message was fastened on, and the pigeons released, watched by Brownies whose eyes grew larger as their birds circled round, then disappeared into the distance. They arrived safely in their lofts at Ratho and the message was delivered. Later, at the 1957 Rally at Stenhouse, 200 pigeons were released with greetings from all present to the Chief Guide—how white they looked against the sky! A touching story appeared in the press—the occasion had been too much for one poor bird and he alighted on a window sill nearby. The inhabitants christened him Charlie and fed him—wise bird, he ate his meals, but would not allow anyone to catch him—until his owner came to fetch him home!

In 1975 at the World Association of Girl Guides and Girl Scouts Conference at Sussex University, Guide delegates from all over the world collected on the campus on Saturday, 28th June, for the thrill of seeing 1000 pigeons being released as part of a pigeon race. The pigeon with the longest flight arrived in Edinburgh at a Duddingston loft on Sunday morning. It was expected on Saturday evening but owing to heavy fog would not "come in"—landing lights not working perhaps!! The message read, "Greetings from W.A.G.G.S. Conference to all Girl Guides in Scotland." Mrs Wilkie, County Commissioner of Edinburgh, replied by telegram, "Best Wishes from all Girl Guides in Scotland for a very happy and fruitful Conference."

SCROLLS make one think of old Egyptian parchments, but they have played a very exciting rôle in the Edinburgh Guide story. The first scroll was formal and has a place in Edinburgh Civic history. Representatives of everyone who planted a tree or took part in the Braidburn Valley Silver Jubilee Gifts, 1935, signed a parchment which was then given to the Lord Provost to place for safe keeping in the Council Chambers—perhaps a Girl Guide of 2000 will be given the chance to see her predecessors' names!

In 1950 the World Conference was held in Oxford and to mark this great occasion and to enable all Guides to share in the Conference, messages of welcome and friendship inscribed on vellum scrolls were sent from all parts of Britain to the delegates at Oxford. Guides and Brownies had tremendous fun planning the most exciting and adventurous ways of conveying the two scrolls which passed through Edinburgh. One actually began its journey in the city on 20th June, and was to be handed eventually to the New Zealand delegate; and the other, for the South African delegate, started in Fraserburgh and arrived on 26th June.

The New Zealand scroll was handed to a group of 1st Class Guides at Scottish H.Q. by Lady Colville, the Scottish Chief Commissioner, and, led by Scout pipers, they marched to the Castle. Here the scroll was signed by the Governor, lowered in a basket from Queen Mary's Room to

Johnston Terrace far below, and taken by car to the canal at Slateford. From there a boat trip with the Sea Rangers, followed by cycle and pony conveyance to Princess Margaret Rose Hospital, where the scroll was left overnight in the care of Extension Brownies and Guides. The next day, by means of a pony, cycle and tractor, it arrived at the Royal Blind School, and, finally, with the aid of a trek cart, it reached Craigmillar Castle where a pageant and campfire had been planned to take place. Unfortunately, the weather was far from friendly and everyone was crammed tightly in a neighbouring hall for these final celebrations at which the scroll was handed over to the Midlothian Guides.

A few days later the scroll for the South African delegate arrived by Admiral's Barge at Granton Harbour and was received by the Sea Rangers. During the next four days it travelled by the most ingenious and unusual ways that could be devised by the Divisions and Districts. From the majestic dignity of travel by elephant at the Zoo to the final trip in a coal lorry for delivery to Midlothian Guides, the scroll was carried round all parts of the city: on the footplate of a train, in the Sea Rangers' boat, in a fish creel carried by a Guide, in a pram wheeled by a Brownie, and in many other ways. Wherever it went crowds of Brownies and Guides shared in the fun which reached its peak at the camp fires held each evening.

15

Royal Visitors

HER MAJESTY THE QUEEN and Her Majesty the Queen Mother are Patrons of the Girl Guides' Association; the first President was the Princess Royal, and she was succeeded by her niece, Princess Margaret. The Guide Movement is very privileged to have the interest and membership of many of the Royal Family, and over the years Edinburgh Guides have been fortunate to have many varied opportunities to express their loyalty.

In the days when Royal Visits were State occasions and within a year of the formation of the Association, Guides were asked to line the streets near Waverley Station to Greet King George V and Queen Mary. In 1934 there were Brownies as well as Guides waiting to see Their Majesties, and Brown Owls were warned to restrain the Brownies from rushing out on to the road! Newspapers to sit on whilst waiting were allowed—"but they must be removed afterwards."

For the Coronation visit of King George VI and Queen Elizabeth in 1937, Rangers, Guides and Brownies lined Regent Road. Miss Crommelin Brown, the North Division Commissioner, says:

"One of the Captains was ill, consequently I was in charge of her Company of Guides. As the Royal carriage came towards their stance, the girls saw Princess Elizabeth, who was sitting in front of her parents and sister, turn round to her father, tap him on the knee, and point to the Guides! She was obviously interested in seeing her sister Guides, who were so excited at this recognition that they jumped up and down and waved to her!"

Once more, in 1953, there were 150 Rangers and Guides on Castle Terrace to greet Her Majesty Queen Elizabeth and H.R.H. the Duke of Edinburgh after she had received the Key of the Castle from the Governor. Another memorable moment.

Although Guides don't line the streets any more, many girls watch the Royal Family as they move around Edinburgh during their annual visits. Four Belfast Guides, invited to North-West Division Camp in 1971 and staying in Guide homes afterwards, made their hostesses realise how lucky are the citizens of Edinburgh. They were all near the Royal Scottish Academy to watch the Queen and Prince Philip go in, and this was the happiest memory taken home to Ireland. With starry eyes they said: "We've seen the Queen!"

The 116th Company Guides were similarly enraptured at their camp at Carberry Tower in 1968 when the Queen and the Duke arrived for a short visit to the house and the Guides were allowed to stand near the front door. For security reasons, an official invitation to be in the grounds had been necessary, and the girls hadn't known about the visit beforehand so it was an enormous surprise. One of the Guiders recalls:

"We watched the cars arrive and everyone was so excited to be so near the Queen. We were honoured with a special smile, and the Duke stopped to chat. He went straight to the girls' hearts when he said: 'Camping in this wet weather! Aren't you getting a bit mouldy?' Since this was a current 'in' word, it raised quite a chuckle! As the car drove away, we dropped all formality, dashed up to it, and gave a great cheer. The Queen had a hearty laugh and such a big wave for us. We floated rather than walked back to the camp site, each Guide quite sure that the Duke had spoken to *her!* Tea was a little late that day."

In Lady Baden-Powell's book, *Window on my Heart*, she pays tribute to the work and enthusiasm of Princess Mary, who insisted on being enrolled and taking the Guide Promise, so that she "could be one of us." As President of the Girl Guides' Association, Princess Mary inspected the Edinburgh Guides on 7th July 1920 at the King's Park. The following account is taken from a Company Log Book:

"About 9 a.m. one cold foggy morning, our Guides and Brownies met at 28 Heriot Row, and were whirled away in two motor buses to the King's Park. Although so early, a great number of Companies had assembled, and gradually the masses of Guides and Brownies became separated, and grouped into orderly Divisions, whilst distracted Captains and Commissioners stopped running about asking questions and on all faces came a look of anxious expectancy. Prompt to the minute the great doors of the Palace swung back, and a girl appeared, to be immediately surrounded by Commissioners and officials. It was a memorable scene and a thousand thoughts and fancies passed through one's mind as the young Princess made her first inspection of Scottish Guides. With simple dignity, the Princess walked round all the Companies, and then took her stand at the saluting base during the March Past. Finally, messages were signalled to the Divisions telling of the whereabouts of three bouquets, which runners from each Company had to interpret and discover, the winning Company in each case having the honour of presenting the bouquet to the Princess. After the singing of the National Anthem, the Princess retired amid loud cheers and the doors of Holyrood hid her from view."

One Brownie remembers this historical event especially because she was allowed to have her very first pair of BROWN shoes for it! She later became President of Midlothian Girl Guides.

Princess Mary visited Edinburgh in 1930 to receive the Freedom of the City, and 50 1st Class Brownies, Guides and Ranger Star holders provided a Guard of Honour.

Again, in 1931, Princess Mary inspected the Guides at a large Rally held on Daniel Stewart's Playing Fields. Instructions for the great day were sent forth. "Begin to smarten up uniforms at once. There is a lot of hair out of plaits. There must be no ringlets, fancy hair slides or coloured ribbons. Neither must there be any white petticoats, white knickers or white socks. Practise marching *now*, in eights, and wheeling in fours." On the morning of the Rally the sky was rather forbidding, and much consultation took place—should the event be held under cover in the Waverley Market? In the manner of the fickle Scottish weather, the sun shone, so the Rally proceeded as planned. Tram cars filled with Guides and Brownies rattled their way to the assembly point and discharged their excited passengers. Then the weather changed again; it rained and rained, and everyone was soaked to the skin. Many were even dyed blue, from the new uniforms, bought for the great day.

Princess Mary changed out of her wet clothes, afterwards remarking to Miss Dalmahoy that she was rather ashamed to have done so, when everyone else was still in their wet uniforms. Thereafter the day went down in Guide history as the "Wet Rally."

A letter was subsequently received at Headquarters from the Lady-in-Waiting:

"The Princess wishes me to write to you, and I can hardly say too emphatically how greatly Her Royal Highness was impressed by the undaunted spirit shown by the Edinburgh Guides and Brownies yesterday in spite of the relentless rain. The Princess does want to congratulate you, one and all, and thought that your performance was a splendid tribute to all that the Guide Movement stands for, and the cheerful way in which the programme was altered at such short notice did you the greatest credit. The Princess does hope that no one will be any the worse for getting wet."

In 1935, the Duke and Duchess of York represented the King and Queen at the Silver Jubilee Rally of youth organisations at Murrayfield, when the pigeons were dispatched with loyal messages to London. Each organisation was allotted 15 minutes for their display. The Guides' choice was tent pitching and a parade of Colours. A member of one of the Division teams wrote:

"The bell tents were pitched in a semi-circle facing the Grand Stand. Weeks of practice meant that the tents were up in 2½ minutes, each team standing at attention in front of their tent. At a given signal all the Colours were paraded between the tents and drawn up in formation—a splendid display! Down came the tents and were in their bags in 1½ minutes. We ran off the field with the tents hanging from their poles, clutching the ends of the ropes in our hands. Not a second left to tie knots. The timing was magnificent. I shall never forget the thrill we all got out of it. The final dipping of the Colours as the Duke and Duchess left the field was most moving.''

And on their Coronation visit in 1937, as King George VI and Queen Elizabeth, accompanied by Princess Elizabeth and Princess Margaret, they were present at another gathering of Scottish Youth Organisations at Murrayfield. This time Guides gave a Keep Fit Display, and looked most attractive in the new bright blue Camp Uniforms. They also proved that "a Guide is Useful," by staffing the Edinburgh schools (at the special request of the Corporation) in which 500 members of Youth Organisations from all over Scotland were accommodated for this Royal occasion.

In 1944, Princess Mary attended a Church Parade of Edinburgh Guides at St Cuthbert's Church. The Lord Provost. Sir William Darling, and Lady Constance Blackburn, the President, were present. After the service, the Princess briefly visited 33 Melville Street talking to some of the

. . . never — oh! never — the two together!

Commissioners before taking the salute on the steps of Headquarters at the march past of 3000 Rangers and Guides which, with District Commissioners and Guiders, made an impressive sight. Many of the Divisions had practised marching, helped by interested members of the women's services, and it really paid dividends! Believe it or not, the Guides enjoyed their practice sessions very much.   When the Division Commissioners were introduced to Princess Mary, they had to remember to curtsey first, salute next, but never—oh! never—the two together!   A Division Commissioner remembers:

"I was cycling down to Headquarters in uniform, ready for the service and was in a hurry as usual, when the front wheel caught in the tram-line! Next thing I knew was being picked up and dusted down by a nice young sailor. My knee was bleeding, my stocking torn and he suggested that I should go to have treatment. 'I can't,' I said, 'I must curtsey to Princess Mary if this knee will let me.'   He looked at me very strangely!"

Two thousand members of youth organisations gathered at the Waverley Market to welcome Princess Elizabeth and the Duke of Edinburgh.   It was a very special day for Margaret Thomson, now Mrs Davies, who says:

"How well I remember the day! It was Thursday, 3rd March 1949. A friend and I had been chosen to represent the 16th Company at a Reception for Young People in the Waverley Market, at which Princess Elizabeth and the Duke of Edinburgh were to be present. The great day had arrived, and right up to an hour before leaving the house for the Waverley Market, I had been polishing my Guide Badge and whistle, pressing my Guide uniform, making absolutely sure that I would be all spick and span for the Royal occasion. To crown everything, I had fused my mother's iron whilst pressing my uniform! My father said, 'You would think *you* were to be presented to the princess.'
    "Boys and girls from every type of school and youth organisation formed a huge double circle in the Waverley Market to meet the Royal visitors.   There were palm trees and flowers in abundance, and a band played popular music. When the Royal couple arrived, you can imagine my amazement when Princess Elizabeth turned and spoke to *me,* and not to the others as expected. She asked, 'To which Company of Girl Guides do you belong?'   Proudly I replied, 'The 16th Company Your Royal Highness.'   She told me she liked Edinburgh very much. What I remember most about those few precious moments is that Princess Elizabeth had a lovely smile, and as she spoke to me the band was playing 'This is my lovely day.' As Princess Elizabeth continued to speak to many other young people, His Royal Highness, looking very handsome in Naval uniform, came forward to talk to a group which included myself. What excitement all in one day! He said that he wondered how we all managed to keep our uniforms so nice and clean.

I just wished I could pluck up sufficient courage to reply, 'Oh, our mothers use Persil, Your Royal Highness.' At the end of the reception, we nearly raised the roof of the Waverley Market when we cheered the Princess and the Duke, with a final cheer for the Royal baby, Prince Charles.

"On arriving home, my father jokingly asked, 'Did they speak to you after all that fuss about your uniform, and fusing the iron?' I had great difficulty in trying to convince my parents that indeed they had! However, the following morning my father, on opening his newspaper, remarked that there was a photograph of a lucky Girl Guide who had been chatting with Princess Elizabeth in a throng of 2000 young

people in the Waverley Market. He then exclaimed, 'My goodness, it's Margaret, and she *did* speak to the Princess.' I was indeed lucky!''

In 1953, the Princess returned to Edinburgh, and once more attended a Youth Rally at Murrayfield, this time as Queen on her Coronation visit. As she entered the Stadium, she saw a huge crown, flanked by ''E.R.'', formed by members of all the youth organisations who, standing there, sang, ''I vow to thee, my Country.'' There followed displays, the one given by teams of Guides was of tent pitching and Colour hoisting; each team marched past the Queen who asked the Lord Provost to pass on her congratulations on the smartness of all present.

It is on occasions such as these that British Girl Guides realise the significance of part of the Promise they make on enrolment.

16

International

FROM THE START, World Guiding has been such an active affair in Edinburgh that only a chronological list of all the events could do justice to its story. In that guise it would be all very impressive—but how dull! and how unfair to reduce it to a catalogue of dates and names and places, when what really counts are the impressions which people remember; the good times which they had; and the kindness and thoughtfulness which others remember of *them*.

If the story were to be told in lists, they would be long—as long as your arm:

—of visitors from every corner of the earth, here for a year or two, or for a few hours—like the party of Australian Guides who arrived from London in time to watch the Tattoo, and left straight afterwards to begin their long journey home;

—of Edinburgh Guides who ventured abroad to nearby countries or half-way round the world;

—of all the units and individuals who corresponded regularly, mostly in English, but sometimes in a common foreign language or, with a neat ingenuity, in Pidgin Dutch or in pictograms;

—of the Brownie Guider from the Solomons, well accustomed to interisland travel at home, who was quite at sea among the islands of Princes Street;

—of international camps at Blair Atholl and Blair Drummond;

—of Thinking Day services, international evenings, trainings and rallies;

—of . . . but even the catalogue of the lists is endless!

The early Edinburgh Guides realised that they were members of a Movement whose scope and potential was as wide as the world itself when, in May 1911, the German Guides invited British Guides to visit Hamburg that summer. A Guide of the 4th Company remembers: "The Scottish representative was Jean Curran from Girvan. As she was sailing from Leith to Hamburg, she stopped in Edinburgh and visited our company. She also visited us on her way home, and told us about her visit. I corresponded with her for some time after."

The news that Guiding had spread to another country caused tremendous excitement and exhilaration, for here, at last, was an idea that was not exclusive to one nation, but was going to be a bond uniting them all. And when a photograph arrived from Germany one day it was passed from unit to unit and every detail observed and discussed. The uniform appeared somewhat the same as ours but, on consideration, "rather quaint."

Guiding was spreading quickly elsewhere, too, and by 1913, the Edinburgh Honorary Secretaries, the Misses Young, felt able to advise gentlemen from South Africa and Italy, to whom, in the confident words of the Minute Book, they gave "all the necessary information."

During the First World War an American girl, instead of joining a Company, had to be content with an "attachment" to it, and with certificates instead of the badges which she had earned because, although Girl Scouting had been officially established in the United States, she could not take the British Guide Promise of duty to the King. Nowadays all Guides from abroad are welcomed wholeheartedly as full members and can make a special promise which recognises their loyalty to two nations, and they are enrolled with the World Badge, adopted only in 1948.

They have come to the City at all ages—a Brownie in the uniform she wore in Singapore; a long-term patient at the Princess Margaret Rose Hospital, from Hong Kong, was enrolled in bed as a Guide; many leaders from the U.S. bringing with them their wonderful energy and liveliness; and a trainer from Uganda who returned home to become her country's International Commissioner. Most have returned home, but they have left a particular sparkle on Edinburgh Guiding.

But the traffic has not by any means been only one way. Many who started Guiding in the City have moved abroad and strengthened the links with all the other Guiding and Scouting nations. Brownies emigrating with their families have been transferred to Packs in their new home-towns and have found things much as they knew them here; Guiders, abroad for a year or two, have helped to overcome the perennial and world-wide shortage of leaders; and all are now accepted on their merits, regardless of race, nationality or religion.

Language has never proved a real difficulty (except at World Conference and World Bureau level, where even a smile cannot convey quite the precise shade of meaning of a particular word or phrase, and here business is conducted in the three official Guide languages—English, French and Spanish). It is no barrier to friendliness, though it may be to understanding, so a new tongue, unrecognised by scholars has evolved— "Desperanto"—which, with gesture and mime, covers all situations. Except, it seems in the cinema in Norway. The 183rd Company, hostelling in the mountains there with their Rangers and Scouts, returned to the sophistications of Oslo, and decided to spend a wet evening at the pictures. With great care, they chose an American film, so that, whatever the sub-titles, they would be able to understand it. Unfortunately, *Tora Tora Tora*, for all it was American, had a Japanese sound-track—and even a Guide could be forgiven for failing at that point and resorting to mirth.

The Scandinavian countries have always had a special attraction and the records are full of references to trips there by units and individuals. Invitations came regularly—and still do—to their huge national camps. One, in Denmark in 1970, accommodated 8000 Danes, 999 from other countries and one Assistant Guider, Linda Young, from North Division in Edinburgh. Belgium, Holland and France also welcomed many in the early days, and occasional visits were made to other European countries. Switzerland, of course, has always appealed to travellers, and many are the companies which have spent holidays there, even after costs began to soar in the '70s; over the years they must have trodden deep paths in the eternal snows to the top of the Jungfrau or in the woods and meadows around Adelboden. Some of the countries which appear in the records sound unlikely to modern ears—Lithuania, where Betty Ballantyne and Betty Dickson attended a large camp in 1938; and Hungary where, in 1939, Honor Pape was one of the Scottish representatives to the World Camp—as was Mrs Wilkie, many years before she became County Commissioner (but that is part of Peeblesshire's story, and not this).

No units seem to have crossed the Atlantic but many individual Edinburgh Rangers and Guiders have done so, mostly to attend specialist trainings rather than straightforward camps, or to learn about some particular aspect of Guiding and Scouting over there.

In 1938, a U.S./U.K. exchange training scheme was set up, and Betty Mackay, who had been the Lieutenant of the St Christopher's Cadets and had just been given her first Company, was sent over to represent Northern Ireland, Wales and Scotland. The English representative was another Betty—"Betty England" and "Betty Sc-a-a-atland" to their hostesses, who clustered at their elbows whenever they spoke to savour their different accents. They spent four weeks there, centred on New York, where they landed from the ship on a day when the temperature was 98° in the shade with humidity to match, dressed in uniform—none of your camp overalls, as in these days, of bright, cool blue— but a thick dark navy serge "suit," white shirt and tie, and wide-brimmed, cockaded hat. They caused a sensation among their fellow passengers!

Their tour of camps took them north to Cape Cod, where the sand, even through shoe leather, was too hot to stand on; where turtles swam in the clear water of the lakes and blueberries were planted in depressions so that, come the harvest, the plots could be flooded and the berries float to the surface. It all sounds idyllic—but trouble occurred at a nearby English folk dance camp which they were taken to visit. They were expected to take part in a Morris dance, and it would not be the last time that the make-up of the United Kingdom had to be explained; it was difficult, too, for the Americans to understand that Morris dancing was a man's job and that women simply did not do it.

These pinpricks were slight compared to the ones which were to come at the next stop—Girl Scout One, the very first permanent U.S. training camp built on the site of a swamp—where Betty used a whole bottle of ammonia in an effort to soothe her mosquito bites. For the first time, two coloured leaders were attending a session, and the two Bettys were dismayed to find themselves being carefully protected by their hostesses from what they imagined would be an embarrassing experience. Far from being embarrassed, they were later to enjoy a visit to the first-ever camp for coloured Guides in New York State.

Their journey home was across the path of a summer hurricane, and during the Munich crisis when war was a distinct possibility. Pitched from one side of the ship to the other, and with an ear always cocked to the radio news-bulletins, they were still able to appreciate the episode in the dining-saloon at the height of the storm, when a whole cauliflower was ejected from the waiter's serving dish, landed on the head of a French monk—Friar Tuck in dress and shape—and slowly rolled down his vast brown front, leaving a path of white sauce in its wake.

With the advent of war politics intervened. But when the clouds rolled away, Guides were back on the road once more—North to camp in Iceland (camping-de-luxe, with hot water available at each site from the thermal springs); or South, as Miss Winnie Wallace went, the only Girl Guide representative in the British Delegation to a World Youth Conference at Dakar, West Africa; West to Our Cabana in Mexico; or East to New Delhi. Over the years the number of travellers decreased as the cost increased.

A Girl Scout invitation for a Scottish Ranger to go to the States to join in the Bicentennial celebrations cost over £500 in 1976. How different was the modest 2/6d a day which it cost the St Giles Rangers to stay at a Belgian convent forty-four years earlier; and they each found a pound of cherries in their packed lunches to complete the sandwich meal!

Edinburgh has always been a Mecca for visitors. They come on holiday, to study and confer, and a great number have been Guides or Scouts. In July 1937, the World Committee came to the city and were entertained to lunch at the City Chambers; at the same time, 100 overseas girls, dispersing from the International Camp at Blair Atholl, were given hospitality in Edinburgh homes before leaving for their own countries. It was a tremendous undertaking and the staff work which it involved must have been terrific—yet it was done with so little fuss that it is only the bare facts of that week which are recorded. Miss Maisie Wood had been appointed Secretary for Overseas Correspondence in 1934, the first of those who are now called Commonwealth and International Advisers, and it must have been she who was largely responsible for the success of the operation.

It is a pity that most visitors choose to come during the summer months, when Companies have closed for the holidays and many of the older girls have temporary jobs. Even in the twenties, it was a problem to find

Guides and Rangers available to help with evening entertainments or to act as escorts for sightseeing and shopping—the two most popular pastimes. If Edinburgh Guides have left a trail up the Jungfrau, Guides from abroad have left a similar mark from the Castle down the Royal Mile via the tourist shops! And if only a few of them were in good enough shape—or time—to tackle Holyrood as well, it was the flesh, rather than the spirit which failed. Indeed, the spirit has been abundant, and the determination of the units to fill every minute has been astonishing.

During a heatwave, a large party of Danish Extensions and their helpers, girls and boys together, having lunched at 33 Melville Street, departed for the Castle by wheelchair, on calipers or on foot. The citizens were visibly wilting, but the Danes maintained their objective and appeared as fresh and gay as when they first set out.

American Girl Scouts at a Ceilidh in the Guide Hall

A ceilidh has always been the other traditional way of entertaining our visitors. It has the merit of being typically Scottish and of providing an opportunity for both hostesses and guests to show off their songs and dances in an informal, cheery way. Occasionally there has been time to join them on expeditions, to foregather with Guides of other counties who see fewer visitors than we do. In 1974 one small band of Winnipeg Rangers, bearing greetings from the Mayor of Selkirk, Manitoba, to the Provost of Selkirk, Scotland, were driven down in the Guide Minibus, and after the presentation and a civic lunch, spent the afternoon up the Ettrick and

Yarrow valleys, where many of the original Manitoba settlers had their roots. It was gentle soothing country after the flat prairie lands they were used to, and they were content to sit quietly on a hilltop in the sunshine, drinking it all in. It was they, too, who, at the planning stage, had decided to hire bicycles to enable them to get about the city "quickly and easily." Their first glimpse of the hills and of the traffic made them realise how different cities could be!

Individual visitors come in all shapes and sizes and uniforms:

—the very large and cheerful leader in the U.S. camp uniform of white blouse and dark green Bermuda shorts;
—the Danes who cling lovingly to their wide-brimmed hats;
—members from the Commonwealth in Headquarters blue which takes on such a vivid tinge against a brown skin;
—the Canadians, always immaculate with their maple leaf scarves;
—the tiny Sri Lankan trainer so elegant in her pale green sari.

They come from countries where Guiding is mature and well established, or from emerging nations where training facilities are non-existent and where they are called on to do the social and educational work which, in Britain, would be considered the task of the professional experts. They come from stable countries or from others whose governments totter at the slightest puff of wind. Some, like the guests from Ethiopia and Bangladesh, have had to suffer the terrible anxiety of knowing that revolutions have broken out while they were here and that their families were in danger. It has been impossible to do more than give sympathy and kindness on these occasions, but they do bring the world and its troubles very near.

They all bring their particular characteristics with them—the French who do not plan ahead and the Americans who do; the Swedes who find it strange that Guides do not camp with the Scouts; the Ghanaians who were used to a very communal life and felt lost when they were given separate bedrooms—and again the world becomes a smaller place.

But for all the excitement of these comings and goings they each affect, at best, only a handful of Edinburgh people. The real stuff of World Guiding is what goes on, year in, year out, in the units, and the methods which are used to kindle the spark in every Guide: the badges, international gatherings, Thinking Day and all the ingenious devices for involving the children in the World Conferences.

Of the badges, the Interpreter's was one of the earliest ones and often it was a passport to unusual adventures. When the International Federation of University Women held their 1932 conference here, Rangers who held the badge were asked to act as messengers and to show delegates round the town—if possible dressed in kilts. Never before or since have Guides actually been *requested* to wear a coloured skirt!

The Friendship badges never seem to have attracted as much notice as they should have, but maybe they were too similar to Commonwealth Knowledge, which must be held by all Queen's Guides. This wide-ranging badge has always set some problems for the candidates, their leaders and their testers.

In 1965 Edinburgh held the British record for the numbers of Commonwealth Knowledge badges awarded, far in excess of even London; and in 1967, there were as many as 135 passes. 1969 again broke all records and by 1970 the testing of this badge was handed over to organisers in each Division. Six years later, at a meeting of these experts and the C.I.A.s from nearby counties, plans were made for a series of international gatherings in the Borders and Fife, where the local Badge candidates could have a chance of meeting Commonwealth citizens staying in Edinburgh, and coming from countries the Guides had chosen to study. Edinburgh Guides are lucky to have so many overseas friends and share them happily.

From the beginning, international gatherings have given Guides of all ages the chance to meet guests from overseas, both Guide and non-Guide. Commissioners and Trainers have met them at small lunch parties; young Guiders and Rangers at evening parties; Guides at rallies and Brownies at revels. Also the Trefoil Guild, helping in the Office one day, became involved with the problems of Ethiopia, when the Ethiopian National Secretary, on a World Bureau Scholarship, was conferring with Miss Turnbull. These gatherings leave a kaleidoscope of memories: the colour of the Thais' silk dresses and the Indian saris, strange music on strange instruments, curry and spices brewing in the kitchen at H.Q., Brownies teaching three gentlemen from Swaziland and Zambia to dance a Scottish reel, and the Ranger and the Indian university lecturer who each thought that the Gaelic words, printed on the table napkins, were in each other's language!

The tradition of celebrating the joint birthday of B-P and the Chief Guide as Thinking Day was not started until 1927, but there had already been a big county service in Edinburgh at St Giles on 22nd February of the previous year, and it was an indication of the way the Movement was growing in Edinburgh that each company and pack was limited to sending only two members. In 1932, a new tradition was born, of "Giving" as well as "Thinking," and every year since then Guides in Edinburgh have joined others everywhere in giving their pennies, their cents or their centimes to spur on the spread of the Movement, and to remembering their sister Guides overseas, known and unknown. Thinking Day services have usually been held in Divisions, simply because no church was large enough to accommodate all the Guides in Edinburgh; but every so often a County service has been held. At the one in 1948, a colour bearer from British Guiana carried the World Flag, and it is her great dignity as she marched slowly up the aisle at St Giles, flanked by Swedish and Scottish escorts, which is still vividly remembered.

In 1955, two units turned thought into action and sent to refugees in the Middle East bags full of tinned food, and seeds, and clothing which they had made. This was the decade in which the plight of refugees in Europe and the Middle East became desperate. Thousands had been uprooted from their homelands as a result of wars and their aftermath, and had collected in vast, inhospitable camps where they remained, forgotten and ignored for the most part, for years until in 1960—World Refugee Year—by an enormous international effort, they were settled permanently in new homes in strange lands. The Guide records of that period are full of references to the help Guides were trying to give, sometimes in small thoughtful ways, and sometimes in great, astounding gestures of generosity and goodwill.

Cards and letters were sent off to Guides in the Displaced Person Camp Companies, and specially to the Lithuanians with whom we had made a link during the international camp there in 1938; gifts were sent to Greek villages which had been ravaged by the Communist rebels; help was given at Netherurd, which was being used as a temporary hostel for Hungarians escaping after the uprising in 1956; and in 1959, as a Golden Jubilee Challenge, a fund was set up to enable 14 Guides to come from Refugee Camp Companies to the County International Camp at Blair Drummond the following year. Each of the eight Divisions undertook to raise £100. South-east and Portobello & Niddrie reached their target quickly, and by the time the fund closed, the latter had added another £400.

The refugees, Latvian, Lithuanian and Hungarian, came from camps in Germany; of necessity, they were excellent linguists, and very understandably bore the marks, both physically and mentally, of their deprivations and hopelessness. They spent a month in Scotland, in homes, after the Camp had ended, and there is a touching reference to them in the Annual Report for 1960: "They looked fitter when they left and, it is to be hoped, less bitter"; and their hostesses were thanked particularly for their infinite care and tact.

The Trefoil School for physically handicapped children has always been a hive of international Guiding. Young house-mothers and fathers, with Guide and Scout backgrounds, came from as far away as Australia, Korea and Kenya, though mostly they came from nearer European countries. In World Refugee Year the School played its part by raising £160 as their contribution and a small eight-year-old Polish child, suffering from the after-effects of polio, joined the School, helped financially by the whole County.

The School's interest in the world is of the curious variety and "Undaunted" (as their motto proclaims), the Guides set off to find out for themselves what Switzerland is all about. Twice, in fact, in 1967 and again in '69, with visits full of activity and excitement.

Other extension units, from the Blind School, have taken themselves abroad on three occasions: the St Cecilia Rangers to Our Chalet in '53, the Guides to Denmark three years later, and for the younger Guides a trip to Eire. A report of the Swiss trip appeared in *The Council Fire* describing their adventures and some of their problems. The chief of these problems seems to have occurred before their departure and was connected with signatures which were needed for passports and currency—but thumbprints were taken instead and a friendly Bank Manager did the rest. In Switzerland, on a day-expedition to Kandersteg organised by Pen of "Our Chalet," only the blind Rangers, together with the Dutch members in the party (who can hardly have been mountaineers by nature), succeeded in reaching the mountain-top; each girl was escorted up the narrow steep path by a Scout from a group which they had met on the way. Another day, on the Lower Grindlewald glacier, the Rangers crossed a narrow wooden gangway by each holding the belt of the girl in front —strange crocodile in unlikely surroundings!

When the time came for fund-raising to begin for the Guides' trip to Denmark, two of these Rangers, who by then had just started to work, arrived at Miss Darroch's door one evening and handed in the contents of their first pay-packets—"so that the Guides could enjoy themselves as much as we did."

Denmark is a country which nowadays is very enterprising in their Extension branch; so it is interesting to find among the archives a letter from the Danish International Commissioner to Miss Darroch which ends, "We were all very impressed with your girls, and I personally take back all my doubts and am very happy to do so."

The Blind School girls came home from these trips with memories of sounds and smells and the tangible qualities of whatever they had come across, things which are ignored by most of us: the intonation of French voices at the frontier, the cool air blowing off a glacier, and the taste of beer at the Tuborg brewery—although a *taste* was all they got, for the *refreshment* was lemonade!

Two World Conferences have been held in Britain, in 1950 at Oxford and in 1975 at Brighton, and both these events were so organised as to make every Guide in the country feel that she was part of them.

At the earlier one, scrolls bearing greetings to the delegates were passed from hand to hand through every county. In Edinburgh a huge number of girls became involved and the means by which the scrolls travelled were wonderful in their ingenuity.

In 1975, Edinburgh Guides were even more closely involved. Some had met Mrs Rajasuriyah, the Chairman, when she had been entertained the previous summer at a supper party; Mrs Keppie, the Treasurer of the

World Committee, was "One of Us" and knew all about counting in the currencies of ninety-three diffèrent nations of the World Association; and two young Guiders, Janet Young and Alison Middleton, worked as Aides at the Conference itself.

Afterwards, on both occasions, delegates from abroad had a chance to visit different parts of Britain and, as always, many came to Edinburgh.

All events in the Guiding World seem to have a habit of being celebrated by special camps of an international flavour, and Edinburgh has had its share. In 1957, the B-P Centenary Year, World Camps took place in four countries—the Philippines, Canada, Switzerland and at Windsor. At each of thesé we had a representative. Maureen Brown's path to the Philippines was maybe not as smooth as it might have been, but there were compensations. The Suez Crisis and the closure of the Canal sent her ship (ordinary mortals did not fly in those days) round by the Cape and added three weeks to her journey. However, she did call unexpectedly at Singapore and there, waiting for her, was her Guide pen friend. The welcome she received was tremendous and the Far Eastern equivalent of the fatted calf was prepared for her—only it wasn't calf. It was chicken, served at a very exact moment in its development, just as it is about to emerge from its shell. An honoured guest is expected to swallow the lot, but may be excused the beak if it is too sharp. . . .

International rallies have taken place twice. In 1966 at Penicuik House, the Victory Shield Competition required each participating company to portray a country which had been allotted to it six months earlier. Although the 41st Company—"Sweden"—won the Shield, "The Ivory Coast" could well have carried off a prize, had there been one, for originality when they proceeded to sacrifice the chicken they were about to cook, with appropriate dance and incantation, before it went into the pot. And what did mother say when the Guide returned home that night whose hair had been set with mud??

The Commonwealth Day Challenge at Dreghorn was another Shield occasion, with 30 companies representing 14 countries. The judges were people who came from these countries, so the standards were expected to be high. "Jamaica" was the winner that year, portrayed by the 173rd Company dressed in the most colourful clothes.

And Brownies, not to be left out, have had their Revels, and revel they did! Very internationally in Ugandan dance, Caribbean song and that old Danish favourite which turned out to be *our* old favourite, "Incy Wincy Spider."

Within the community from the first, Guides have made an effort to do what they could to give help to those other organisations who are working towards good international relations and racial tolerance. Some units befriended young "au pairs" and nurses working here, far from their homes, and often very lonely; Local Associations offered a reliable baby-sitting service to the families of overseas students; Divisions welcomed all Ugandan Asians who settled here, particularly in the Wester Hailes area, after their expulsion from their homeland in 1972, and it was disappointing that for various reasons (our lack of leaders and their very natural suspicion of our way of life were two of them) the children could not be drawn into the local units—though one or two who already were Brownies were soon transferred to Edinburgh Packs.

Several Guides who began their careers in units here have moved into the wider world of the Movement and their names have become well-known in many countries beyond our own. Jean Keppie, of course, on the World Committee; Sheila Thomson, who became a C.H.Q. Trainer and, more recently, was co-ordinator for the 22nd World Conference Hostess Country's Planning Committee; Greta Collyns, Chris Lumsden and Andrina Wilson, three more of the senior Trainers who passed on their experience to overseas Guiders; Margaret Harvey, the present Guider-in-charge at the New Zealand Training Centre; and Irene Thomson, who over the years has made her second home at the Chalet—to sing, or to ski, or just to be there—and now must have friends in every country which has sent Guides or Scouts to Adelboden! They are all Edinburgh Guides interpreting Guide friendship in a truly International spirit.

17

Funds and Finance

THE GENEROSITY OF THE first Committee, who paid for every Proficiency badge gained by Guides and Brownies for years, has been matched by everybody connected with the Girl Guide Movement from the new recruits to the Trefoil Guilds, from tradesmen to tycoons!

Money has inevitably played an important part in the story of Edinburgh Guides because it costs a great deal to keep so large an organisation running smoothly. Therefore, funds and finance are the subjects of this chapter—boring? No, not at all!

The first record of "finance" was when the Committee was formed in June 1909 and each member agreed to pay 1/- subscription for current expenses. By 1st October that year, Guiding was in business with a balance of 2/4d. By July 1910 things were really moving when £9 was raised at a demonstration in Bruntsfield School. Out of this sum £1 was paid to Scottish Headquarters and £1 to the Local Committee. By the middle of 1912 it was back to square one with "no funds," so the ladies of the Committee agreed to raise their subscription to 2s/6d; this brought in a total of £1 12s 6d. Even in those days there were problems regarding the Guides' contributions to Headquarters' funds, but a minimum subscription of 3d was agreed in that year. There is a record of a capitation fee being paid to Headquarters from ten Companies—total £2 10s on the 6th May 1915.

At the County Commissioners' Conference in Perth in November 1918 it was decided that Counties should give £5 per annum to Scottish Head-quarters for central expenses. Later, Miss Dalmahoy suggested that a fund be set up for an Edinburgh Headquarters building. As County Commissioner, Miss Dalmahoy realised that with the rapid growth of Guiding after the war a permanent Headquarters was required for the Movement in Edinburgh. Bazaars and exhibitions were the accepted ways of raising money at that time. So an especially big money-making effort for the building was made at the Handcraft Exhibition in 1928, held for two days in the Music Hall. For nearly two years Guiders, Rangers, Guides and Brownies worked towards this by first of all attending classes in such crafts as embroidery, leather work, raffia work and toy-making, and then using the skills acquired in making articles to sell. The work had to be of a very high standard and the Commissioners went round units examining it; if it was poor it was brought to Headquarters for the County Commissioner's inspection! The Council ran a provision and household stall

152

and the parents also rallied round and donated gifts and produce. Miss Anna Buchan, Lord Tweedsmuir's sister, was asked to open this Exhibition and for the first time a Brownie, Helen Harvey of the 170th Pack, was chosen to introduce her. When the great day came, Lord Tweedsmuir unexpectedly arrived too but the small Brownie was undaunted and introduced him as well! The Brownies were well to the fore—each division had a toadstool with a Brownie hiding underneath and as soon as the exhibition was open, at a signal out they all came. Over £2700 was raised which in those days was a tremendous amount, and this money was used the following year for the purchase of 33 Melville Street as a new county headquarters. After this really splendid effort, Miss Dalmahoy visited each unit to thank them for all their hard work.

It should be mentioned that in this year all members of the Movement in the Empire were asked to raise money to build Imperial Headquarters in London and despite their own commitment to the Handcraft Exhibition, Edinburgh Guides and Brownies saved their pennies and subscribed £666 5s 3d towards the "Equipment Room," which was their responsibility.

As has been pointed out, there have always been problems over the financing of day-to-day expenses of the County, 2/4d did not go far in 1909 and considerably more was needed to maintain a building and administer a growing organisation. No wages or salaries were paid to anyone (not even to the caretaker of No. 33) for years to come, but there were office accounts for the telephones, postage, paper and equipment; house bills for rates, heating and lighting, cleaning, repairs and insurance. In 1926 it had been suggested that units should give one week's subscription per annum towards Headquarters expenses and Leith units, who supported their own small Headquarters, gave half their subscriptions. (At this time the "Juvenile Organisations Committee" were appealing for other Youth Club Leaders—paid at 7/6d per night!) To encourage units to send in their subscriptions—Guider 6d, Rangers 3d, Guides 2d, Brownies 1d—the new Headquarters was open every evening one week in November 1929 when Patrol Leaders were asked to bring the company contribution. £60 9s 9d was raised—not nearly sufficient to cover the expenses. By 1936 the contributions rose to £102 9s. Fortunately good friends helped, the Council raised money in various ways and legacies were used for the most pressing needs in the building.

Eventually the principle that all members of the Movement would pay the same annual subscription was accepted, and by 1976 it was 75p. Surely that must be the smallest contribution to belong to the largest "club" in the world giving the best value; or, with apologies to Winston Churchill yet again, "Never has so much been done by so many for so small a sum."

The subscriptions received in March each year are usually divided equally between Edinburgh, Scottish and Commonwealth Headquarters and used extensively on behalf of the girls. For instance, in London, an extremely comprehensive insurance policy is renewed annually covering every member (which may interest parents), when involved in a Guiding activity, provided that the conditions laid down in "Policy, Organisation and Rules" have been observed. The regular income from subscriptions has been augmented through the years by grants from numerous Trust funds catering for different activities. Local Authority grants were first applied for and granted in the 1950s—particularly for trainings; an administrative grant in 1970 allowed Edinburgh County to employ the first full-time paid Secretary. Apart from a part-time secretary, no other adult is paid.

All property owners have faced the problem of insurance and this item has figured largely in the County budget, the cover for No. 33 having increased ten-fold in the ten years up to 1976.

So much for finance. Fund-raising has always been greatly enjoyed by Guides and Brownies; given a good cause, they have turned to with a will. During the Second World War, Edinburgh Guides as part of their war work raised large sums of money which bought a mobile canteen for the Church of Scotland, and helped to buy two air ambulances and a lifeboat. They also helped the Baden-Powell Memorial Fund and assisted the G.I.S. Fund for the rehabilitation of refugees in the Displaced Persons' Camps. In all, over £3700 was raised for other people between 1939-45. After the war the County's own financial needs were pressing and all members undertook a big money-making effort. This was the Christmas Sale held in 1947 in the Music Hall opened by the Scottish Chief Commissioner, when over £1500 was raised.

1957—the Centenary Year of Lord Baden-Powell—was obviously going to be an expensive one with local celebrations and many foreign visitors to entertain. Therefore, in 1956, a special Centenary Fund was begun for this purpose. When the year was over enough money was left to buy a projector and screen, an electric clock and a large coloured picture of the Founder for Edinburgh Headquarters.

Three years later it was World Refugee Year and each division was asked to raise £100 to help with the expense of bringing fourteen Guides from companies in refugee camps as guests to the International Camp at Blair Drummond to be held in 1960. Jumble Sales and fashion shows helped to bring in more than £1000 and some of the money that was left was used to help with other refugee projects and the Thinking Day Fund.

By the 1960s it was becoming obvious that more space was needed in Melville Street for the many activities which went on nearly every day and so plans were made to build a new hall at the back. For this purpose, a Christmas Market was held in 1961, again in the Music Hall, when there were stalls such as the Brownies' Sunshine Stall, the pet stall, a Fun

Fair and a Lucky Dip; there were Brownie singing games, a Guide Camp-fire and turkey lunches served by the Local Associations. The result was a magnificent £2926 towards the new hall. Over and above this, each division was required to raise a quota of money in proportion to its number of members; the varied and ingenious methods of reaching their targets showed that Guiders and girls were not at a loss for ideas! Generous grants from the Scottish Education Department and the Edinburgh Education Authority were received and the fine new Hall was ready for use in September 1964. Another £1000 was well spent in 1972 when a kitchen was made from one of the cloakrooms and the Trefoil Guilds equipped it with all the right things. When the Guilds provide anything for the County, infinite trouble is taken to find exactly what is needed, of good design, well finished and up to date.

The next project was the building of the Adventure Centre at Stane-muir, a purpose-built house equipped for anything from Pack Holidays to Guiders' trainings, and including facilities for handicapped girls. Fund-raising followed the same pattern and another dream materialised in June 1971. Edinburgh Guides are unusually fortunate to have the use of these excellent buildings and, judging by the numbers constantly coming and going, they appreciate them.

Fund raising for others. Toffee apples for sale in aid of the Scottish War Blinded.

The spirit of helping others is never absent from the Guide story and, although it would be impossible to include the hundreds of events by which money is raised for other people, there is one fund-raising project shared by all branches of the Movement in Edinburgh. The idea of collecting

silver paper, milk bottle tops and foil and selling it in aid of a Guide
Dog for the Blind was started in West Division in 1958. However,
progress towards the £250 total was rather slow, so in 1961 the whole
County was invited to join in and the collection centre moved to 33
Melville Street. The first dog was achieved in 1964 and named Rory, the
second in 1970 was Randy, and their photographs can be seen at Headquarters. The third £250 was raised by 1974, but by that time the total
required was £500, and by March 1976 nearly £400 has been reached
towards this. The tin foil is packed into sacks by Guides working for their
Service Flash and bought by various scrap-metal merchants (even one
in Wales who paid the transport and 42/- per cwt!). The present rate is
£1.25 per cwt. Many non-Guide people bring in silver paper or ask
for it to be collected, and yet there are still many Guides who do not
know that silver paper is collected at Edinburgh Headquarters!!

Raising money for unit funds or camp expenses has always been part of
the Company or Pack activities at some time or another. Jumble sales
provided and indeed, still do, the most lucrative means of doing this.
In the 1920s preparing for a jumble sale was like preparing for a battle!
First of all the notices had to be delivered about the dates and times of
collections, then on the night before and the morning of the sale, helpers,
Guiders, Rangers and Guides set up the stalls. Next, barricades in front of
the stall were made of benches joined together. Two men manned the
doors, one or two intrepid ladies with sticks took up positions in front of
the stalls and the mob was allowed in—some to buy the best early, others
to beat down prices, and those who stayed to the bitter end in the
hope of getting something for nothing before the junk man came to remove
the apparently unsellable hard goods. A few Guiders and Rangers survived
to clear up the mess!

Concerts were another popular means of making money. These were
time-consuming affairs with rehearsals and costume-making, but on the
whole great performances and good advertisement. Less elaborate money-
raising efforts were sweet-making, small sales of work, doing odd jobs
and so on. One Ranger Company made marionettes and a little theatre
and wrote their own plays for it. Coffee evenings, Bring-and-Buy stalls
all helped to fill the coffers that were never full enough for the things that
Brownies, Guides and Rangers wanted to do. But having to work so
hard made the final outcome much more worthwhile.

Expenses for individuals working with Guides have been kept to a
minimum and it has always been the policy that a Guider may take postal
and telephone charges out of unit funds. In 1965 a small allowance
towards similar expenses was brought in for Commissioners to help to lift
the burden on the housekeeping purse.

It must be obvious, with this emphasis on money, that good housekeeping has been, and is, essential. Ideally, unit accounts have been

kept and audited, Guiders have attended trainings in simple accounting and this knowledge has been passed on to Patrol Leaders. The girls perhaps have learnt the value of saving, and thrift may become a fashionable word again when the "throw away-blow away" phase of the Seventies passes.

The County funds have been looked after by a Treasurer and Finance Committee since 1938, the latter, with professional advisers as members, has met at least twice a year. The former has maintained a constant vigil to ensure that Edinburgh Girl Guides' finances have remained sound and secure.

18

More Organisation!

IT COMES AS A SHOCK sometimes when the census forms come into the Guide Office each March to read the actual numbers of girls in the different branches of Edinburgh Guiding.

It is much more of a shock to move out of the comparative peace of 33 Melville Street and see those figures take physical shape!

PICTURE those dull census figures as 2000 small Brownies, with bright faces, at their Jubilee Service and planting heathers in Princes Street Gardens afterwards.

IMAGINE the 1000+ figures in running kit at Meadowbank.

CONVERT the rows of numbers into swim-suited figures in the lanes of the Commonwealth Pool, with families and friends in every single seat.

COUNT the 30 or more Queen's Guides every term receiving their Certificates, watched by proud parents and Guiders.

GUESS at the number of unknown Good Turns and all the community service they have done.

RECALL how in the War, a Patrol of Guides met the Mobile Canteens every night through every week for over six years to wash up and clean up—the co-operation in districts and units must have been excellent.

VISUALISE those colourful census forms as canvas tents with figures of sleeping (?) campers underneath.

REMEMBER that Companies and Packs are small—much organisation is needed to bring even 100 children together.

THINK of all that has been written in previous chapters and then WONDER at the title of this one!

The wonderful example of good Guiding through the early years has been followed in Edinburgh by thousands of women with every imaginable kind of talent. Those few whose names are given in this book would be the first to acknowledge that the ideas, support and good humour of others have added to the satisfaction they derived from their own appointments. It is sad that many more people cannot be mentioned but it speaks volumes for the Guide Movement that if every adult was named, this book would need to be the size of the Edinburgh telephone directories which have listed so many well-known and well-loved Guiding names.

The War years of '39 to '45 saw many women on active service but not only those who were in the Forces. There was nothing INactive about bringing up a family without the father at home, or taking a man's position at work in order to release him to the Services, or doing one's own job (often a reserved occupation) and caring for elderly parents at home AND THEN running a Unit, District or Division for Girl Guides. How *did* they do it all?

As in the past the example was set by the County Commissioner, Miss Verona Wallace Williamson, who also served on the Imperial Executive Committee, helped to found the Trefoil School and was Advisory Officer with G.I.S.

Because Guiders were becoming so scarce Greta Collyns wrote and distributed her now famous "Lone Wolf letters" to Patrol Leaders in the city to encourage them to stand on their own feet and carry on. The first went out in October 1939 and later were distributed throughout Scotland, being published in book form after the War.

In spite of heavy commitments, Edinburgh Commissioners served further afield: Verona Wallace Williamson and Doris Morison Inches served on the Imperial and Scottish Executive Committees respectively and so many others wore two or three "hats"—a tradition which still continues!

With peace in Europe on the horizon in May 1945, all members were asked to attend Thanksgiving Services and when the "Cease Fire" sounded in the Far East "Thanks be to God" echoed from many more hearts. The County team came together again, re-established the committees, modernised the indexing of Companies and Packs, renewed the annual competitions for the Shields and held the Annual Meeting of Guiders, showing them a parade of the suggested new uniforms. Guiding was really back in business with girls coming forward all the time. Adults, however, were reluctant! Many had been in uniform for six years and not even the new designs tempted them back to Guides!

Not surprisingly, Edinburgh County was having financial problems. To gain public support it was decided that an Annual Report should be compiled incorporating the Work of Guides in Wartime. Three thousand copies were printed and distribution began at an Annual General Meeting in the Music Hall in 1948. An A.G.M. has been held and a Report printed ever since. After 13 years, Lady Constance Blackburn retired as County President and the Duchess of Hamilton and Brandon was warmly welcomed in her place.

Another change came in September that year with the first paid part-time Secretary working in E.H.Q. Having agreed in 1941 that uniformed youth organisations should take advantage of Government grants, Edinburgh Girl Guides accepted this help gratefully.

In 1950, at the end of her very busy term of office as County Commissioner, Miss Verona Wallace Williamson became Chairman of the

Scottish Executive Committee for the ten years that Lady Colville was Scottish Chief Commissioner.

She recalls:

"Looking back on the last ten years I realise what a wonderful job Guiders did ensuring that girls could still enjoy the fun of Guiding and share in any war work suitable for their age. This was particularly noticeable in the eagerness they showed in restarting camping, first in day camps and later in weekend camps on small sites with camouflaged tents and solid shelter nearby. It is amazing to think that in 1942, 991 Guides and Rangers camped and that by 1945 the number had risen to 1778.

"It seemed that during this period everyone got to know each other better, not through the usual unit meetings, but because they were Guides meeting each other through the different forms of service they were giving. This spirit of friendship was shared with others as the Guides moved in the community around them.

"At a time when, as a County, they were raising large sums of money for the various national Guide appeals, individual Packs and Companies took it for granted that they should continue to be self-supporting. Grants were available only for special items and at County H.Q. there were anxious discussions before anything was bought or repairs undertaken. It was a great help when the Church of Scotland Huts Committee mended the kitchen floor where much urn-boiling and other work had taken place! The Government offered grants to organisations who would be willing to cater for unattached young people who were causing anxiety. After careful thought, Edinburgh Guides accepted a grant which was used to launch the 'Square Centre' at Granton.

"This period seemed to develop a maturity in members of the Movement in Edinburgh which showed, first in the happy resumption of friendship with Guides in other countries through giving hospitality, and later in exchange visits and international camps. This led to units wanting to go abroad and to a general interest in travel. At home there were more opportunities to go to national conferences and trainings where young Guiders were particularly welcomed. For many, their horizons had been widened by war experiences and they brought enthusiasm and new ideas back to Guiding in the City."

Although years later it was suggested that a County Commissioner's Cockade was in every Brownie's pocket, Miss Doris Morison Inches had never been a Brownie when she succeeded as County Commissioner in 1950. This surely was the only branch she had not personally known as she brought a wealth of experience, as Captain of St Giles Guides and Rangers, Division Commissioner and Scottish Ranger Commissioner, to her new post, along with her many other interests and delightful sense of humour.

The Conference of the World Association of Girl Guides and Girl

A beautiful album consisting of an illustrated page from every unit in Edinburgh was given to Miss Wallace Williamson on her retirement. This was the frontispiece of the album.

Scouts was held in Oxford in 1950 and many activities concerning it involved organisation in Edinburgh. Two Scrolls of Friendship passed through the city, Aides to assist the delegates went down to the Conference —equipped with bicycles—and after it many overseas guests were welcomed and given true Scottish hospitality. An International Adviser was first appointed in 1945 so Edinburgh was prepared for visitors who arrived in the upsurge of travel once wartime restrictions were lifted.

Edinburgh Trainers, Guiders and girls were indeed lucky when Major Thomson presented Netherurd House, near West Linton, to Scottish Guides for a Training Centre with two camp sites in the grounds. To have all these facilities so near has been much appreciated by many, and happy camps and excellent training weekends have been arranged and remembered through the years. Guiders even join visiting units for an evening when friends from afar are camping there, and the Kingdom is often United round the Campfires at Netherurd.

With training in mind, a library was started in No. 33 for the use of Guides and Guiders, and another great asset was the "Acting Chest" full of exciting costumes and props for the use of units putting on plays. The 1st Class Club and the Melville Club were both flourishing during these years.

1953 was a busy year not only for Coronation celebrations but for the Trainers' Conference held then! The girls were all involved in Coronation Camps and other festivities, and "Extensions" were at all the celebrations including the planting of an avenue of trees in the Meadows. Following on from her great interest in the Trefoil School, Doris Inches encouraged Extension Guiding in all branches. Guides were asked to steward at a Conference on Home Economics and also, during United Nations Week, at a meeting in the Usher Hall.

"Imperial" became "Commonwealth" Headquarters in 1955 and that was the year when the "Birthrate Bulge" after the War hit the Brownie age group—Oh to have enough Guiders, just for once! The County Commissioner stressed in her annual reports the importance of finding more Guiders to lead the increasing number of girls wanting to join "Guides." She realised that to the Brownie Guiders who had to say "No room for you yet" to the eager little girls at the hall door on meeting night, each number on the waiting list represented a sad little face.

One of the originals in the County team, Miss E. Tod, handed over one of her "Hats"—Finance Secretary—to Miss Doris Vickary, and two years later she passed "Badges" to Miss Kitty Watson who, in 1976 has just completed the same length of service as Miss Tod—20 years.

The City of Edinburgh recognised the Golden Jubilee of the Girl Guides' Association by inviting 1000 representatives from Edinburgh and Midlothian Counties to a Garden Party at Lauriston Castle on 17th June 1960—a perfect summer day.

The Duchess of Hamilton and Brandon, County President, Miss Hamilton Bruce and
Miss Inches, County Commissioner, at the Garden Party.

Planning had started early for this anniversary as a Birthday present was to be given—not received. It coincided with World Refugee Year in 1960 and all Divisions were asked to raise over £100 each to bring 14 refugee Guides from Europe for a month. Much organisation was happily undertaken and Doris Inches agreed to remain until July when most of the festivities would be over. Staying at the camp at Blair Drummond was her swansong (appropriate phrase as it was so wet, and an appropriate place as she was always a keen camper). She "never forgot nor allowed other people to forget that . . . Guiding is first and foremost an outdoor game for girls." Later in the year Guiders and Rangers gathered in Moray House for a party and gave their present to her. Two albums—each illustrated page contributed by a Pack or Company—made a particularly appropriate present for Doris Inches because she took a deep interest in all the girls, visiting as many units as possible, and these pages gave her much pleasure.

She says of her years as County Commissioner:

"This decade saw the biggest growth in the Guide Movement everywhere and as the numbers grew in Edinburgh (to over 11,000 in 1956) the emphasis was on giving the divisions more scope and responsibility and stressing the importance of the Pack, Company and individual child, encouraging all to grow to their full potential. There were many County Competitions—Athletic, Signalling, Swimming, Embroidery and Victory Shield—but also many 'local' division affairs and events which needed much work in organisation but were more personal and involved more children in their own setting.

"The Queen's Guide Award was quite something! Having been introduced in 1946, we had two in 1949, increasing to 38 in 1958. This badge made great demands on girls, Guiders and testers. I made a point of presenting these when asked, as the companies considered a County Commissioner's visit was merited and it gave me the chance to visit different companies.

"Camping was very popular with Patrol Permits, 'Light Weight' and Ranger Permits in fashion. Trefoil Guilds and Local Associations were strong all over the city and backed up the divisions well. There was a continual struggle to recruit Commissioners and Guiders, and the latter were urged to attend trainings—which brings me back to the importance of the girls, their units and their leaders."

The new County Commissioner in 1960 was Mrs Jean Keppie, already well known in Edinburgh Guiding as Captain of the Colinton Company and County Secretary until 1954 when Mrs Miller took over from her, followed by Mrs Rose Russell Logan who coped most ably with the extra activities of Jubilee Year. Mrs Keppie asked Miss Verna Ellingsen to be County Secretary; both had great experience, especially in camping and training, and both continued with their Guide Companies.

There are no new problems; just variations of old ones, and the Executive Committee decided that old, well-tried solutions were often the answer—so they planned a "Christmas Market" to solve the financial problem, which it did, to the tune of nearly £3000. The unvarying problem, which began in 1909 of finding more leaders, hasn't been solved in 1977!!

In 1964 the whole country put the "Spotlight on Guiding" and in Scotland's capital city Edinburgh Guides showed what they could do for a whole week. Lady Primrose had just become the new County President and she and Lord Primrose became very involved in this big enterprise. Many readers must remember that week; how many came back to start new Packs and Companies?

With an increasing workload, Jean Keppie appointed the first Assistant County Commissioner, Mrs Persis Aglen, whose experience covered Guiding in the Sudan. "Notes for Commissioners," to help newcomers, were compiled and have proved most useful. Organising the Johnstounburn Adventure Centre and buying a minibus were the Committee's extra ploys in 1965 and the following year the girls joined the Scout "Gang Show" for the first time; more organisation but a different challenge for all.

During these years plans were being made at Commonwealth Headquarters to revise the whole programme and to produce new Handbooks for all the Branches. Advice was sought from all the Counties and many consultations were held. Some approved the new ideas, some did not and resigned, but the Working Party pondered for two years, produced a report in 1966 and the New Programme was launched in March 1968. This was a great day for the Movement; an interdenominational Service was held in the Usher Hall, and nearly 3000 braved a snowstorm to be there. Divisions and Districts held imaginative and exciting functions for distributing the long-awaited Handbooks and the Annual General Meeting was attended by the Lord and Lady Provost, showing that the strong link with the City was maintained.

That summer all the Guides and Brownies experimented with the New Programme featuring the Eight Points stressed by the Founder. The Athletic Shield was competed for and with two years' preparation behind them the Camp Committee held a very successful International Camp at Blair Atholl, near Pitlochry.

All this activity made it a very busy first year for the new Treasurer, Mrs Agnes Keymer, who coped so ably with the financial side of distributing 8000 Handbooks. Planning a custom-built Brownie House began now and this became a reality in 1971 as Stanemuir Adventure Centre.

With the Diamond Jubilee only two years away, the "Three Cheers Challenge to give a cheer to a person, a place and yourself" was taken up by everyone, which ensured a successful year. Another memorable Service in the Usher Hall, a Folk Fest there too—all Edinburgh performers, and the "wheelchair dancing" by the Trefoil School Scouts and Guides under Miss Varcoe's direction was a star turn. Headquarters was "open" for a week, seats presented, trees planted and a Commonwealth Challenge Day camp held at Dreghorn for the Victory Shield.

What a year for Jean Keppie to end her term of office! Amidst all the hard work, her joy in the out of doors and the fun she saw as an essential part of Guiding have been passed on to all who worked with her. At the Jubilee Dinner Dance in October the County said "Thank you" by giving her a new screen on which to show her many slides of happy Guiding days. Jean Keppie says:

"What are my impressions of my ten years as County commissioner?

"The first is of being stimulated—stretched— active—alive—and enjoying every minute.

"The next—you can't escape it in this Movement!—is of teamwork, fun and friendship, in the County and indeed throughout Scotland, because the County Commissioners of Edinburgh and Glasgow have the privilege of being members of the Scottish Executive Committee.

"And then the memories come flooding in—happy, nostalgic, amusing, even a few sad ones.

"The Christmas Market in 1961, especially the Brownies' Sunshine Stall; the candles and the lovely singing at the Campfire; the Fashion Show with its Brownie Chairman; and the wonderful sight of the Assembly Rooms and Music Hall full of Country Dancers on the last night.

"Spotlight! So many memories, such vivid impressions!

"The First Class Club Good Turn camps.

"The 'Bally Flash' presented at the Scottish Commissioners' Conference in the Pitlochry Theatre with Andrina Wilson as the Ballerina, supported by four Edinburgh Commissioners/Trainers as the Corps de Ballet.

"The Rover/Ranger Burns' Suppers; Mary Nixon addressing the Haggis.

"Extension Thinking Day Parties, and the Dinner Party in 1970.

"Enrolling 15 African Nuns at Craiglockhart College of Education.

"Handbooks!! (March 1968). The Hall completely full of the new Handbooks, and the monumental task of distributing them in two days.

"The International Camp at Blair Atholl—the staff trying out the trampoline—after dark!

"The Brownie Matinée—and the wonderful sight of our indefatigable County Arts Adviser leading a vast number of Brownies round the hall, all miming one enormous DRAGON.

"The Diamond Jubilee celebrations in 1970; the County Service in May, and Dr Selby Wright's inspiring address; the equally memorable Scottish H.Q. Service in July, and the vast undertaking of providing hospitality for hundreds of Guides from all over Scotland; and the privilege of representing the County at the National Service in Westminster Abbey.

"Finally, a memory which will remain with me all my life—the evening in November 1965 when the Scottish Chief Commissioner presented me with the Silver Fish. It was a total surprise, such a tremendous honour and such warmth in the happiness of all those who were there to share this great experience with me."

The new session began with the news that Jean Keppie had been appointed Treasurer of the World Association—a great honour for this Edinburgh Guide and a wise appointment. There was also a new Division, the tenth; Wester Hailes was formed from the new development there plus parts of West Division. And the new Commissioner to look after this expanding County was Mrs Kath Wilkie, who had been a Guide in Peeblesshire and latterly the Assistant County Commissioner with special interest in Ranger affairs, and also Press and Public Relations Adviser; thus her warmth, vitality and enthusiasm were already well known within and outwith the Movement. She appointed Miss Mararet Turnbull as County Secretary, who had been District Commissioner and Camp Adviser, and was an experienced Secretary, so the Office was in good hands. For the first time this became a full-time salaried appointment, thanks to the increased grant for administration from Edinburgh Corporation.

Kath Wilkie invited the Division Commissioners to meet her for a Working Lunch twice a term. These have been most useful meetings for sharing advice and views on current problems. She also meets each Division Commissioner in June to discuss their Division activities and future plans.

The County settled down to its main purpose—taking Guiding to the girls—something which is never forgotten, and meetings, badge tests, camps and all the other activities continued as usual. Just as usual the Executive Committee was looking ahead—when should the Shield Competitions be held and how often? 1972 was the year everybody swam in spite of the "fuel crisis," everybody sang too for the B.B.C. Guide Song Contest, and already preparations were going ahead for the Athletic Shield Competition to be held in 1973—at Meadowbank, no less!—a brave venture crowned with success.

Commonwealth Headquarters were already informing the Counties of plans for the World Conference to be held in Sussex in 1975 and asked for gifts which could be given to delegates. All the Brownies, Guides, Rangers—everyone—turned to handcrafts and the Victory Shield was awarded in 1974 for the Gift Competition.

All these varied events required much organisation especially for Guiders and the girls who participated. Although paper work was kept to a minimum (and the Guide network has always been an excellent "Post Office") there was much to be done in the Office. The welcome gifts of a photo-copier, two electric typewriters and the purchase of an electric Roneo machine brought the equipment up to date.

Local Authority Regionalisation in Scotland posed a problem for the Girl Guides as the "Counties" were to disappear and become "Districts," whereas England has kept "Counties." It was considered wiser for Scottish Commissioners to retain their customary titles, thus simplifying communications throughout the United Kingdom.

Throughout the year before 15th May 1974 the County Commissioners, Assistants and Treasurers of Edinburgh, East, Mid and West Lothians met regularly to discuss the boundary changes, any problems of the units concerned, and the method of applying for grants which varied greatly from County to County. All the Guiders were told of the changes by their Commissioners.

For Edinburgh it was quite an upheaval; although all the new units were to the west of the city, central Divisions had to be altered to maintain a balance in size between the 12 Divisions being planned. As the points of the compass names were in disarray through previous boundary changes these were dropped and all Divisions chose a new local name. From these, the reader should be able to place the Divisions in their correct parts of the city: Blackford Hill, Braid, Dunedin, Forth, Harlaw, Inveralmond, Leith, Pentland, Portobello & Niddrie, Raeburn, Turnhouse and Wester Hailes.

The Edinburgh Guide Council members most kindly gave a welcoming party in May 1975 for all Commissioners and Guiders of the areas which were coming into Edinburgh District—Currie, Balerno, Ratho, Newbridge, Kirkliston, South Queensferry and Dalmeny. They all came to meet the Council, the Executive Committee and Commissioners of Guide districts adjoining theirs—country and city spent a happy evening getting to know each other.

Like her predecessors, Kath Wilkie has set the example—Girl Guides in Edinburgh give a warm welcome to newcomers and to all visitors from near or far. Delegates to the World Conference and Guides passing through to the camps were welcome visitors that year.

After a whole year of working together, becoming involved together in running a Young Leaders' Camp at Balerno, and the Swimming Gala in the Commonwealth Pool when every seat was filled, it would seem that the larger County has shaken down well.

More organisation—yes! Plans are being made to give Edinburgh folk a chance to meet the Girl Guides again at "Focus on Guiding" in April 1977 in the Assembly Rooms—a familiar venue in this story! And Edinburgh Guides will meet the World at an International Camp in July when visitors from overseas come to "Dalmeny 77."

Through Pow Wows and Councils, each Brownie, Guide and Ranger becomes involved in these plans which result in fun for themselves along with the work which gives joy to others.

Looking forward to these events and on to the future, Kath Wilkie writes:

"The six years I have completed as County Comissioner have flown past and how I have enjoyed all the fun, friendship and challenge of this appointment. I have got to know so many Guiders from students to busy mums and how I do enjoy meeting them all. It is wonderful to have so many more married Guiders in the Movement now.

"There have been some exciting moments for me—my first Annual General Meeting—the opening of our Adventure Centre at Stanemuir—our first Athletic Shield Competition at Meadowbank when a Guide exclaimed, 'Fancy me running on the tartan track!'—all those Brownies at St Cuthbert's Church followed by the planting of heaths in Princes Street Gardens—the privilege of having delegates to the 22nd World Conference as our guests here afterwards and the fascinating reports brought back by our Aides.

"I enjoyed working with our neighbouring County Commissioners before regionalisation; the happy relationships built up then have been continued and we still meet each term to discuss common issues. It is good to see many from Edinburgh's new units joining in County events, and it was a special thrill to fill every seat at the Commonwealth Pool for our Swimming Shield Competition.

"Following Edinburgh Guides' tradition of always looking outwards, I have become involved with other youth organisations within the Region. On regionalisation in May 1975 a Deputy Community Education Officer was appointed to liaise with all the youth organisations and we turned the tables by inviting the first occupant of this post to become a member of the Edinburgh Guide Executive Committee to help with any problems, as had the Principal Youth and Community Education Officer for Edinburgh during the previous year. This liaison has been most useful, as is that between Division Commissioners and their local Community Education Officers.

"Edinburgh Girl Guides are represented on many local committees from the Council of Social Service to U.N.I.C.E.F., the Netherurd House Committee to the Board for Information on Youth and Community Service—Public Relations. The list in the Annual Report lengthens yearly.

"Only good can emerge from all this co-operation, both within and outwith the Movement. The airing and sharing of ideas and the working together towards the same goal will surely benefit all the young people in our care."

19

Exploring the Arts

"Come, come light up the fire,
Come, come join in the ring
Here find dreams to inspire, stories to tell,
music to sing."

THIS INVITATION TO SING has appealed to Brownies, Guides and Rangers over the years, either in small groups round a campfire or at larger organised events. In June 1921 a choir was formed from members of various youth organisations to sing at a large gathering, and afterwards the Guide members formed their own choir led by Mrs Maitland of Heriot Row, who at that time was very well known in amateur musical circles. She was the first conductor of the choir and the weekly practices were held either in her house or in St John's Church Hall. Such was the girls' enthusiasm that in June 1924 the choir had 84 members. Each year they gave concerts at the Music Hall with guest celebrities, and even broadcast in March 1928. By the early 1930s enthusiasm began to wane and soon it was so small that they could not afford the services of a paid conductor any longer. Despite efforts by interested volunteers to revive the choir, by 1937 it had ceased to exist.

It was not until the late 1950s that the choir was restarted, and perhaps the fact that it soon became a combined Guide/Scout choir was an added incentive! The choir gave several successful concerts culminating in a performance of *The Mikado* in April 1961. After this the boys seemed to have lost interest, the choir became "Guides only" and sadly in 1963 when the conductor left Edinburgh it disbanded altogether.

The Guide choir may have come and gone but Guides and Brownies in their units never stopped singing, sometimes for themselves, sometimes to entertain parents and friends; and over the years Brownies, Guides and Rangers have taken part, singing, playing instruments or dancing, in the annual Edinburgh Musical Festival, either as individuals or in groups.

Despite various attempts to form a Guide Orchestra in the 1930s, it was not until 1974 that one was formed under the leadership of Yla Stephen, an Edinburgh Guider, and this played at one or two County events after having had a "Making Music" Weekend at Stanemuir. However, in 1968, a Portobello Guide did win the Chief Guide's Violin, "Sybil" for two years—a coveted honour. Long before this, Edinburgh had its own piper, Bessie Watson—a Guide who had played the bagpipes since the age of seven.

"Stories to tell" conjures up a variety of pictures in the mind! As far as Edinburgh Guiding was concerned, the stories were told in pageants, concerts, displays and folk festivals. One of the most spectacular occasions

Making music.

was when 650 Guides joined 650 schoolgirls to dance and to form part of the crowd at the Craigmillar Historical Pageant organised by Edinburgh Corporation in 1927. Transporting over a thousand girls from all over the city by train to Duddingston was a formidable task; then the girls had to walk uphill to Craigmillar Castle. The return journey was hectic, making sure that every one of them got to Duddingston in time to catch the train. On the final evening they missed it, and buses and private cars had to be stopped to take the girls back to town. The girls worked really hard, particularly on the last day, Saturday, when there were two performances. The final tableau nearly resulted in tragedy on the Saturday afternoon when the Prince of Wales was on the platform. The Fisherwomen's Choir was behind the children and they suddenly dashed forward to get near the Prince and dancers were jostled in all directions.

The Guides presented another pageant called *A Pageant of Scottish Women* especially written by Miss Mary Crawford for the visit of the Chief Guide in October 1948 for the Conference of Local Associations in Edinburgh. Four years later, when the Chief Guide again visited the city, she saw a Pageant of Scottish History enacted by Guides from all over Scotland, in which Edinburgh Guides played a large part. The recently-appointed Drama Adviser, Mrs Halliday Croom, helped in this production, and during the fifties she did much to encourage an appreciation of drama among the girls.

To celebrate B-P Centenary Year in 1957, Guides and Scouts had a special week in June, when displays and tableaux were put on every evening at the Ross Bandstand in Princes Street Gardens. The highspot of the week was a massed campfire on Calton Hill

In 1968 one of the Eight Points of the new programme was "Exploring the Arts" and this inevitably led to the girls taking a more active interest in art and music. The County's first Arts Adviser, Enid Nicholson, was appointed in 1968 to help encourage all forms of art, and at once she involved the whole County, starting with the Brownies whom she inspired by sheer magnetism to do their best on the stage of Gillespie's School in the "Brownie Matinée." All who were there will remember that magic afternoon. She organised many highly original competitions, including an international doll dressing competition, though she will best be remembered for founding the Edinburgh Club in 1969. The idea behind this was to explore the wealth of the history of our capital city. The club meets four times a year and has had a series of interesting speakers, and visits to historical houses such as Lauriston Castle, Gladstone's Land and St Cecilia's Hall. Membership is open to all members of the Movement, including husbands and boy-friends.

Folk music flourished, and from 1971 to 1975 as part of the Festival Fringe a Folk Fest took place in Edinburgh Headquarters and many groups participated.

"Dreams to inspire"—for some Edinburgh Sea Rangers their dreams surely came true when they participated in, and won their section of the National Guide Festival of Song in 1972. The quartet from S.R.S. Forth represented Scotland at the final in London by first of all winning the

Edinburgh Contest, then the Area finals in Glasgow and lastly, the Scottish finals held in the Assembly Rooms, Edinburgh. Let one of the Rangers take up the story:

"We had a great send off at Waverley Station and all knew that we would do our best. We were met off the overnight train at King's Cross Station by Lady Baden-Powell and driven straight to C.H.Q. for a meal, after which we volunteered to wash the mountain of dirty dishes used by the Brownies who were competing that morning, whereas our contest was at 4 p.m. We had a final singing practice in the kitchen! This verse of a song—sung to the tune *The Smoothing Iron*—tells all!!

> With faith like that what could we do?
> We sang as if each song were new,
> We sang as if each song were new, and then the judges said,
> "Though Wales and Ireland both are near, that Scotland's
>   top is surely clear."
> Anne was screaming to deafen ears;
> Hilly and Chris burst into tears;
> Janette mopped up her hysterical peers and so the
> honours came home.

There was a concert after all the judging in which the best items featured. We wore uniform with tartan sashes and felt very proud to be Scottish.

"Next day we kept on singing at the B.B.C.'s Maida Vale studios, first for the record *The National Guide Festival of Song,* then for a radio broadcast put out nationwide in May, and also we were asked to sing something for the *Get Together* record of folk hymns.

"Then the long sing was over—in one sense; in another it was only just beginning and we had a great deal to do to enlarge our repertoire beyond the contest songs. The Song Festival was an experience we wouldn't have missed for anything but it was strange to think we'd entered for a joke!"

Edinburgh Guides made history in November 1967 when they were the first Guides in the world to take part in a Gang Show. Earlier in the year the Scouts, who had been producing an annual Gang Show at the King's Theatre for some years asked if the Guides would join their show, an innovation that undoubtedly caused a stir! There must have been many occasions during rehearsals when both Scout and Guide members wondered whether it had been a good idea. Happily such doubts were soon dispelled by the show's unqualified success, and since then Guides have taken part in the Gang Show every year. There is keen competition at the auditions in the summer and once in the show, no one wants to leave. Rehearsals start in May and go on to the end of June, breaking for the summer holidays; after that it is "all systems go" until the show in November. The cast certainly earn the right to wear the coveted red neckerchief, a privilege enjoyed only by Scouts and Guides who have actually performed in the Gang Show. During January and February the cast perform various "mini-shows" for charity, and finally round off their hard work enjoying themselves at their annual reunion in March.

20

Camping and Enjoying the Out of Doors

"WE GO TO CAMP not only because we enjoy it so much, but also to gain experience. A Guide likes to try her hand at making things and finding out how to do a thing herself in a way she can't do at home." This was written in the *Handbook for Girl Guides* in 1912 and gives the first clue why "to go to camp" is the highlight of the Guiding year.

The early Companies certainly "tried their hands" and "gained experience" by using their own initiative.

The first known camp was in 1912 when the 2nd Edinburgh Company went to Archerfield, near Dirleton, in a horse-drawn furniture wagon, using it and a striped awning for sleeping. The Captain of the 12th Company challenged her Guides to make their own arrangements to get all their kit to the station; she was a little taken aback when the triumphant girls arrived in a hearse—one of their fathers was an undertaker. The 4th Company set off on foot with their equipment in a covered trek cart.

In July 1919 the 12th Company too went on foot; they marched from Edinburgh to Rosslynlee. As they passed through Roslin, the Captain, Miss Gilchrist, was asked if they would join in the village Victory Parade that afternoon. She said "Yes"; they went on and pitched their camp, returned to Roslin for the parade and entered in the sports afterwards. It was a very hot day and tea and cakes were much appreciated before the Guides marched back to camp.

Transport methods have changed in six decades, but the excitement felt by a Guide when the Company assembles to set off on what is her first camp, is still the same spirit that spurred those early campers to venture forth on unknown pursuits.

Perhaps the mother of today's Guide also feels just the same as *her* predecessor!

The camps in those early days had a military flavour. Army bell tents were pitched in a semi-circle with the Colours in the centre; the Guides learnt the meaning of the Colours and that they must not be left unguarded. There was also a reference to the posting of night sentries but no doubt B-P had others than the Colours in mind when he recommended this!

Father's old kit bag from the war held a Guide's possessions for one or two weeks' camp and its cylindrical shape had a devastating effect on items of uniform. No crease-resisting fabrics then!

Edinburgh Guides have been fortunate in having many good local sites available for camps of all sizes; large gardens, paddocks and fields have all been used. In 1916 there were camps at Grange Dell, Penicuik; Ashgrove House, Musselburgh; Carnwath; Leadburn; and Heriot. Many companies used huts, barns and farm cottages for sleeping, so enjoying the fun of living together as Guides.

"Time spent on reconnaissance is seldom wasted" and many Guiders learnt the wisdom of this on entering the farmer's "ideal" camping field for the first time, to find that his cows passed through it twice a day to be milked! The Guides learnt to be a friend to animals (however big) through these close contacts. One friendly horse was obviously used to being fed by a company, as she chewed up the bunch of cherries decorating a visitor's hat carelessly laid on the grass—shades of *Home Notes*!

Friendly farmers often ringed their otherwise delightful fields with barbed wire and members of the 7th Company were recognised for years by the neat "L"-shaped darns in the backs of their tunics due to mis-judging the height of the wire. Officers wore uniform at all times, but ties were removed and tunics undone on the camp site. Frequently too, wet skirts were taken off when wearing a waterproof—a fact not always remembered when the rain stopped! Commonsense prevailed in wet weather and the girls wore only gym shoes as legs dried more quickly than lisle stockings; wellington boots and waterproof coats were expensive and many didn't have them. Wide-brimmed felt hats suffered greatly in camp but a hot iron and brown paper soon restored them to shape once back home.

Having transported all equipment and kit to the site and pitched their tents, there came the moment when many city Guides felt camp had truly started. Long sacks were taken up to the farmer's barn and there began the hilarious game of filling them with sweet-smelling straw—puffing into a "Li-lo" is not half the fun of stuffing a palliasse! Usually a sleeping bag made from two blankets sewn together was laid on the top of the palliasse; there were no terylene bags then and girls were made of sterner stuff as is evident from a Ranger log book:

"They set off while the snow was on the ground, equipped only with two blankets and a Scotsman to sleep in a draughty barn in Peebles-shire!"

The "sweet-smelling straw" will evoke memories of other scents and aromas:

—of the freshness of the early morning as one stumbled from bed to join the Cook Patrol;
—of bacon sizzling in the pan which stirred the appetites of the campers;

"Officers wore uniform at all times."
Miss Hotchkiss, Captain of the 1st Company.

—of wild flowers, blossoming hedges and pine woods on hot summer days;

—of wet earth;

—of wet clothes in the tent,

—of wet hessian (so familiar but not so fresh) with overtones of carbolic!

—of campfires—each so different.

The pioneers had learnt a lot by experience which, added to enthusiasm and commonsense, resulted in enjoyable camping. However, the safety and welfare of the girls were of prime importance and the Guide Movement appointed a Director of Camping in 1920. Three years later Camp Advisers were appointed in the counties and a licence test for Guiders before they were allowed to take girls to camp was introduced. Parents' consent forms and doctors' certificates in certain cases were required and the regulations laid down then, with subsequent amendments, have ensured a high camping standard ever since. Thanks to the strict adherence to early ideals, a Guide Company in the Seventies will find a welcome back from farmers who appreciate that the Country Code is understood, and all that the Guides will leave behind them will be their thanks.

Dundas Castle grounds were used for the first training camps and many photographs bear evidence of the happy times spent there—indeed "A lesson learnt through fun is a lesson well learnt." For years the Guiders' annual weekend training camp at the Trefoil Site has been called "Fun Camp." Then, as now, Guiders spent precious holidays in camp (one week per annum was the average holiday for working girls in the 1920s). Training for and taking the licence test at a special camp involved at least a year's work; the County Camp Adviser for many years was Miss Thomson Clay who inspired many with her own keenness and high standards. Many companies waited patiently whilst their Captains earned the qualifications needed to give the girls the chance to "try their hand" in camp.

In 1924 the first World Camp was held at Foxlease; Patrol Leaders from the 4th and 12th Companies represented Edinburgh at this, being the fore-runners of all those who have since travelled far and wide to International Camps making friends with others bound by the same Law and Promise.

The necessity for strict regulations, the difficulty in finding Guiders willing, or able, to take their Camper's Licence, and the financial crisis, all made it increasingly difficult for companies to go to camp. As Edinburgh was a depressed area, grants became available and experienced Guiders were asked to take unemployed girls to camp with their companies. (The 7th Rangers took two girls from Fife who never forgot this wonderful holiday.) Camp Advisers ran large camps for companies whose Captains did not have a licence, and ingenious ways of covering the cost of a camp were found. One Ranger Company camping at Boghall for a weekend charged 2/6d, six potatoes and some jam per head.

With the outbreak of war, camping faced new problems and difficulties. In 1940 all Guide camping was banned, but in succeeding years camps were held on small equipped sites which could easily be reached for weekend camps. One week's camp was held at Craigmillar Castle, the Guides carrying out their camp duties and taking part in all camp activities during the day and then going home every night. This was in response to the Government's appeal to all patriotic citizens to have "holidays at home."

A thorough training in "Blitz" cooking was given and there were public demonstrations on brick fireplaces in Melville Street and Princes Street Gardens. Quartermasters had the added problem of all foods being rationed or on "points" and Guides, like everyone else, came to know the meaning of thrift. Hayboxes came into their own during the war and, much later, companies in Edinburgh were being asked for advice on how to make and use them in homes during the fuel crisis in the Seventies.

From 1941 Guides attended berry-picking camps, and Rangers and Guides worked in forestry and harvesting camps where their training in B-P's ideas proved useful. The call of the outdoors was strong and the number of campers in Edinburgh County had doubled by the end of the war in spite of all the difficulties. By 1948 the County records show 600 more campers than any other Scottish Guide County.

The Trefoil School had moved to Gogarbank and the field below it became Edinburgh's camp site, a hut for storing equipment being opened here in 1948 by the Scottish Camp Adviser, Miss Betty Beveridge. The Trefoil site has become well known for Fun Camps for Guiders, division and company camps, a testing ground for Camper badge, Patrol Permits and, of course, Camper's Licences. Many happy camping holidays have also been spent there by Guides from all over the United Kingdom. Getting to know the Trefoil School children during the term was always a joy and interest for all campers.

When Netherurd opened as the Scottish Training Centre more camping facilities became available, two company sites and two patrol sites. The burn running between them made raft making and bridge building more than hypothetical exercises!

A small site at Carsewell, near Penicuik, has been used for many years by Edinburgh Rangers.

The introduction of the Patrol Camp Permit would have gladdened the Founder's heart. With a responsible adult nearby, a Patrol Leader was, and is, able to take her Patrol to a suitable site and they all loved, and still do, their little camps where they were self-sufficient and dependent on each other. By 1957, 65 Patrol Camp Permits were held but still there were Guides who wanted to camp and not enough licence holders. Miss Inches, as County Commissioner, was herself a keen camper and encouraged many Guiders by her own example; the pages of her album bear witness to numberless visits to camps.

The camping season of 1958 is still remembered as one of storm and flood but 2136 girls went to 161 camps, so they had been undaunted by the weather. Many had quite a thrill from their experiences and refused to strike camp. The 43rd Company wrote in their log book after a week of thunder, lightning, gales and rain: "So ended the largest camp in the worst conditions the company has ever had but we think that the weather doesn't make any difference." Might B-P have said, "Well done"?

In spite of the weather Guides do "go to camp . . . because they enjoy it so much," and more clues to the reasons why may be picked up by stalking down Memory Lane. Not very far down the road—do you remember?

—the long sunny days of 1976 when supper came *after* camp fire because it was too HOT to eat earlier;

—at the other end of the Lane, the glorious summers in the early days when short-sleeved camp overalls and bare legs were NEWS!

—the strange feeling of sharing a tent with other girls and being away from home for the first time;

—the "dark" darkness and the quietness;

—the wild night of wind and rain, and the comfort of hearing Captain testing the guys and saying, "Are you all right in there?"

—the thrill of actually seeing the brilliant blue of a kingfisher;

—the "shiver down the spine" hoot of an owl;

—the food—never mentioned in a record of the 1912 camp; it was not done to discuss what one ate!

—how one talked nostalgically of it in the war!

—cooking!

—the sudden awareness of the meaning of the Promise through a "Guides' Own Service;"

—the songs and stories at Camp Fire, groups with combs and whistles, or recorders and guitars; and the calm after "Taps";

—the fun of devising strange games for parents and visitors;

—the fancy dresses and last night pranks;

—the Guiders, nicknames, and the catch word, phrase or song which identified a camp for years to come.

The Lane is just not long enough!

National events have inspired special camps like the Coronation Camp at Penicuik House in 1953. A Guide who was there writes:

"There were 26 Patrols in tents whose names began with a different letter of the alphabet relating to royalty; one tent was "U" for Unicorn. I shall always remember the large camp fires and the Sunday Service by the loch side which was wonderful."

Jubilee years have always been good encouragement for campers. The first big County International Camp was held to celebrate 50 years of Guiding, the second was in the year the New Programme was launched.

The Golden Jubilee Camp in 1960 took place on the Blair Drummond Estate, on what is now the Safari Park. As well as the refugees from the D.P. Camps, the visitors came from Canada and the United States, from Scandinavia, Holland and France, and from Spain which only three years earlier had been recognised as a Tenderfoot Member of the World Association—350 Guides and Girl Scouts altogether, divided into 12 sub-camps, named after national training houses and separated from each other by great stands of trees.

Among the Challenges offered were two which were obviously born of long experience of camping with girls—that the Guides should refrain from speaking from 9.30 at night until 8 o'clock next morning, and that they should carry out early-morning good turns without waking anyone in the attempt.

The *Evening Dispatch* of 8th August devoted the entire front page to pictures from Blair Drummond—several showed girls wearing their national dress on visitors' day; others an attractive little totem pole, and the bands performing on their improvised instruments; and one was of a small group of Guides unhappily posed at the home farm round four plump piglets busy with their dinner: the piglets had broken loose one night, had raided the store tent and helped themselves to the breakfast sausages—cannibalism! No wonder the girls looked unhappy.

It was the first Edinburgh event at which the flags of so many nations had flown beside the World Flag, and they really did make an enormous impression—all the more so for the efforts of the camp staff, who had raised all those 60-foot poles one evening, before the girls arrived. Each pole had to be snugly seated in a hole two feet deep and no wider than the pole itself. What a sight it must have been—all those Guiders kneeling, bottoms-up, like a lot of burrowing rabbits!

The second camp was held at Blair Atholl in the summer of 1968, only a few weeks after the Olympic Games in Mexico City. It was known, therefore, as "The Camp of the Flame" and the 12 groups were named after the cities which had been host to previous Games. The activities were all sporty, and the first camp fire was lit from a torch—whose manufacture had posed serious problems—after the torch-bearer, running from group to group, had summoned the whole camp into the arena.

Each Guide had the chance to learn two of a wide range of sports, and a "Gold Medal" was awarded to the most proficient group. "London" and "Paris" tied for first place, and the outcome was decided, inter-nationally, and in the crowded marquee because of the weather, by making the two teams play Chinese Ladders.

The Army Youth Team became almost a part of the camp. Twenty men and "Sir," their officer, set up the trampoline, the climbing net and laid out a commando course—and even raised the flagpoles, too! They helped with all the activities, and on one occasion took the Rangers, including one who was blind, on a canoeing expedition.

Gateway to the Camp of the Flame.

One account states firmly that "Central" group, *i.e.* the Staff, did not compete in the sports. Another version, however, has it that the small Guide who was discovered at midnight trampolining happily by herself was not the only person to do so!

A third camp is to be held at Dalmeny in 1977 to celebrate the Queen's Silver Jubilee, and invitations have gone out to neighbouring countries and to those with whom we have had personal links over the last few years. The camp is sure to spark off as many reminiscences and anecdotes as the other two to add to the Edinburgh story.

"Guiding is a jolly game largely played in the out of doors where Guide and Guider go adventuring together picking up health, happiness, handcraft and helpfulness."

Once more B-P puts in a few words all that is meant by "ENJOYING THE OUT OF DOORS."

The first Edinburgh Brownies, Guides and Rangers played the game by meeting out of doors whenever possible, but with the growth of the city, it has not always been easy to hold a meeting outside even in fine weather. However, groups of brown or blue-clad girls have been seen playing Wide Games or rounders in local parks, tracking in the streets, having a barbecue on nearby beaches or hiking in the hills.

Any outdoor pursuit has appealed to Guides, from games to a hike with a meal cooked in the open, through light-weight camping to more sophisticated and organised excursions to go canoeing or ski-ing.

Both these activities have been enjoyed by Guides and Rangers for years, but in 1972 a canoe club and a ski club were formed within the County. Both have flourished; members of the Ranger Canoe Club, having built their own canoes, have tested the waters from Fisherrow Harbour to Machrihanish, they have taken part in races, white water slaloms and national competitions. Through the encouragement and instruction received in Guiding, some members have joined the British Canoe Club and entered the wider world of canoeing.

The County Ski Club established a store of equipment in Edinburgh Headquarters, hired it out to interested Guides and set off for the slopes of Glenshee, usually in the minibus. As Rangers had co-operated with Scouts in the Glenshee Ski Rescue Service there were instructors available from both Movements, and many girls have been able to learn to ski. In March 1975 a party of 40 went to Glenshee, 21 were beginners, some were quite young Guides who, adventuring together with the Guiders, must have learnt to know each other better by the time the minibus returned to "No. 33." Safety and Fun is the motto of both these clubs.

There is a new sport particularly suited to the Scout and Guide Movements as it involves all levels of ability, all ages from 8-80 years, needs very little equipment and uses the old Scout/Guiding skills of compass work and map reading. This is Orienteering, which originated in Scandinavia and has been described as "a car rally on foot," "the thought sport" or "cunning running." The aim is basically to cover a course in the fastest time by running, jogging or walking, aided by a map and compass. As the fastest route is not necessarily the shortest, good map reading and compass work is required.

In the Guide Movement, Orienteering covers many of the Eight Points. It obviously involves "enjoying the out of doors," map and compass reading and decision making require "thinking for yourself." The girl who takes part soon finds herself "getting to know people" especially as she fords burns and negotiates marshes with her partner, and she will certainly "keep fit" as her skill improves.

Two Edinburgh Guiders have set up a practice course at Netherurd and, after learning map reading and how to use a compass, many Guides, Rangers, Guiders and even Commissioners are taking the opportunity to use these skills in a new way. There is a great sense of achievement in reaching B from A with map and compass!

Times change, old skills are passed on to be adapted to new ways. If a company is to have an annual camp, the Guider's small children may have to go too—usually to the mutual joy of all concerned! Calor gas cookers are often used to cut out some of the chores which take too long, as small girls of 10 years cannot manage to do all that older girls did in earlier days. Convenience foods like "Smash" are often used so that maybe the whole camp may take part in a challenge; or simply so that both Guides and Guiders will have time "to stand and stare together."

The Guides wake up each morning, wondering what excitement the day will bring. Will it be a long and interesting trail through the woods, or collecting leaves, grasses and flowers for making collages? Perhaps there will be time just to lie face downwards in the grass discovering the fascination of watching insects busy in their own secret world, or the beauty of a tiny wild flower often trodden heedlessly underfoot. Let the Guides themselves describe some of the new experiences that crowd each day in camp.

"Why do I like camp? That's a thought? Well, I think I like camp for a bundle of reasons, like we do our own cooking not like at home where we get the food placed before us; we make new friends, as not only your company goes but others as well; and everyone mucks in together doing all the activities of the day thought up by the very brainy adventurous and back-breaking Guiders. I will talk about my memories of camp to my children hoping they will join Guides and find out for themselves what a good time Guiding and camping is!"

—Gail.

"Washing the dishes is an experience at camp as you never know until you start whether the water will be hot or cold! Most people like night-time as you go visiting to other tents and have a good time. At camp you make new friends and try to keep them afterwards."

—Rosalind.

"Then in the morning the Guiders come round at 8.30 and say, 'Right—up you get, it's a glorious day,' even when its foggy. But I think the Guiders work quite hard to take our Mothers' places."

—CAROLINE.

Different? Yes! But the ideals are the same whether the game is played just outside the Hall door, in the park over the road or amongst the heather and the hills. The out-of-doors is there to be enjoyed.

21

The Trefoil School

THE WARTIME EVACUATION SCHEME was to finish at the end of 1944—
what was to become of all the pupils at Cowdenknowe's Special School.

It had been demonstrated that, complementary to the skill of doctors
and orthopaedic surgeons, a good education was necessary for the
economic independence of disabled people, and that even the severely
physically-handicapped child could rise to challenges, both physical and
mental, and had much to contribute to society. The untiring efforts of
Miss Crawford, Miss Hamilton Bruce and Miss Wallace Williamson,
working with committees concerned with the welfare of handicapped
children and the Director of Education, brought about the recognition
of the now grant-aided school by the Department of Education.

A new house had to be found, and in the spring of 1945 the school
moved to Polkemmet, near Whitburn. A new name was needed too, and
"The Trefoil School" was chosen because of the strong link with the Girl
Guide Movement through its founders—"the small band of twelve
Edinburgh Guiders who went to St Abbs on 4th September 1939."

Everyone concerned with the school longed for a permanent home
and the dream came true when the move to Kirklands House, near
Hermiston, took place in April 1951. On seeing the old stone house in its
beautiful grounds, one of the boys said, "It's lovely, but is it paid for?"
Not then—but the faith of the Council, formed in 1945, was justified soon
afterwards when the Council and Executive Committee became the
owners of Kirklands House and grounds.

The finances of the school had always been a form of miracle but also
a tribute to the response of people who saw the need, as yet only partially
recognised, of the right to a full life for every handicapped child. During
the war years the Guider Staff was on a voluntary basis: then the school
was recognised by the Scottish Education Department and a small salary
was paid. The Director of Education at that time declared that "the
Guides are the brightest jewel in the Education Committee's crown."

Basically, ever since the beginning, the school has depended on generous
donations from Guide friends, Trusts and others, supplemented by grants
(60% on any deficit) from the Scottish Education Department and
payment from Local Authorities whose children were pupils. Eventually
it was possible to raise salaries to the appropriate scale.

Miss Hamilton Bruce, who was awarded the M.B.E. in recognition of
her work as one of the founders of the School, was Guider-in-Charge

until 1956 and was succeeded by Miss Dorothy Varcoe. She in turn was given the Guide Beaver Award in 1962, and was succeeded by Miss Blackwell who had the magic touch with all things mechanical. This was increasingly useful because as disabilities became more extreme the equipment to cope with them became more sophisticated. Polio and surgical T.B. became blessedly rare but even more heavily handicapped pupils arrived, dependent on wheelchairs.

Though a good deal had been done for the mentally handicapped by this time, physically handicapped youngsters had either been left at home with the minimum of school teaching, or taken to the local school where, too often, they led a backwater existence, treated as mentally sub-normal and missing most of the fun. Trefoil School provided specialised treatment to make up the leeway: small classes, pleasant relaxed environment, carefully selected helpers and—dare it be said?—no nonsense. At a recent Former Pupils' Reunion, one lad, now himself an official of the Scottish Education Department, and preparing to sit his final exam for an Open University Degree, confessed that in his first arithmetic exam he had scored a big 0 and 5% in geography.

Miss Morison had already been Head Teacher for several years at Polkemmet providing stimulating education for pupils at different stages. She remained with the School until her retirement in 1967. Her successors also showed the ability and devotion necessary to help the children to make the effort to achieve a good standard despite their handicap.

Constant adaptions were contrived in dormitories and classrooms to suit the changing needs and to overcome every obstacle so that each child shared fully in all the activities. When sufferers from the new disaster, thalidomide, arrived, complete or partial absence of limbs complicated the problem so electronic devices had to be acquired and mastered in and out of school. This involved training in the Self-care Unit under the Professor of Bio-engineering at Princess Margaret Rose Hospital.

One little girl, born without arms but most dexterous with her feet, could even sew, and dress her doll. Artificial arms were provided, powered by a CO_2 cylinder, so that by different movements of her shoulders she could manipulate a knife and fork. Her toes were far better at the job, which was quite acceptable in school, but is society ready to accept it in public? Many days were spent acquiring these skills, but as she said, "If I don't have arms, how can I push a pram?"

Many a child, inspired by others equally handicapped, found themselves able to do quite a surprising number of "impossible" things. One frail boy said, "Could you teach boys like me to brush their hair?" The Housemother could and did!

Earlier a garden classroom had been built in memory of the School's first Treasurer and the raised garden plots (buttressed by stone which started life as setts in Charlotte Square) was another good idea. Children were able to work from their wheelchairs with the specially adapted tools and to experience the primitive pleasure of handling the soil and growing things for themselves. The gardener, Mr McCallum, had an artificial arm himself but this did not prevent him from growing fine crops of vegetables and flowers, showing the children how to sow seeds, take cuttings, prune and learn other items of the gardener's craft, culminating in the final pleasure of eating the results. Everyone was delighted when he was awarded the B.E.M. before retiring.

All these and other activities helped to generate skill and confidence, each one rejoicing in his own and others' progress. Perhaps the greatest thrill was Morag's wonderful electric wheelchair which worked on a "sook-blaw" principle—to reverse she sucked in her breath, to advance she blew into the tube. Nothing could equal the bliss of going about entirely on her own for the first time in her life.

In the grounds sports and games have been a great delight and being in a team was an exciting experience for newcomers. All sorts of games were devised or adapted so that no one was left out. A football-cum-hockey pitch was soon made and a five-a-side match played against Westerlea School. There was archery, clock golf and quoits. More recently, as fewer people could kick or run, wheelchair basketball was introduced and proved very exciting, involving much speed in the handling of the chair and not a few spills. Croquet was played by those with weak arms using light plastic mallets. When at last it became possible to have a resident physiotherapist, outdoor games played an even larger part in treatment.

The star athletic pupil was Barbara. Her record runs: 1974, Dunedin Commonwealth Paraplegic Games, two golds; Heidelberg Paraplegic Olympics, three golds; 1976, Toronto Paraplegic Olympics, one gold. Not bad for a lass in a wheelchair *and* she passed her exams too!

When it was seen that active games such as football were out of the question, another fund-raising effort was launched. This was magnificently supported by members of the Scout and Guide Movements and the public in response to a B.B.C. appeal. In 1970 the Hydrotherapy Pool was finally declared open by Bobby McGregor, O.B.E., Olympic Gold Medallist. He then delighted children and guests by taking the first plunge in the pool and demonstrating various strokes. Then a boy crippled by rheumatoid arthritis was lowered into the water on the hydraulic lift and swam a length to great applause. A girl paralysed below the waist and another without arms swam out with the school crest and motto "Undaunted" on a rubber ring. The thrill of being water-borne to a physically handicapped child is beyond anything we can imagine.

Another sporting personality who became a friend of the School was the boxing champion, Ken Buchanan. He not only visited the school and raised money for it, but with great generosity took two of the boys by air to spend a night in his hotel in London and to have ringside seats from which they watched him win his World Lightweight title. The social poise of the boys was noticeable then, and again when they were invited to attend the Civic Reception for him in Edinburgh City Chambers.

Though unable to participate in athletics, football or rugby, the boys and girls followed their special heroes or team. Some discussion on strength was going on in a dormitory when a boy, weak because of muscular dystrophy but of great mental ability, was heard to say, "But being strong isn't just being able to run or jump." All the pupils had the strength of courage and fortitude.

There had been cruises and trips abroad for one or two selected Guides and Scouts from the School but for a long time Miss Varcoe had dreamed of taking the Guides to "Our Chalet" and in 1964, thanks to a generous gift and to the Falk Memorial Fund, four Guides, five ex-pupil Rangers and two helpers set off with her. Three of the girls walked with calipers, four were in wheelchairs but the school motto is "Undaunted." The flight from Edinburgh went smoothly, thanks to Miss Varcoe's invention of small carrying seats which fitted into wheelchairs, plane and bus seats so that the girls could be carried from one to another without loss of dignity or danger of injury. These had been made at Linburn and caused great interest among staff in the planes, trains, buses, boats, a jeep, and even chair lifts, for the party did almost everything there was to do. Falk would have been pleased to have seen willing hands at "Our Chalet" helping the handicapped girls, heard the laughter and known of the new friendships made.

The Guides already had an international outlook, for there had always been Swiss Guiders working as housemothers at the School and some came to "Our Chalet" to renew old bonds and lend a hand. Many also had come to the School from Denmark and other continental countries, from Australia and New Zealand, Bermuda and Korea, to gain experience in work with disabled children. Two other trips were made to Switzerland as new generations of Guides became old enough. Then Miss Varcoe thought the children should see more of their own country and instituted an annual Scottish Heritage Tour. Each of these studied and explored different areas and aspects of life in the country. The "van," the gift of the Trefoil Guilds, accommodated ten pupils in their wheelchairs and six who could walk. With Miss Blackwell at the wheel the van sped through the glens as far as the Isle of Skye. With the hydraulic tail lift it was possible to get everyone in and out with comparative ease to spend nights at Youth Hostels, "just like everybody else," and giving the party an opportunity to mingle with other young people and swop yarns.

A shorter but no less exciting journey was when, some years ago, a group of children went to Holyrood Park to see our Patron the Queen who, on seeing the van, came over to speak to them.

Miss Varcoe had a great love of music and the school music group reached a high standard in recorder playing, twice winning the Shield for Group Music at the Disabled Week Talent Contest. A graceful "wheel-chair dance" she evolved has been taken up by other schools and clubs. Another musical outlet was a Folk Group with voices and guitar which gained second prize in another Talent Contest, while another group, playing stylophones and drums, took part in a concert in the Usher Hall. Incomplete arms did not debar children from making music, a xylophone trio was formed, the players holding the stick in their mouths—very effective in the annual Carol Service with their bell-like tones.

Interest in music, painting, crafts and literature is of special value if one must be largely housebound later. Discovery of artistic talents led to one girl training as a painter of designs on pottery, and to a boy becoming a wood carver. Some of his work can be seen on the crest above Lord Bilsland's stall in the Thistle Chapel in St Giles.

Then there were various clubs: The Pets Club, Garden, Handicraft, Homecraft, the Saturday Club for seniors and, of course, meetings of Brownies, Guides, Rangers, Cubs and Scouts. One seven-year-old said, "The best thing I ever did in my life was to come to Trefoil School."

Happy days.

Drama had been an important item in the original curriculum and continued to be so. Every child loves to "dress up," though often boys won't admit it, except one whose interest was so great that later he trained to be a tailor. When, as at Trefoil, a great collection of fascinating apparel is at hand, concocting plays as an excuse to wear these costumes is inevitable. Miss Crawford's historical plays, giving rein to love of historical pageantry, have a universal appeal, and have been used by other groups of handicapped people.

In recent years Parents' Day entertainment has included puppetry, Gilbert and Sullivan and modern musicals. Always a part was found for every child, and in each the costume was adapted to conceal as much as possible any "ironmongery" (calipers) or other appliances. Often a last-minute change of cast had to take place because someone was whisked off to hospital for further treatment or surgery, but doctors and surgeons were most understanding and did their best to avoid such disappointments.

The friendship with the "Men of Linburn" is of long standing and benefits both groups. Trefoil children made excellent hosts and hostesses to their blind partners at the annual Hallowe'en Party, guiding them and describing the ghosties and ghoulies, witches and spiders that hung from the ceilings and brushed the guests' faces. One of the parties proved a turning point in the life of a hitherto self-centred girl who had never before known the satisfaction of helping others.

Each year a Christmas party for the children was given at Linburn and after what can only be described as a sumptuous repast, a riotous evening was spent with amusing games and a hilarious performance given by the men. Finally, Father Christmas produced a present for each child, showing a considerable amount of research as well as great generosity.

The other big annual social event was the New Year Party given by the Corstorphine Friends at which the guests were entertained by members of the Scout and Guide Gang Show with excerpts from their current production. Through these friends' kindness the Recreation Room alongside the pool was built. They also arranged a Sports Day at West Linton during the summer term. So impressed was an onlooker by the spirit of the children that a donation of £500 "for the comfort of the children" was sent. This was used to buy mattresses, much appreciated by those who were unable to move in bed; a sewing machine on which the girls made some elegant party frocks; and a billiard table. Other gifts of equipment have poured in. Each year some exciting new device would arrive. Sometimes paintwork suffered, as one boy said, "It's difficult not to chip the paint when you are flying along in a wheelchair!" The thalidomide children careering about on their "buggies" were a terrifying sight until one realised how cleverly they handled them.

There was "give" as well as "take". For many years, until too few had strong hands, the Sale of Work raised money for other people. A Guide Dog for the Blind was paid for and money was sent to the Muscular Dystrophy Society for Research, and so on.

Gradually pupils were aiming at O-grade exams with considerable success, one girl achieving O-grade passes by typing her answers on an electric typewriter by a stick held in her mouth. Some, having left aged 16, went south to do A-levels and then proceeded to Technical College.

In World Refugee Year (1960) the Girl Guides' Association raised £2500 to sponsor a Polish girl from a Refugee Camp. This was more than sufficient to pay for Krystyna Zgorski's education and maintenance at Trefoil School, and hospital treatment for polio, so her parents were brought over also. After eight happy years she left school with O-grade English and German and a training in Commercial subjects. By now her parents had gone to Germany, so after a job in this country, Krystyna joined them and has since married and has a daughter.

The future now seemed assured and indeed, for twenty-five years, all has been activity and progress in and out of the classrooms. Pupils have taken part in a great variety of outside activities where their social poise and independence and lack of self-consciousness have greatly impressed everyone they have met. This out-going and cheerful attitude was due to the happy atmosphere in the school where members of staff encouraged self-help and never "talked down" to the children. (Some outsiders are apt to do this when conversing with intelligent young people who are crippled. Worse still, people have been known to talk to the pushers of the wheelchair as if the occupant hardly existed or was incapable of thought or speech.)

Each year, Seniors about to leave have visited Edinburgh Castle through the kindness of Scottish Command, when soldiers gave them a personally conducted tour. Field studies were made also at Stirling, Bannockburn and other historic spots, the lighter moments written up in the School Magazine.

In an Architectural Heritage Year competition, Senior "A"class chose "Three Centuries of Building History in East Lothian." This involved three expeditions of discovery in the school van and then a final check and completion of a scrap book showing the variety of 16th-18th century buildings which can be seen in one day's drive from Edinburgh. This project won Special Commendation and the class was invited to the Assembly Rooms to receive a prize of £15 from Princess Alexandra, followed by a sumptuous luncheon.

Edinburgh Girl Guides in founding the school in wartime and consolidating it in peace-time have shown the way. They have proved that disabled people can play an active part in the community and in industry. This pioneering effort by a voluntary body has become known world-wide.

Miss Wallace Williamson, O.B.E., Honorary Secretary of the Executive Committee until 1970, was the moving spirit in many of the extensions and improvements gradually made to the buildings, culminating in the addition of the swimming pool in that year. Her resignation was received with regret, but her knowledge of the school continued to be of great value to the Committee.

The visitors' book boasts an imposing array of names. The Chief Guide,

Guides and Scouts from all over the world have come and we have had many visits from educationalists and officials from as far away as Japan and India, many of whom paid us the compliment of reproducing our methods when they returned home. The Princess Royal's photograph hangs in the hall, commemorating her visit in 1954—the boys won't forget how they rigged up a telephone so that the chicken-pox victim could speak to her! The Countess Bernadotte came in search of inspiration for a similar school, and many other notable visitors were welcomed.

Others who brought outside interests and a male point of view were the Scouters, the White Fathers, the Corstorphine Rotary Club, Church Youth Groups, the Bible Class at Ratho and the Captain of our adopted ship, *M.V. Crinan.*

In recent years in Scotland, some Regions have built or are planning residential schools for severely disabled children. Others are providing easier means of access to classrooms in local schools. Numbers applying for admission have therefore steadily been falling and "Trefoil" is no longer needed by enough children to justify continuing as a school. We are proud of the past achievements of the School and although this chapter ends in 1976 we hope that the pioneering work of the founders which has benefited so many disabled young people since 1939 may take a new but equally useful direction. A new chapter will surely begin soon: look out for our next instalment.

Although the news of the closing of Trefoil School has been received with great sadness by everyone connected with it, its last few weeks were gay and happy. On Parents' Day there was an exhilarating performance of *Joseph and his Technicolour Dream Coat* by all the pupils. On the last day of school, at bedtime, a fly set off the new fire alarm system. To the ringing of fire bells, children emerged in night attire, or fresh from the bath, wrapped in blankets. Within minutes three fire engines arrived but all was well. It was a balmy evening so while everything was checked, the firemen chatted to the children whose costumes were now completed by firemen's helmets.

Next morning all the children set off for the last school camp. It turned out to be one of the very best. Weather, neighbours and farm animals all co-operated to perfection. Old friends, formerly on the staff, joined the school staff for a very happy camp. The horse gave rides and came to supper, nuzzling a little girl's cheek to her delight. The cow inspected a tent and the dogs were ever ready for games. At a final campfire, some of the staff gave a demonstration of fire-walking on the embers. The following day everyone went home but looked forward to meeting again at the October reunion.

The School After-care Committee will carry on, ready to give help and advice to ex-pupils if needed. They follow with interest the successful lives of many in careers which include accountancy, hotel ownership, secretarial posts, electronics, to name but a few. Three are studying for degrees in the Open University, others are playing an inportant rôle in organising activities for the disabled. Mrs Margaret Grant, herself in a wheelchair, for her work in starting the Brittle Bone Society, was designated "Disabled Scot of the Year 1974."

The Trefoil School Association of former pupils and staff will, of course, continue as a very live group. It is a great delight to see the beautiful, healthy and well brought up "grand-children" who come with their parents. Nearly 100 members attended the 1976 reunion when the film of Trefoil School was shown, recalling old times.

To echo the words of an Old Boy years ago, "It makes such a difference having been at Trefoil School because people care what becomes of you."

22

Reaching Out

GUIDING, LIKE SCOUTING, creates through its programme, an interest and an aim in life. Through the unique patrol system, that small closely-knit group within which the whole of the Guide programme can be carried out, a girl progresses until she is able to recognise and accept the responsibilities as well as the adventure which life holds. With such a foundation, Guiding, from the beginning has reached out with confidence to the wider world outside.

As early as 1913, and for 19 years, Miss Dalmahoy presided over a Scottish committee of all those "Kindred Societies" who were affiliated through their headquarters with Scottish Guide H.Q. (Five years later, there were as many as twenty-six societies affiliated at a U.K. level with C.H.Q. in London.) They included the Y.W.C.A., the Girls' Brigade, the Scottish Mothers' Union and the Catholic Women's League, the influential International Council of Women—and the pleasant-sounding Loyal and Ancient Order of Shepherds. These were other organisations whose ultimate purposes were similar to that of the Girl Guides though they achieved them in different ways and attracted a different type or age of person. Many of them had been in existence for a long time when Guides appeared on the scene, and the encouragement and practical help which these older and more experienced societies gave to the newcomer was both generous and useful.

Of all the organisations, the one which has always been very close to Guiding has been the Y.W.C.A. With experience dating back to the Crimean War, they had given a great deal of practical help to B-P with his new Movement. In the thirties in Edinburgh, companies were formed in the Y.W.C.A. Clubs, adapted slightly to conform with their specifically Christian principles, and many women with an Edinburgh Guiding background seem to have slipped quite naturally into positions of responsibility in the "Y.W." How easily the stories of the two organisations merge was discovered by Sheila Moyes, the present General Secretary of the Y.W.C.A. in Scotland.

She went to Copenhagen with the St Giles Rangers. Accommodation there was difficult and a Danish Commissioner put her flat at their disposal though she was not to be at home. To say thank you for this kindness and trust, they left her a Scottish pebble brooch. In 1975, eleven years later, there was a "Y.W." Conference in Vancouver at which Sheila was a delegate. One evening in her hotel she came upon the Danish delegation, entered into conversation and mentioned her visit to Copenhagen and the trust of their hostess there. "But *I* was your hostess," exclaimed one Dane, "and I still have the brooch to prove it!"

An even closer partnership has been with the Scouts. Although in the early days joint activities were not encouraged, nevertheless many troops and companies found themselves involved together in church functions. This led to some Scouters reaching out to take a Guider's hand in marriage though many have been too shy to admit it! There were also cruises for Scouters and Guiders in the thirties, an idea of the Chief Guide. The first, in *S.S. Calgaric* in 1933, visited the Northern capitals in the Baltic, the third went to Iceland in 1938 and an account of the second cruise follows:

"The *S.S. Adriatic* left Liverpool on the 29th March 1934 for a two-week cruise to the Mediterranean with the Chief Scout, the Chief Guide, their family and some 400 British Scouters and Guiders.

"Races and games on deck made one forget the rough Bay of Biscay, it was the Rock of Gibraltar that seemed so unsteady to those marching in the Parade when we landed there.

"We called at Villefranche, Malta and Algiers where we walked through the narrow streets on our way to a Camp Fire on sand, under the stars, with camel noises for an accompaniment.

"At Lisbon Lady Baden-Powell asked the four Guiders in my cabin to take four Portuguese Guiders round the ship. We all wanted to see more 'local-life' than had been possible from the 'charabanc' in France so we asked these Guiders for their help! Both parties spoke D grade 'O' level French and not each other's language. They found a large, open taxi which took us through the town by the back streets, into the country, to Cintra where we bought food in the market to add to our packed lunches, and on to the Pena Palace. There we had all the officials to ourselves; two helped me up on to a high window ledge and held my ankles while I took photographs. We picnicked in the gardens before driving to the coast, and so back to Lisbon.

"We had seen much more of the countryside and the Palace than had the bus tour, with the cost for the eight of us the same as ONE tour ticket. Lady Baden-Powell had done us a very Good Turn!"

By the seventies, Scout/Guide camps had become an accepted activity, at least in one Edinburgh division.

"Joint camping is being advocated now in 1976, but we in Portobello and Niddrie have been weekend-camping with our Scouts for some years now. It all started in 1969, out of a fairly casual, but friendly, relationship between the troop and the company; we all felt it was a good idea, and decided to give it a try. There was a great deal of "talk and coffee" between the Leaders before we got organised, but the basic plan was to take P.L.s and Seconds and all the Leaders who wanted to come, the more the better, and to make it a Fun Camp! Well, fun it was—and is—but the standard of camping nevertheless tends to be very high. After all, neither group can let their side down, can they? The Guides usually look after basic arrangements—including food, and the Scouts see to the programme. This has scarcely ever varied: Friday, pitching and supper; Saturday, a full programme of activities of a challenge nature and a camp fire, of course; and Sunday a Scouts'-Guides' Own Service, and games. One formality we always have is Colours. One morning we do it the Scout way, and the other it's "à-la-Guides"—this in uniform, and no nonsense!

"Practical jokes abound! Once the Scouts managed to strike our store tent, and remove it and all its contents, to the extreme end of the site where it was pitched and set out exactly as it had been. And this without our hearing a thing! They heard *our* retaliation though—off-key Christmas Carols, with full tin plate percussion, at 7 A.M.!

"It was at one of these camps that our Ranger Unit was started. On the Sunday afternoon, we had a serious moment, thought deeply, then ejected the older girls and all their equipment to another part of the field, where they set up the first Ranger camp. For these particular girls, this couldn't have happened in a happier way. Several of them are Guiders now.

"Last year we found that the older Scouts and Guides couldn't come, so we opened it to the younger folk, and instead of having two separate camps as before, we made a third daytime camp, with mixed patrols for cooking, eating and activities. Now that really *did* work out well! Happily, it's a huge field, so it was easy to place Scouts here, Guides there, and all the camp staff in the middle. The boys were able to be tough about wooding, and the girls were very happy to potter about the kitchen area, and to show off their cooking skills.

"We'll carry on like this, till we feel like another change, then perhaps we'll try something else.

"These camps are really easily run, but the Leaders get very, very organised well beforehand, and the Scouts and Guides are left in no doubt that any "untoward behaviour" will lead to instant leave-taking. No warnings once we're in camp—just an escort to the bus stop! In fact, such an occasion has never arisen. We thought at the beginning that parents might be doubtful, but it seems we have their full support and confidence, which is an enormous compliment. Perhaps this is partly because we are both experienced camping units, and go away regularly. Anyway, it's all great fun—it helps relationships within our church and between the two units—it keeps us all on our toes—and it helps us all to see that Scouting and Guiding are two halves of one great organisation, based on a super idea. And that isn't at all a bad idea to grow up with.''

The game of Scouting and Guiding was devised to attract the children, not as a means of imposing adult ideas on them. Just how strong this attraction was proved itself in a venture undertaken by Edinburgh Guides in 1940.

What is a Square Centre? This question has been asked not only in many parts of Scotland and England but even overseas. In response to a Government appeal, the idea of starting a centre for girls of 14-18 came to certain far-seeing members of the Scottish Executive Committee who, while realising that Guiding in its usual guise would have no appeal, felt that with its principle of character-training through self-government and service it had much to offer to the girl who was not attracted to any organisation.

The Granton Square Centre was opened in 1940. Edinburgh was fortunate in having a suitable location, the old church hall in Granton Square, still more so in having an ideal leader—Greta Collyns, already one of the leading Scottish Diploma'd Trainers who gave up her outside professional work and undertook its launching. Her methods produced an immediate response from the members, who appreciated the sense of co-operation in being asked to share in the forming of the Centre. From the first night the girls took possession and looked on the Centre as their own.

The first members were mostly factory girls working long hours on monotonous jobs, wild and noisy with unbounded energy which required an outlet, and crying for self-expression. None were attached to youth organisations and hitherto their chief distraction had been the cheap dance halls, the fish and chip shop and the cinema.

Contrary to their expectations, in the Square Centre they were treated as grown-up intelligent people expected to manage their own affairs, to think for themselves and stand on their own feet. Could they make their Centre into something of which to be proud?—"Of course we can—we will make it the finest centre in the country."

They made their own badges. One girl sat all evening laboriously making hers. When she had finished she sewed it firmly on to the lapel of her coat and with sparkling eyes and an air of satisfaction and achievement said triumphantly, "I'm a life member now, Miss."

They formed their own committees, planned their programmes and entertained their own visitors. The Princess Royal took a great interest in this experiment in Guiding and visited the Centre on two occasions in 1944, giving great encouragement to all those who had taken part in building up the Centre.

All sorts of activities and interests were promoted and encouraged:

dancing, hairdressing, personal grooming and dress-making—every activity starting from the needs of the members. The first concert, all too hastily planned by the girls, led them to give their own verdict—"Terrible, but we can do better than that." After some months the girls asked, "What about the laddies?" which resulted in boys being introduced to the Saturday dances followed by their own request for a boys' night. This led on to the adoption of a mixed committee of boys and girls to run the Centre —the chairman a boy and the secretary a girl.

With the introduction of an "under 14 group" came an interesting request from a small group—"Could we be Guides, Miss?" which the leader met by stressing the difficulties and the high standard required. This immediately whetted the appetite, and before long there were two Guide Companies, Brownie and Cub Packs; and, in due course, a Ranger Company was formed with the girls attracted by the "Home Emergency Service" programme of training and tests as a means of being ready to serve their country.

An "Epilogue" closed the evening programme for those who wished to stay for it. When it was explained what an Epilogue was, one girl said, "I'm not religious but it's no' a bad idea," and a later comment was, "I don't go to church but I like you."

The "How and Why" Club proved most valuable in encouraging the boys and girls to discuss social problems, current events and standards of conduct, to think and reason for themselves and to listen to each other.

The Centre aimed to become financially self-supporting and the members paid 1d a night and 1/- for their weekly dance. As numbers grew larger and better premises were needed so a building fund was started—farthings, halfpennies and pennies were saved and in little over a year £167 was raised. As the Government Youth Service developed, grants were received from Local Authorities and other sources towards the salaries of leaders. Edinburgh Guide County formed a support committee and they raised funds for the Centre as needed.

There were outdoor activities including swimming, hiking, cycling, treasure hunts, etc., and the annual summer camps, looked forward to all the year, very brave ventures undertaken by the leaders.

Very soon the success of Granton influenced other Guide Counties to start Centres of their own in Coatbridge, Methil, Alloa and Musselburgh, and subsequently in Melbourne, Australia. Miss Collyns started training courses for leaders which lasted for six months, for those over 25 years who had some form of previous experience. They consisted of an equal balance between practical work in a Centre and theoretical work; there was training also for those under 20 years with a qualification as Assistant Leader following a year's training. There were also part-time courses lasting a year for three nights a week for those who did not wish to become full-time leaders or who were unable to give up their employment to take full-time training. At the start of this scheme the Government grant allowed for a salary of £200 p.a.

Here is an interesting excerpt from a press article in 1945:

"Only those who were present during the first few months of the Centre's life could have a full idea of what has been achieved in four years. Compare the first night when everyone shouted and ran around at the same time with a normal night when the members' committee take upon themselves the responsibility of maintaining discipline; compare those early nights when the girls would keep their coats on the whole evening no matter how hot and stuffy so as to hide what they had on below or for fear of having them stolen, with their present smart appearance; compare the early days of the Epilogue when a gang would try and come in to wreck it, with the present days when there is seldom a serious interruption."

The work accomplished in the Square Centre which gave such opportunity to those young people to gain a wider knowledge of life, poise and self-reliance, is the outcome of taking Guiding and Scouting out into the wider world.

It is good to remember that Guiding through Square Centres met the need and the challenge of the moment to be followed later by the more elaborate forms of the expanding Youth Service.

Again, thirty years later, the Guide response to the problems of the time was yet another practical gesture. In September 1970, Miss Betty Robertson, an Edinburgh Diploma'd Trainer was appointed for a term of three years as Trainer for Community Development at Scottish H.Q. At that time no other youth organisation had such an appointment.

Her broad remit was to find means of helping Guiders to become more involved in their own communities, to recognise and adapt themselves to the conditions they found in their own neighbourhoods. She was also asked to suggest ways in which the Eight Point Programme could be made relevant for an older age group.

She spent her first year making contacts both in and out of the Movement and finding opportunities for Guiders to meet leaders of other organisations working in the same areas, who were interested in sharing resources and talents.

Under her guidance projects were undertaken at West Pilton, in collaboration with the Y.W.C.A. and the Sisters of Charity, to provide help and facilities for young mothers who wanted to meet and to discover new interests. Starting with simple cooking and handcraft classes, the group also enjoyed outings and holidays; various activities were established within the "Y.W." Centre at West Pilton—a cookery class still meets there, at which students from Queen Margaret's College provide the expertise, and the links with local families are still maintained. Guiding has been seen to be concerned with the difficulties of that part of Edinburgh. Elsewhere Betty encouraged many Guiders to look outwards to their communities and gave them ideas for appropriate service.

In other ways, too, Guiding has reached out beyond the Packs and Companies enjoying the programme, to parents, friends and indeed everyone in the community. "Guiding is Good News!"—the very first Edinburgh Guides talked or wrote to their friends to pass on this message, but today the good news is spread by every modern means of communication, and now we have become accustomed to mass advertising and country-wide coverage of news in the Press, on television and radio and know how great is their influence. It has perhaps never been so necessary to ensure that the right image of Guiding is shown, in particular that the Law and Promise are all-important. Every news item and picture that focuses attention on the Movement can help to attract girls and adults to join in "this great game of Guiding."

Edinburgh Guides on the move in the "Evening News" Centenary procession.

In 1909 the first report of a Guide meeting appeared in *The Scotsman*, and in 1911 in the minutes it is recorded that "it would be a good thing for paragraphs to appear from time to time in the *Dispatch*. From then on Edinburgh Guides had good press coverage, particularly in later years from the *Evening News*. Many Guide and Brownie events have been visited by a press photographer to the children's excitement and the slightly mixed feelings of the Guiders, who may well have had hastily to re-time the evening programme (many a cake has been cut twice!) to fit the unpredictable timing of the photographer's arrival.

Edinburgh County Committee were quick to take advantage of that exciting new invention—radio, and in 1926 the County Commissioner persuaded Miss Maud Anderson to give a broadcast talk about Guiding. Two years later a Guide choir took part in an evening broadcast and from 1932 items of Guide news were included in a weekly B.B.C. bulletin. Much later in 1951 an even more exciting broadcast was made. The B.B.C. invited Shelagh Cuthbertson, an Edinburgh Commissioner, to bring six Guides to Glasgow to take part in a radio performance of her play, *The Trefoil Brooch*. Professional actors played the principal rôles, while the Guides had small speaking parts and sang at the camp fire featured in the play. Shelagh remembers the occasion:

"In those days one went on the air live: no mistakes—or else! There were no tapes and no re-play, and Auntie Kathleen of the B.B.C. Children's Hour explained all this to us. As I sat, the trembling author, behind the glass screen maintaining strict silence, it was all I could do to prevent my teeth chattering. The excitement was intense. Thinking Day was the reason for the play being written and the story was about a girl whose ambition was to sing in public. She achieved this through her contact with a Guide Company, and the Camp Fire was her opportunity. Thanks to the producer, the actors and the Guides, the whole broadcast was a success."

The seventies have given even greater opportunities for radio publicity because in January 1975 Edinburgh's local station Radio Forth was launched. This gives excellent coverage of Guide events and during the station's opening week Joan Warrack, the Assistant County Commissioner, was asked to join Nancy Mitchell in her topical programme to appeal for news items and photographs for this book!

The popularity of the cinema in the thirties prompted a foray into that field and in 1933 Guides from the South-West Division were filmed packing Christmas parcels for poor families. This was included in a larger film about Guiding which was shown to the public. In 1937 the 4th Leith Company won the Victory Shield and because of this was chosen to take part in a film which was shown in the Scout and Guide Hall at that year's great Empire Exhibition at Bellahouston Park in Glasgow. The then youngest member of the company remembers, when she saw it, clearly seeing her shaking hand as she made her Promise during the shot taken at her enrolment ceremony. Other films followed and in 1957 Mrs Simson Hall made one of the Guide Rally held in Edinburgh and five years later another, called *A Guide Log,* was shown at Edinburgh

H.Q. to parents and friends. During the sixties some Edinburgh Guides took part in *Perpetual Spring* which was widely shown in the U.K. Now in 1976 many Guiders make their own ciné records of unit activities, Camps and Pack Holidays, and these as well as being great entertainment are invaluable in showing what Guiding is all about.

This account of the part publicity has played in the Guide story in Edinburgh must also include the occasions when the Guides have put themselves on show in the city. These really tremendous events are written about fully elsewhere: the Guide week in May 1939, the "Spotlight on Guiding" exhibition held in the Waverley Market in March 1964 and the inauguration of the New Programme in 1968.

To bring the story right up to date—another exhibition, "Focus on Guiding," is planned to take place on 23rd April 1977 in the Assembly Rooms, which is the publication date for this book, and the Edinburgh story of the Girl Guides moves into the future.

The Founder of the Movement stated its ideals very clearly in 1937. The wording may seem old-fashioned after 40 years but the principles stand as true now as they did then:

"Through her daily Good Turn, playing the game for her side, and her active patriotism for the community, the girl becomes Christian by practice rather than by profession, and develops within herself that love and charity for others that is the love of God. . . . The object of the Scout and Guide Movement is to provide health-giving recreation for boys and girls, and spread amongst its members the spirit of brotherhood, without regard to differences of country, creed or class."